African American History Reconsidered

THE NEW BLACK STUDIES SERIES

Edited by Darlene Clark Hine
and Dwight A. McBride

*A list of books in the series appears at
the end of this book.*

African American History Reconsidered

PERO GAGLO DAGBOVIE

University of Illinois Press

URBANA, CHICAGO, AND SPRINGFIELD

A version of chapter 3 originally appeared in the *Journal for the Study of Radicalism* Vol. 3, Iss. 2, 2009, pages 81–112. Copyright © 2009 by Michigan State University.

Portions of chapters 4 and 5 previously appeared in the *Journal of African American History* and are reprinted by permission of the Association for the Study of African American Life and History (ASALH).

Library of Congress Cataloging-in-Publication Data
Dagbovie, Pero Gaglo.
African American history reconsidered / Pero Gaglo Dagbovie.
    p.   cm. — (The new Black studies series)
Includes bibliographical references and index.
ISBN 978-0-252-03521-0 (cloth : alk. paper)
ISBN 978-0-252-07701-2 (pbk. : alk. paper)
1. African Americans—Historiography.
2. African American historians—History. I. Title.
E184.65.D34   2010
973'.0496073—dc22   2009041751

For my courageous sons, Perovi, Kokou, and Agbelé,
and in the loving memory of their mother, Juliet TShaka
McQueen Dagbovie, who taught others and me so much.

It is the centrality of the Afro-American experience that makes its past so significant, a past that has a sobering but redemptive quality for our nation, not as an escapist journey to some gossamer glory of bygone days but possibly as a vehicle for present enlightenment, guidance, and enrichment.

—Benjamin Quarles, *The Negro in the Making of America*

Contents

Preface

Legitimized as a scholarly discipline by the mainstream U.S. historical profession sometime during or immediately following the dynamic Black Power era, African American history as a concept, profession, and cultural facet has been an important component of African American life arguably since the creation of African American people. The African people from whom African Americans were and are descended tended to view history as a pragmatic socializing agent that played vital roles in people's day-to-day existence, education, and identity and community formation. For the masses of enslaved African Americans, knowledge of the past and memories were important reservoirs of hope, faith, and self-knowledge, embodying a communal interpretation of history and a vital tool of survival. Initially byproducts of African Americans' enduring struggles against racism and oppression, conceptualizations and interpretations of African American history as a philosophy, source of identity, and repository of resistance have undergone numerous monumental changes and phases since the publication of James W. C. Pennington's *A Textbook of the Origins and History of the Colored People* (1841); William Wells Brown's *The Black Man: His Antecedents, His Genius, and His Achievements* (1863); and George Washington Williams's *History of the Negro Race in America, 1619–1880: Negroes as Slaves, as Soldiers, and as Citizens* (1883).

During every period of the African American historical experience since the scientific study of black history was systematically professionalized in the first half of the twentieth century, black history has evolved as a discipline, as has black history's meaning. The evolution of the black historical profession since W. E. B. Du Bois earned a PhD in history from Harvard University in 1895 has been marked by countless important turning points, including the founding of the Association for the Study of Negro Life and History in 1915, the ascendancy of "Woodson's boys," the initial publication of John Hope Franklin's *From Slavery to Freedom* in 1947, the various enduring transformations ushered in by the modern civil rights era and the Black Power movement, the black studies movement, the black women's studies and black women's history movements, Vincent Harding's *There is A River* (1981), the post–Black Power era rise of many prominent black historians in the U.S. historical profession, and the emergence of hip-hop generation black historians. Today black history is an established, dynamic, and growing subfield of the U.S. historical enterprise.

While the last major phases of popular black historical revivalism emerged during the Black Power era, the "golden age" of hip hop, the Afrocentric movement, and the 1990s, black history continues to shape African Americans' worldviews and America's political, social, and cultural identity. Though perhaps not as effective as the Negro History Weeks of the early black history movement, contemporary Black History Month celebrations constitute important threads in the American cultural and educational fabric. Vestiges of black history are everywhere in contemporary American society. As Du Bois pronounced more than a century ago, "We [African Americans] have woven ourselves into the very warp and woof of this nation." A knowledge of black history is crucial to our understanding of the present state and the unknown (yet slightly predictable) future of African American culture. Many black leaders, spokespersons, and public intellectuals realize this and continue to view black history as a central core value of black life. Cornel West's and Julianne Malveaux's critiques of President Barack Obama in 2008, for example, highlight the significance of African American history and memory in the twenty-first century. On August 28, 2008, during the *Tavis Smiley Show,* these black public intellectuals chastised Obama for failing to weave the history of the black struggle into his historic acceptance speech at the 2008 National Democratic Convention, which attracted more than 30 million viewers.

West insisted that Obama should have acknowledged the historical black struggle "that has gone in [*sic*] for him to be where he is." The "Obama people," in West's view, were "trying to escape from history, appeal to the white center, and in doing that," he surmised, "I hope that they don't lose the wind at their backs. You can't change the world without acknowledging a tradition, memory, and history." Celebrating her token reference to one of the most famous black female freedom fighters, West proceeded to credit Hillary Clinton with tapping into the reservoirs of black history more than Obama had. "Well, I mean no mention of Martin, no mention of the black freedom movement. It made sister Hillary to talk about Harriet Tubman." Malveaux's critique of Obama's lack of historicism was equally as harsh. "My heart's broken, actually," Malveaux told Smiley. "I hoped to hear more about Dr. King . . . I think the brother dropped the historical baton. . . . The fact is that he basically perpetrated a whitewash of our history."[1]

West and Malveaux wanted, and seemingly expected, Obama to place his monumental, unprecedented, and now historical moment within the context of African American history, memory, and struggle. By not publicly commemorating hundreds of years of black resistance and agency, Obama failed, West and Malveaux concluded, to make the most of his historical moment. While I understand the logical bases of their critiques of Obama, episodes in black history, especially before the modern civil rights movement, were not the best or most effective communicative devices for a black man who was then striving to become (white) America's next president. Since 2008, countless scholars and social critics have examined the real challenges that Obama faced as a black man running for president and will now face as president. West's and Malveaux's commitment to black history could have perhaps been better articulated by their placing Obama within the historical context of post-Reconstruction black politicians and black leaders like Booker T. Washington who carefully negotiated their unavoidable relationships with various groups of whites. While Obama shares many things in common with Washington—a complex "b(l)iracial" identity, as black cultural and literary critic Sika A. Dagbovie has theorized, a unique celebratory status, impeccable oratory skills, polyvocality, as well as a nuanced, compromising disposition—Obama, though astute, culturally bilingual, and adept at code-switching, has arguably not fully developed the Washingtonian art of pleasing a diversified, nonhomogeneous, and often competing clientele. As America's first black president, he will certainly be challenged to further develop his approach and already outstanding communication and oratory skills.

West's and Malveaux's comments also insinuated that Obama totally ignored black history during the last stages of his campaign, yet in July 2008 at the 99th Annual Convention of the NAACP in Cincinnati, Obama incorporated black history into his speech. "It is always humbling to speak before the NAACP. It is a powerful reminder of the debt we all owe to those who marched for us and fought for us and stood up on our behalf; of the sacrifices that were made for us by those we never knew; and of the giants whose shoulders I stand on here today." Obama continued, "They are the men and women we read about in history books and hear about in church; whose lives we honor with schools, and boulevards, and federal holidays that bear their names. But what I want to remind you tonight—on Youth Night—is that these giants, these icons of America's past, were not much older than many of you when they took up freedom's cause and made their mark on history."[2] Whatever the content or the tenor of the criticism from various quarters, relevant, thought-provoking debates like those raised by West and Malveaux will inevitably continue within black public intellectual circles, and African American history will continue to constitute an essential element of black life and culture.

* * *

Embracing Edward Hallett Carr's straightforward assertion that "history means interpretation," this book probes the seemingly countless interpretations, perceptions, and applications of black history. More specifically, it is about the evolution of black history's multiple meanings; the past, present, and future teaching of black history; the diverse worldviews of black historians; the black historical profession and black historiography; and numerous analytical frameworks for understanding and delving into a variety of dimensions of the African American historical experience. My study contributes to many issues, subjects, and subfields in African American history and historiography and black studies, primarily black intellectual thought and history. Many scholars and historians have theorized black history, but no comprehensive examination of black history as a multifaceted philosophy has been published.

* In part engaged by Manning Marable's intriguing essay, "Living Black History: Black Consciousness, Place, and America's Master Narrative,"[3] in this study I unpack a century of thoughtful definitions of black history.

* Scholarship on the teaching and learning of mainstream U.S. history has largely ignored African American history, and historians of the African American experience have not devoted a great deal of research to teaching the subject matter. Acknowledging past and recent strategies, I discuss new and innovative ways to teach African American history to diverse groups of college and university millennial learners, focusing on the millennial hip-hop generation.

* While scholarship on "the father of black history" Carter G. Woodson is advanced, I examine and contextualize a recently discovered manuscript written by Woodson entitled "The Case of the Negro" (1921). Foreshadowing dimensions of his 1933 classic *The Mis-Education of the Negro,* Woodson's 1921 polemic clearly places him within a tradition of black radicalism, helps us more fully understand his ideological development, and sheds more light on the philosophical underpinnings of the early black historical profession.

* Three major books, *Black Women's History at the Intersection of Power: ABWH's Twentieth Anniversary Anthology* (Rosalyn Terborg-Penn and Janice Sumler-Edmond, 2000); *Women and the Historical Enterprise in*

America: Gender, Race, and the Politics of Memory, 1880–1945 (Julie Des Jardins, 2003); and *Telling Histories: Black Women Historians in the Ivory Tower* (Deborah Gray White, 2008), have examined the unique experiences of black women historians. I offer a comprehensive analysis of black women historians from "the nadir" through the modern civil rights era and a bit beyond.

* By critically assessing the exhaustive historiography on Booker T. Washington, I not only suggest new ways to interpret Washington, but I also demonstrate the value of historiography—essentially epistemology and the social construction of knowledge—in black history.

* Today there exists a host of useful frameworks for analyzing the African American historical experience. Building upon the frameworks developed most by political activists, a small group of social scientists, black studies practitioners, and a group of radical Afrocentric scholars, I explore the value of using the hotly debated concept of genocide as a window into understanding and framing African American history.

African American History Reconsidered does not claim to provide a complete reinterpretation of the African American historical experience. Instead, it reconsiders many important themes, intellectuals, conceptualizations, and phenomena in African American history and historiography. The chapters address a wide range of topics that deserve further consideration and seek to contribute to the development of black intellectual historiography and the "multidiscipline" black studies. By inquiring into and considering the ideas of numerous twentieth-century black intellectuals, this study constitutes a restoration project in black intellectual and historical thought. I hope that my ideas contribute to how we interpret the meaning of African American history as we proceed into the new millennium.

Acknowledgments

I am grateful and humbled by the generosity that I received while I wrote and rewrote *African American History Reconsidered*. Numerous family members, friends, students, colleagues, and administrators have supported me. Darlene Clark Hine, V. P. Franklin, James B. Stewart, Derrick P. Alridge, and Frances R. Dagbovie provided especially careful and crucial readings of and comments on the manuscript as it underwent its various incarnations. The former chairperson of the Department of History at Michigan State University, Mark Kornbluh, supported my research and professional activities. My senior colleagues in the African and African American Studies Program have encouraged my research, teaching, and commitment to "academic excellence and social responsibility." Numerous conversations with fellow historians and scholars Daina Ramey Berry, Sowandé Mustakeem, Nwando Achebe, Aime Ellis, Jerry Garcia, Dylan Miner, Thabiti Asukile, and Ben Smith have helped me maintain my sanity. Thanks are also due to the Office of the Vice President for Research and Grants at Michigan State University for providing me with an Intramural Research Grant's Program grant during the fall semester of 2008 that facilitated the final revisions. Michigan State University's Lilly Teaching Fellows Program served as an important turning point in my interest in the teaching and learning of African American history. I thank Joan Catapano, Angela Burton, and the University of Illinois Press for supporting this book project from its inception. It was a pleasure working with the press's various staff members once again. I benefited greatly from Julie Gay's exceptional editorial skills. I thank the Association for the Study of African American Life and History (ASALH) for providing a social and intellectual space for me to develop many of the ideas that are explored in this book. More than a few graduate students with whom I have worked have listened to me as I worked out the ideas that appear in this book. I thank Bayyinah Jeffries, Rachel Laws, and Tracy Robison for tutoring my children as I completed this book, as time was of the essence.

For their encouragement and unwavering support, I owe a great deal of thanks to MAOOH (the Most High) and my ancestors; the Dagbovie family at home and abroad; my parents, Prospero Yao Dagbovie and Frances R. Dagbovie; my sister, Sika A. Dagbovie; my children, Perovi, Kokou, and Agbelé; and the Combs, McQueen, Patterson, and Jones families. I thank my uncle Frido Dagbovie for providing me with a home away from home as I made my final revisions. LaShawn D. Harris, my best friend and pillar, patiently listened to me talk about black history and culture every day and had my back while I was finishing this book. I give thanks to generations of black historians and countless unselfish freedom fighters who essentially *made* what I have made the subject of my life's work.

African American History Reconsidered

Introduction

Afro-American historiography, with its own conceptual and methodological concerns, is now poised to illuminate the Afro-American past in a manner that will broaden and deepen our knowledge of black people in this country. The writing of Afro-American History is no longer undertaken principally to revise the work of wrongheaded white historians, to discern divine providence, to show black participation in the nation's growth and development, to prove the inevitability of black equality, or to demonstrate the inexorable progress made by Afro-Americans. It is conducted as a distinct area of inquiry, within the discipline of history, with black people as its primary focus to reveal their thought and activities over time and place.

—Robert L. Harris Jr., "Coming of Age: The Transformation of Afro-American Historiography"

Today Afro-American history is a respected and legitimate field of American history . . . As we approach the twenty-first century, the time has come to assess and evaluate the historical outpouring of the last few decades. But beyond assessment and evaluation is the challenge of charting new directions, raising new issues and concerns about the future context and nature of black history . . . Much of the new scholarship, the fresh interpretations and insights, have not been incorporated into the textbooks used in schools around the country. Thus, it would appear that we have only just begun our work.

—Darlene Clark Hine, *The State of Afro-American History: Past, Present, and Future*

The paradox of extolling the academic impact of a movement
while ignoring the academic voices within that movement raises a
fundamental intellectual concern, for, although African-American
historiography has reached full adulthood, there remains an
ambivalence about its place. That ambivalence, a consequence of
an evolving, special relationship with what may be characterized as
mainstream history, manifests itself in the psychological bedrock of
many historians . . . as well as in the categories of formal research
and discourse.
—David Levering Lewis, "Radical History: Toward Inclusiveness"

The above musings of Robert L. Harris Jr., Darlene Clark Hine, and David
Levering Lewis testify to the unique stature of African American history
during the 1980s, arguably one of its golden ages.[1] Equally important, these
thoughts also speak to and illuminate pertinent issues affecting the present
nature and position of African American history in academic and popular
culture in the United States. We are now undoubtedly witnessing the most
advanced phase of the systematic study of the African American experience.
Historians of black America can no longer ignore the relevant and numerous
complex, interconnected, and influential factors—geography, varied strategies of resistance, religious orientations, intraracial dynamics, age, gender
and sex, class, and legal and extra-legal forms of oppression, just to name
a handful—when framing their analyses and interpretations of black life
and culture over time and space. At the same time, as our predecessors
of the 1980s and earlier decades acknowledged during their times, we still
need to engage in revisionism and advance black historical knowledge while
unpacking and addressing the multiple, historically rooted, contemporary
challenges facing African American history's role and place within U.S. academic circles and discourse, popular culture, and educational institutions at
its different levels; the function and meaning of African American history
to the diversified African American community; and the construction and
interpretation of black America's past throughout the ever-expanding African
diaspora and the world.

This book is essentially about black history, its multiple meanings and
social constructions, its scholarship and pedagogy, its scholars and interpreters, its evolution as a profession, and its overall intricately intertwined
past, present, and future. The chapters in this study explore a wide range
of issues, themes, and topics concerning paradigms for understanding and
analyzing African American history, dimensions of the twentieth-century
black historical enterprise, the teaching and learning of African American
history for the twenty-first century, the millennial and hip-hop generation's

unique relationship to and interpretations of the African American historical experience, historical paradigms for black studies, and the social construction of knowledge in African American historiography. Ultimately, *African American History Reconsidered* seeks to contribute to the further development and expansion of scholarship on black intellectual history and the philosophy of black history, subfields of African American historiography that are still in their formative years.[2]

As the insightful observations that begin this introduction suggest, the decade of the 1980s was an exciting and optimistic period for the study of African American history. During this decade, the study of black history, the black historical profession, and African American historiography—the representation, and various processes involved therein, of African American history in verbal images and written discourse—had reached a noteworthy level of recognition and "legitimacy" in the U.S. academy.[3] Black history as a concept, set of ideologies, philosophy, coherent documented record of African Americans' collective past, and as a field of scholarly inquiry has certainly represented an essential component of African American culture, identity, and intellectual thought since the antebellum era and concretely by the Progressive era, "the nadir" for African Americans. From Robert Benjamin Lewis's *Light and Truth: Collected from the Bible and Ancient and Modern History; Containing the Universal History of the Colored and Indian Race* (1836, 1844) and James W. C. Pennington's *A Text Book of the Origins and History of the Colored People* (1841) until the publication of W. E. B. Du Bois's *The Negro* in 1915, at least a dozen history books on black America's collective history were published in the United States. Spearheaded by Carter G. Woodson, his disciples, and countless of his co-workers at the Association for the Study of Negro Life and History (ASNLH), the early black history movement of the first half of the twentieth century gave rise to the formative years of African Americans' collective historical consciousness and the scientific study of African American history. More than a few historians have acknowledged the seemingly sudden and unprecedented heightened interest in black history during the civil rights and Black Power movements and the 1970s. This serious academic intrigue and excitement in African American history among black and white historians was an expression of the monumental changes in blacks' enduring struggle for human rights and in U.S. race relations in the aftermath of the 1950s and 1960s. It was part of "a stream of modern American historiography" that blossomed in the mid-1970s and was "convinced that there can be no real sense of the whole without the parts."[4]

As we proceed into the new millennium, the significance of the transformations in African American history in the 1980s becomes more discernable and contextually significant. Though inextricably bound to the important advancements in previous stages of development, 1980–1990 represents a pivotal decade in the maturation of African American historiography. Like their predecessors, black historians of the 1980s seem to have been keenly aware of their discipline's growth. Late in 1987, Robert L. Harris Jr. located a key juncture for the study of African American history in the early part of the decade. "The Conference on the Study and Teaching of Afro-American History," held at Purdue University, October 6–8, 1983, "represented the flowering of Afro-American history," Harris said. "This conference and the subsequent publication of its papers marked the arrival of Afro-American scholarship from the periphery to the core of historical scholarship in the United States."[5] The sentiments of Harris, Hine, and Lewis that open this introduction embodied leading African American historians' optimism, hope, and pride in the advanced state of their field in the post–Black Power era. By the mid-1980s, African American history scholars were arguably "on the cutting edge of the profession." At the closing of the decade, David Levering Lewis surmised that African American historiography had "reached full adulthood."[6] The period represents a sort of a golden age of African American history.

During the 1980s, scores of groundbreaking black historical studies were published.[7] This maturation and innovation was epitomized by the development of African American women's history. For instance, building upon key historical studies of the 1970s, leading African American female scholars in the 1980s continued to theorize black women's history: the essential black women's studies reader, *All the Women Are White, All the Blacks Are Men, But Some of Us Are Brave: Black Women's Studies* (Gloria T. Hull, Patricia Bell Scott, and Barbara Smith), appeared in 1982; Paula Giddings published one of the first broad accounts of African American women's history (*When and Where I Enter: The Impact of Black Women on Race and Sex in America,* 1985); Deborah Gray White published the first comprehensive and widely acclaimed monograph on African American female slaves (*Ar'n't I a Woman? Female Slaves in the Plantation South,* 1985); Jacqueline Jones produced *Labor of Love, Labor of Sorrow: Black Women, Work and the Family, from Slavery to the Present* (1985), a study of black women as laborers; Henry Louis Gates Jr. edited the writings of many important nineteenth-century black female authors; and Darlene Clark Hine published a 1989 study on black nurses (*Black Women in White: Racial Conflict and Cooperation in the Nursing Profession, 1890–1950*), edited significant black women's historical resource guides (for example, *The Black Women in the Middle West Project: A Comprehensive Resource Guide, Illinois and Indiana; Historical Essays, Oral Histories, Biographical Profiles, and Document Collections,* with Patrick Kay Bidelman, Shirley M. Herd,

1986), and called for an authentic black women's historical discourse.[8] The foundations for the institutionalization of black women's history are thus rooted in the 1980s.

The period 1980–90 was also a fruitful decade for research on the study of black history. As John Hope Franklin has noted, two seminal studies on the black historical enterprise and the multi-tiered status of African American history in U.S. culture were published in 1986: the controversial *Black History and the Historical Profession* (August Meier and Elliott Rudwick) and *The State of Afro-American History: Past, Present, and Future* (Darlene Clark Hine, ed.). In Franklin's estimation, these studies pioneered the exploration of the lives, ideas, contributions, identities, and collective scholarship of numerous historians of the black experience.[9] At the same time, the various contributors to *The State of Afro-American History* as well as other scholars concurred that during the 1980s, African American history still had much progress to make in terms of its breadth and scope and its inevitable, symbiotic relationship with so-called mainstream U.S. history and historiography.

Despite the prominence of leading black historians in the 1980s, blacks still faced considerable challenges and historically institutionalized racism—overt, covert, subtle, and hard to pinpoint—within the American historical profession. In a review of Meier and Rudwick's study, Earl E. Thorpe openly discussed the racialized politics of the publishing industry during the 1980s. "Book publishing, at the major commercial and university press levels in particular, has been white. Racism has been very much at work here also. Even the university press publications . . . are suspect." Of the twenty-one volumes published in one of Meier's series, Thorpe noted, "only two were by black historians."[10] Thorpe's observations may have been considered taboo for many during the 1980s, yet they raise many not-to-be-overlooked realities in the sanctioning processes of historical knowledge in the U.S. academy. As revealed earlier with regard to Woodson's often-tumultuous relationships with white academic institutions, during and following the modern civil rights movement the debates surrounding who would control black history were important matters of concern for more than a few black historians. Maintaining autonomy and espousing an authentically descriptive African American–centered approach while also gaining recognition within mainstream, white historical arenas has for at least a century constituted a major challenge for the black historical enterprise. In varying degrees and in different manners in different eras, black historians have grappled with balancing their roles as members of Du Bois's "Talented Tenth," committed to social change and black consciousness raising, and as rigorous academics recognized by white America. During the Black Power era, black studies advocates sought to solve this problem by forming their own independent institutions within white dominated educational infrastructures, such as several scholarly journals (namely *The Journal of Black Studies, The Black Scholar,* and *The Western Journal of Black Studies*), the Institute of the Black World, and the National Council for Black Studies. Countless black studies scholars have critically reflected on the challenges and limitations of this strategy.[11]

An examination of the treatment of African American history and the representation of African American historians in the leading American historical journals during the 1980s sheds some light on the white historical profession's willingness to embrace African American history. During the 1980s, approximately ten articles were published in *The American Historical Review* that focused on African American subject matter, one of which was authored by a leading African American historian, John Hope Franklin. Franklin's article, "Mirror for America: A Century of Reconstruction History," appeared at the dawning of the decade. As Earl Lewis pointed out, Franklin's article represented only the second article by an African American historian to be published in *The American Historical Review,* the first being W. E. B. Du Bois's "Reconstruction and Its Benefits," published seventy years earlier.[12] The fact that Du Bois and Franklin represented African American historians in the oldest American historical journal deserves to be scrutinized. Though separated by nearly five decades, Du Bois and Franklin were acknowledged (Franklin more so) by the white-dominated U.S. historical profession for similar reasons.

Both were exceptional scholars, earning doctorates from Harvard University (Du Bois in 1895, Franklin in 1941). Both men were prolific. When his article was published in *The American Historical Review* in 1910, Du Bois had already written numerous essays and four major books, and two of these studies, *The Philadelphia Negro* (1899) and *The Souls of Black Folk* (1903), were groundbreaking. By the time Franklin's essay appeared in the *American Historical Review* in 1980, he had published countless articles and book reviews, as well as nine books. While Du Bois was clearly an established scholar-activist by 1910, Franklin, despite his civil rights activism, adhered to a philosophy of hyper-objective black history writing. During the 1950s, he openly advocated a stance that would not pigeonhole him in any way as being a *black* historian. In fact, Franklin did not identify himself as being a *black* historian. "Very early," Franklin noted, "I decided that I was going to remove the tag of Negro from any consideration of my work, whether teaching or writing."[13] Both Du Bois and Franklin were among the few black historians whose scholarship was considered worthy of consideration in white academic publishing institutions during the era of Jim Crow segregation. Beginning in the 1940s, Franklin was among the few black historians to gain acceptance within the white, mainstream historical profession.

During the 1980s, more than twenty articles were published in the *Journal of American History* that discussed African Americans at varying levels. Fewer than twenty of these articles focused on dimensions of African American history. The black historians, mainly prominent scholars, who published in the *Journal of American History* in the 1980s included Armstead Robinson, David Levering Lewis (who published two articles, one in 1984 and one in 1989); John Hope Franklin, Vincent Harding (who published two articles in 1987); Nell Irvin Painter, Deborah Gray White, Clayborne Carson, Nathan Irvin Huggins, James H. Cone, and Robin D. G. Kelley (who co-authored an article).[14] Black historians were virtually absent from the pages of the *Journal of American History* in previous decades. Benjamin Quarles and John Hope Franklin were among the only leading black historians to publish articles in the *Journal of American History* from its founding in 1916 as the *Mississippi Valley Historical Review* through the 1970s.[15] Both Franklin and Quarles wrote in nonthreatening tones that would not necessarily challenge the status quo of mainstream white historical journals. During the 1980s, it appears that Daniel C. Littlefield was one of the few black historians to publish an article in the *Journal of Southern History* (founded in 1935). At the same time, the *Journal of Southern History* did publish numerous book reviews in the 1980s on African American subject matter, many of which were authored by black scholars. Further, as August Meier and Elliott Rudwick have noted, the *Journal of Southern History* published six articles by black scholars between 1953 and 1960. Nonetheless, John Hope Franklin and John W. Blassingame were among the only leading black historians to publish articles in the *Journal of Southern History* during the 1970s.[16]

Now, several decades after the eighties flowering of African American history, scholarship on the African American historical enterprise, black historians, African American historiography, and the teaching and learning of African American history constitute some of the most significant yet underappreciated components of research in African American history. What is the role of black history in the twenty-first century, and how is this linked to and informed by previous conceptualizations of black history? *African American History Reconsidered* fills what I consider to be a void in the current scholarship. There are certainly more than a few significant studies that critically explore the black historical profession, black historians, and the philosophical underpinnings of black history. Moreover, John Hope Franklin's recently published *Mirror to America: The Autobiography of John Hope Franklin* (2005), the only major published autobiography by a black historian, symbolically represents the mainstreaming of the study of the black historian.[17] Despite the significance of the existing scholarship on black historians and African American historiography, there are some meaningful ways that this scholarship can be expanded, explored, and re-envisioned to address the current issues faced within the field. The insightful critiques by Earl E. Thorpe and others of Meier and Rudwick's exhaustive study on the black historical profession still need to be addressed and elaborated upon.[18] We can still strive to better understand the diverse schools of thought among generations of black historians; how the meaning of black history in U.S. academic circles and popular culture and black communities has transformed over time; the potential theoretical frameworks for more holistically explaining the African American experience; African American history's role as an educational device; and the bases of our contemporary—and often taken for granted—knowledge of the black past, especially before the classic civil rights era.

If, as David Levering Lewis proclaimed, African American historiography "reached full adulthood"[19] in 1989, then today African American history is certainly and logically—based on the inevitable progression of historical research and thought in modern U.S. society—at its most advanced state, especially considering the monumental advancements of the 1990s and early years of the twenty-first century, in terms of groundbreaking publications, the overwhelming amount of resources and information available on the internet, and multimedia digital technology. African American history and its historiography stand at an important crossroads. It is now timely to explore how we can reconsider, revisit, and analyze dimensions of African American history and the profession with the twenty-first century in mind. Decades ago, Thorpe and Franklin emphasized this point in asserting that every generation of historians "must make its own studies of history" and "provide its contemporaries with materials vital to understanding the present and planning strategies for coping with the future."[20] Such sentiments are especially important in writing and teaching history to a generation of young Americans who are often biased toward the present in their orientation and dependent on limitless, intimidating, and often confusing historical outlets that were not available before the 1990s.

A recent issue of the *Journal of Blacks in Higher Education* revealed that "very few" black students "are majoring in black studies." For instance, in 2003 less than 0.7 percent of all bachelor's degrees awarded to blacks were in black studies, and for the same year only 1.3 percent of blacks to earn bachelor's degrees were history majors. On the other hand, 24.7 percent of all degrees awarded to blacks in 2003 were in business. Similarly, in an article attacking black studies, published in the *Chronicle of Higher Education* in April 2005, Valerie Grim (then interim chair of African American and African Diaspora Studies at Indiana University—Bloomington) commented on the so-called ahistorical culture of African American millennial learners. "The clock has turned back," Grim observed. "The students we have today don't even know who Martin Luther King Jr. is."[21]

Viewed in pragmatic and economic terms, it is not surprising that very few black students nationwide pursue bachelor's degrees in African American studies and history. Moreover, given the overarching ahistorical ethos of American culture during the new millennium, young blacks' lack of interest in history is part of a larger set of young Americans' cultural beliefs and tendencies. Instead of chastising the millennial hip-hop generation for their lack of historicity and their disconnect from African American history, professors of history and African American studies should develop new and refreshing strategies for stimulating their students' interest in the African American past. How we teach, interpret, and present African American history should balance rigorous scholarship with an accessible approach.

How have those of us black historians of the hip-hop generation fashioned a historical delivery, methodology, pedagogy, and consciousness that enables our contemporaries and students to best understand the complex contours and implications of African American history? How have we enriched the approaches and scholarship of our mentors, elders, and predecessors who were being socialized before, during, and directly after the modern civil rights era? While recent publications by hip-hop generation historians have offered new and alternative views of African American history, fewer have called for renovated approaches to writing, presenting, and especially teaching black history in general terms.

Beginning in the 1990s, Robin D. G. Kelley offered young black historians alternative blueprints and frameworks for approaching the African American historical craft. For many of us born during the Black Power era, Kelley's scholarly approach and historical worldview was invigorating and exciting. His first monograph, *Hammer and Hoe: Alabama Communists during the Great Depression* (1990), was widely praised for its innovation and revisionist nature.[22] After establishing himself as arguably the leading African American historian of his generation, Kelley continued to push the boundaries of traditional African American historical scholarship, focusing on writing history "from below" and unpacking post–civil rights era black history. The essays in *Race Rebels: Culture, Politics, and the Black Working Class* (1994) were very creative for their time and interpreted nontraditional topics in African American history. Kelley, for instance, is the first and one of the only established historians to contribute to the emerging field of hip-hop studies, authoring one of the first major scholarly essays on gangster rap. Kelley is also among the few active, professionally trained black historians in recent times to advocate a brand of contemporary history and wide-reaching intellectual history. In the mid-1990s, he was the only historian of his generation to join the ranks of the leading black public intellectuals of the day—Cornel West, bell hooks, Michael Eric Dyson, Manning Marable, and Henry Louis Gates Jr. During the 1990s, Kelley was a highly sought-after lecturer throughout the United States. Focusing on the period from the 1970s until the 1990s, Kelley, in *Yo' Mama's Disfunktional! Fighting the Culture Wars in Urban America,* openly defended and unapologetically gave "voice" to the urban black working class. Reminiscent of Woodson's and his contemporaries' sociological-historical studies, Kelley's work has conceptualized black history as a very recent phenomenon. He is a leading figure in establishing a post–Black Power era African American history and historiography.[23]

William Jelani Cobb's approach to African American history is refreshing. In his recent book of brief social, political, and cultural think pieces, *The Devil and Dave Chappelle and Other Essays* (2007), Cobb focuses on critically deconstructing relevant contemporary issues within the black community. At the same time, he historicizes them. He is a historian-journalist. In "The Hoodrat Theory," for instance, Cobb adroitly places the 2004 controversy over Nelly's "Tip Drill" video at Spelman College within a broader historical context, sampling from Deborah Gray White's discussion of the Jezebel stereotype in her classic 1985 study *Ar'n't I a Woman?* In the fourth part of his book, he showcases works that explore "contemporary events through a historical lens."[24] In an essay in *The Black Male Handbook: A Blueprint for Life* (2008), Cobb linked black history to the present challenges facing the masses of black men: "Bitter and painful history has led us into this situation, but the solutions we seek and the examples we need also live in this history. So this is the task, to mine our souls for those jewels that will sustain us, and leave the rest to pass into dust."[25] Cobb's creative sampling from the past is a practical device for introducing African American history to a hip-hop generation that often suffers from historical amnesia. His book is ideal for young black college and university students who are in the processes of developing a black historical consciousness. Since 2000, numerous hip-hop generation black historians, including Jeffrey O. G. Ogbar, Peniel E. Joseph, Yohuru Williams, Komozi Woodard, Rhonda Williams, and Scot Brown, have contributed to a new and dynamic Black Power–era historiography. While their interpretations are critical, most have also drawn inspiration from their research subjects. Directly and indirectly, they have challenged their contemporaries and younger readers to consider where they fit into the enduring black struggle in comparison with one of the last major periods of black consciousness. As V. P. Franklin has recently argued, the hip-hop generation can learn a great deal from the shortcomings of the Black Power era, especially the Black Panther Party, in avoiding "those ideas, beliefs, and practices that contributed to the untimely demise of one of the most heroic and tragic organizations in the history of the black liberation movement."[26]

Recently, at least one leading historian who came of age during the civil-rights and Black Power movements, Manning Marable, has passionately theorized how African American history can be repackaged to meet the intellectual, social, cultural, and political environment of the twenty-first century. "Living history," he writes, evokes a genuine "multidisciplinary methodology employing the tools of oral history, photography, films, ethnography, and multimedia technology" with the ultimate goal of retrieving "authentic" historical narratives that recognize the many, often competing and complex, "alternative pasts" in the African American experience.[27] Like his optimistic, forward-looking, 1980s predecessors, Marable is calling for a new-fashioned version of black history that is especially relevant for researching, studying, teaching, and learning black history in the new millennium. Marable champions:

> Let us therefore approach the construction of a new black history from the vantage point of the evolution of black consciousness over time. The state of being critically self-aware prefigures both a sense of power and a capacity for action. . . . As racialized populations reflect upon the accumulated concrete expression of their own lives, the lives of others who share their situation, and even those who have died long ago, a process of discovery unfolds that begins to restructure how they understand the world and their place within it. . . . Historical amnesia blocks the construction of potentially successful social movements. As the gap between the past, present, and future diminishes, individuals can acquire a greater sense of becoming the "makers" of their own history.[28]

Keeping Marable's plea in mind, the chapters in this book seek to contribute to a "new black history" that focuses on the role, function, and meaning of African American history over time. How have generations of black scholars, mainly historians, defined black history? How have scholars theorized the teaching of African American history since the early twentieth century? In what ways can history professors today help their students—primarily diverse groups of hip-hop generationers and millennial learners—intimately understand African American history? What can we learn from Carter G. Woodson's recently discovered "The Case of the Negro" (1921) about his nonstatic views of white America and black America's past and future during the latter part of "the nadir," and how does this think-piece contribute to the tradition of black radical thought? Where are black women historians situated in the black historical enterprise, and how does centering their worldviews, scholarship, and experiences challenge the normative, male-centered interpretations and narratives of the black historical profession? How is historical knowledge in African American history generated, disseminated, legitimized, and sanctioned by scholars and those in power, and what can we learn from critically deconstructing the historiographies of important topics in African American history? How have our conventional thoughts about African American history been influenced, shaped, and formulated over time? What are the strengths of looking at African American history through the lens of genocide? These are the fundamental inquiries this book sets out to undertake.

In 1971, Earl E. Thorpe noted that "no effort has been made to evaluate the basic ideas which have produced and inspired black historiography or even to define black history."[29] In the more than three decades since Thorpe's observation, the philosophy of black history still remains an understudied subfield of black history and historiography. Addressing this void, chapter 1, "Conceptualizing Black History, 1903–2006," explores how a significant group of scholars, intellectuals, and especially historians have philosophically conceptualized black history from the advent of the twentieth century until the dawning of the new millennium. I analyze the ideas of those thinkers, most often professionally trained black historians, who have explicitly grappled with and offered insightful perceptions of what black history constitutes.

Defining black history is a prerequisite to teaching it. In 2005, the School Reform Commission of Philadelphia, Pennsylvania, introduced a potentially precedent-setting mandate on the teaching of African American history in the city's public high schools. "In an effort to close the largest academic achievement gap in the district, now be it resolved that the district: ensure that all students and teachers gain the intellectual respect for children of African descent through the infusion of African and African American history and culture in the total curriculum, grades pre-K–12; mandate an African and African American History course in all Senior High Schools by September 2005."[30] Philadelphia public schools' black history mandate is refreshing, justifies the activism of more than three thousand of Philadelphia's African American students in November 1967, and represents a milestone for African American history's status in American culture. Acknowledging these recent developments in Philadelphia, the pronounced multicultural nature of American society in the twenty-first century, the growth of PhD programs in African American studies at major research universities, and the significance of African

American history at many major colleges and universities, it is now timely to reflect seriously upon the teaching and learning of black history. Scholarship on the teaching of African American history in higher education dates back to the early twentieth century, and an analysis of it helps lay the foundation for the adoption of relevant pedagogies for the new millennium. Chapter 2, "Approaches to Teaching and Learning African American History," critically examines approaches to teaching African American history during the twentieth century and suggests relevant strategies for teaching it in the twenty-first century, especially to hip-hop generationers and millennial learners.

Certainly Carter G. Woodson's most famous and widely read book is *The Mis-Education of the Negro* (1933), an open and harsh critique of "highly educated Negroes," the black middle-class, and self-proclaimed black leadership. This diatribe has served as a consciousness-raising manifesto for generations of radical black leaders and counter-normative spokespersons, especially scores of Black Power–era activists and Afrocentric thinkers. A decade ago hip-hop "nation-conscious" emcee and soulful R & B singer Lauryn Hill sampled from Woodson's classic in naming her debut and Grammy Award–winning album *The Miseducation of Lauryn Hill* (1998). Though not as influential as *The Mis-Education of the Negro,* Woodson's "lost-now-found" manuscript, "The Case of the Negro," is an important document of early twentieth-century African American intellectual history. While providing a revealing window into Woodson's expressions of early radical thought and rhetoric, it also helps us better understand the wide spectrum of black scholars' interpretations of blacks' post–World War I status and a changing American society during the early 1920s. This newly discovered collection of essays clearly places Woodson within a trajectory of black intellectual radicalism or black radical thought. In chapter 3, "*Carter G. Woodson's Appeal,* Black History, and Black Radical Thought," I specifically discuss "The Case of the Negro" as a precursor to *The Mis-Education of the Negro;* as an expression of Woodson's early radicalism; as an optimistic, black-pride-inspiring byproduct of the dawning of the Harlem renaissance; and as a part of the vindicationist tradition of African American intellectual thought or "heretical" black radical thought.

The history of black women historians from the era of segregation until the post–Black Power era constitutes a dynamic narrative, challenging us to revisit the lives, works, and ideas of lesser-known black women scholars; reconceptualize conventional definitions of what makes one a historian; and rediscover valuable historical insights. While fewer than a dozen African American women earned doctorates in history prior to the mid-1950s, many black women published historical scholarship and engaged in the historian's craft before the modern civil rights movement. The first formal organization for profession black women historians, the Association of Black Women Historians, Inc. (ABWH), was founded in 1979, thus marking the beginning of a significant phase in the black female historical enterprise. Beginning in the 1980s, black women historians and the field of black women's history made enormous strides. As Deborah Gray White pronounces in *Telling Histories: Black Women Historians in the Ivory Tower* (2008), today's leading black women historians are the "spiritual descendants" of pioneering black women writers of history who operated during the era of Jim Crow segregation. Chapter 4, "'Ample proof of this may be found': Early Black Women Historians," unearths the unique history of a diverse group of black women historians, professional and self-taught, from the 1890s through the modern civil rights movement and a bit beyond. In centering the lives, scholarship, and philosophies of African American women, we gain a clearer, more nuanced and complex view of the African American historical profession.

Chapter 5, "'Shadow vs. Substance': Deconstructing Booker T. Washington," critically explores significant scholarship on Booker T. Washington published since the beginning of the twentieth century. Washington, black America's first celebrity spokesperson, was perhaps the most powerful, influential, and controversial black leader of the Progressive era and twentieth century. References to Washington flourish in today's African American political and social commentaries, almost always within the context of black conservatism. Our contemporary views of Washington have been molded by one hundred years of writings, scholarly and polemic. The historiography on Washington is vast, can be subdivided and analyzed in several ways, and is characterized by debates concerning the role of black leadership. Chapter 5 looks at both the chronological and thematic evolution of Washington historiography, explores overarching ways in which we have been encouraged to view Washington, and offers the beginnings of a framework with which historians can assess and further problematize Washington and teach "millennials"—today's college and university students—about his role as a black leader. A detailed analysis of the scholarship on Washington showcases the various processes involved in how scholars have fashioned ideas in African American history. In many ways, what historians have written about Washington tells us as much about their own generation as about Washington himself. Deciphering Washington's "shadow" and the "substance" of his leadership and celebrity continues to challenge and polarize scholars and black intellectuals.

Chapter 6, "Genocide and African American History," explores the benefits of using genocide as a window into the black historical experience by delving into the relationship between genocide and African American history. After Jewish lawyer Raphael Lemkin coined the term "genocide" in 1944, this loaded word has been adopted to describe actions that result, "in whole or in part," in the "destruction of a nation or an ethnic group." The 1948 Convention on the Prevention and Punishment of the Crime of Genocide attempted to define the term further and sparked debates among a small group of scholars through the 1970s. During the 1980s, genocide studies emerged, and by the 1990s this sub-field underwent significant transformations and growth. While the experiences of various groups of continental Africans have been analyzed in terms of genocide, scholars have not extensively explored notions of genocide within the context of African American history. The African American experience can be productively analyzed through the lens of genocide studies. This chapter unravels the ideas, social activism, and struggles of those African Americans—William L. Patterson and the Civil Rights Congress, Malcolm X, the Nation of Islam, numerous Black Power activists, the National Committee of Black Churchmen, the National Committee to Petition the United Nations, the Black Panther Party, Afrocentric scholar-activists, and most recently the National Black United Front—who have boldly challenged the United States government and American culture and society for committing genocide against African Americans. Drawing from the ideas of leading black conspiracy-theory scholars and genocide studies scholars, chapter 6 also reveals the dehumanizing historical injustices perpetuated against blacks, incidents that have historically conjured up notions of genocide within African American communities and popular culture, such as the slave trade, slavery, segregation, lynching, the Tuskegee Syphilis Experiment, birth control, and sterilization experiments.

African American History Reconsidered seeks to broaden our knowledge about how we understand and conceptualize what African American history meant to previous generations of African American historians, scholars, activists, youth, and working-class people; to interpret what African American history represents in the present and can encompass in the future; and ultimately to contribute solidly to the comprehensive yet undertheorized field of black intellectual history. During the civil rights and Black Power movements, historians created "Negro Thought" scholarship by expanding upon and further problematizing earlier categorizations of and musings on the worldviews of diverse groups of black thinkers and leaders. While they analyzed and subdivided black thinkers' approaches, they really did not define the field of historical inquiry that they were engaged in. In 1996, the *Journal of Negro History,* now the *Journal of African American History,* published a volume titled "Vindicating the Race: Contributions to African American Intellectual History" devoted to the "race vindication strategies" of many significant, once overlooked African American intellectuals. Editor

V. P. Franklin defined African American intellectual history as "an ongoing and systematic analysis of the contributions . . . of members of the African-American intelligentsia to telling the truth about the history and contributions of peoples of African descent in the United States and throughout the world." In the mid-1990s, Franklin asserted that this historical endeavor was in its "beginnings."[31] Similarly and during the same period, John Hope Franklin concluded that what was lacking in African American history was "any critical examination of what the group—historians, novelists, theologians, sociologists, psychologists, and others—were thinking and saying." Franklin added: "As far as I know there has been no . . . comprehensive, overall history of African American intellectuals."[32] More recently, in 2004, Wilson Jeremiah Wilson offered a thought-provoking definition of black intellectual history. "It is the task of the historian to discover the processes by which thinkers seek to reconcile or, some would say, to rationalize their own contradictions. This work is tacitly, or expressly, concerned throughout with identifying such attempts at reconciliation. Obviously, written in this context, 'contradiction' is not a term of opprobrium; in fact the term 'contradiction' need not imply any value judgment at all—except the value judgment implicit in my acknowledgement that the thinking of a given author contains sufficient tension or friction to generate life-giving struggle and to awaken my interest."[33]

This book unravels and analyzes the ideas of numerous well-known and lesser-known mainly twentieth-century black intellectuals. In exploring these thinkers' ideas, this study strives to contribute to African American intellectual history and suggests that the broad subject of African American history, its historians, historiography, philosophy, epistemology, and future, merits more attention and scrutiny in U.S. academic and popular culture.

1. Conceptualizing Black History, 1903–2006

In an unpublished essay written in the late 1970s, Harold Cruse acknowledged many of John Hope Franklin's contributions to U.S. and African American history, but he surmised that "the student looking for the 'seminal ideas,' the challenge of unique 'interpretations,' or anything resembling the unorthodox in the philosophy of history would be hard-put to find such intellectual qualities in Franklin's body of work."[1] Cruse apparently overlooked, ignored, or underestimated the value of several thought-provoking essays that Franklin published during the 1940s, 1950s, and 1960s that addressed the deeper philosophical underpinnings of black history and history in general. However, Cruse's observations did highlight a significant void in African American historiography that existed and still does. Using the scholarly record of one of the most widely recognized black historians of the 1970s as a point of departure, Cruse argued that the philosophy of black history—the study of the broader, fundamental meanings, purpose, functions, and characteristics of the African American historical experience and black history as a discipline—constituted an under-theorized area of black historical inquiry. From the late 1950s through the early 1970s, Earl E. Thorpe and many of his predecessors and contemporaries, as well as numerous black historians who came of age after the civil rights and Black Power eras, posited intriguing philosophical definitions of black history. Thorpe remains one of the pioneering and most important theorists of black history as a philosophy, discipline, and scholarly enterprise. His monographs on black history and historians are still essential starting points for exploring the scholarship on the black historical profession and black intellectuals in more general terms. Yet, before releasing his classic *Negro Historians in the United States* (1958), in 1956 and 1957 Thorpe published four articles in the *Quarterly Review of Higher Education among Negroes* that did not explicitly consider black history and instead focused more on conceptualizing and complicating the philosophy of history from Eurocentric intellectual frameworks.

In 1971, Thorpe observed that "no effort has been made to evaluate the basic ideas which have produced and inspired black historiography or even to define black history."[2] Though Thorpe may have exaggerated his claim— and since the 1980s more than a few important studies have been published on numerous innovative black historians and the black historical enterprise in general—to date, groups of black historians have not devoted complete books to defining and theorizing history as a philosophy. On the other hand, for generations of white American and European historians, the philosophy of history has been and is an established subfield. In African American history, for instance, there is no equivalent to Edward Hallett Carr's provocative *What is History?* (1961). This, of course, does not mean that black historians have not introspectively and intellectually invested in creating philosophies of black history. African American historians from each of the at least five stages of the African American historical profession have indeed developed distinct philosophies of black history. At the same time, they have not devoted extensive scholarship to critically addressing the abstract dialogues that often characterize the philosophy of history.

How do we explain this apparent void in African American historiography? Before and since the mainstream professionalization of black history and the black historical enterprise during the 1960s and 1970s, historians of the African American experience have been most concerned with establishing a black historical record, creating a discipline and with it new interpretive models, and essentially making new historical discoveries. However divergent in their approaches, politics, and worldviews, from the antebellum era through the Black Power era, even if they did not extensively theorize the deeper meanings of their people's past, the vast majority of black historians tended to define and enlist black history as a corrective supplement to mainstream U.S. history, a fundamental component of black consciousness and identity formation, and as an important element of African Americans' struggles for liberation, equality, and human rights. Since the antebellum era, generations of chroniclers and interpreters of the black historical experience have also embraced "contributionism," an ideology that recognizes and contextualizes African Americans' contributions to American history, especially in economic, cultural, and political realms. As Earl Ofari Hutchinson first proclaimed in a 1999 *San Francisco Chronicle* article calling for a critical reassessment of Black History Month (and reiterated in an online essay in February 2009), "Black contributions to society should be celebrated every month. . . . When the experience of blacks is accepted as central to the American story, black history will be what it always should have been—American history."[3] The post–civil rights era legitimization of African American history in the mainstream academy and of the black studies movement has opened the door for more than a few alternative (or resistant) narratives of American history.

Since the 1960s and 1970s, when black history supposedly became mainstreamed in the estimation of many historians, it seems as if black historians assumed that they all agreed upon what black history meant or, less likely, that philosophically defining black history was unimportant. The lack of philosophical treatises on black history also suggests that black historians have been preoccupied with researching historical events, leaders, periods, groups, and themes. Others, especially during the Black Power era, were perhaps more concerned with engaging in more practical endeavors. Whatever the case may be, discussions of black history in basic and abstract philosophical terms are long overdue. Scattered throughout African American historiography in the prefaces, introductions, and conclusions of their monographs as well as in important essays and articles, many black historians, intellectuals, and leaders have conceptualized African American history in provocative philosophical terms. During the twentieth century, dozens of professionally and nonprofessionally trained black historians, as well as a few white historians, have offered some intriguing definitions of black history.

This chapter brings together this collection of ideas and chronologically documents, dissects, analyzes, and compares and contrasts how many different generations of historians, as well as intellectuals who have occasionally attempted to practice the historian's craft, have philosophically conceptualized black history from the dawning of the twentieth century until the first years of the new millennium. In selecting whose ideas to showcase, I have decided to draw from those thinkers, most often professional black historians, who explicitly attempted to grapple with the question *What is black history?* It is beyond the scope of this chapter to detail and cite every scholar's description of black history. Instead, I focus on those scholars who have offered thought-provoking musings about what black history constitutes. Cognizant of the fact that professionally trained scholars who are not historians have offered insightful perceptions of black history, I have opted to concentrate on how professionally trained historians have defined the philosophy of their discipline.

Early Definitions of Black History

Though a significant group of self-taught, amateur black historians published influential narratives of the African American historical experience during the eighteenth and nineteenth centuries, in *The Souls of Black Folk* (1903)

W. E. B. Du Bois posited some of the earliest concrete definitions of black history. According to Manning Marable, "*Souls* was to the black American petit bourgeoisie . . . a framework for understanding history. It was a philosophical statement establishing group identity and social location with an unequal society, and also an appeal for collective action and resistance to oppression and exploitation." Marable declared, "It is no exaggeration to say that *The Souls of Black Folk* has remained the most influential text about the African-American experience for a century."[4] Before Du Bois earned his doctorate in history from Harvard University in 1895, between 1836 and the 1880s Robert Benjamin Lewis, James W. C. Pennington, William Cooper Nell, Martin R. Delany, James Theodore Holly, William Wells Brown, William Still, Joseph T. Wilson, George Washington Williams, and other black intellectuals were primarily concerned with challenging the prevailing notion that blacks had no history, a foundational justification for early U.S. racism. These early amateur black historians' cause was to create a black historical record that highlighted their people's contributions to U.S. culture. Critically theorizing black history was, simply put, beyond the scope of and impractical for black historians writing during the antebellum era, Reconstruction, and the early years of "the nadir."[5]

From the immediate aftermath of World War I through the 1950s, Carter G. Woodson, his protégés and co-workers, John Hope Franklin, whose various definitions of black history reflected his own intellectual growth, and Earl E. Thorpe, the father of black historians' history, contributed most to concretely conceptualizing black history. During the 1960s and 1970s, some of Woodson's disciples, by this time seasoned historians, continued to theorize black history. Ideologically influenced by Malcolm X, a new school of black cultural nationalist historians explicitly linked black history to Black Power ideologies. Since the legitimization of black history in the mainstream U.S. academy and during the 1980s—a pivotal decade in defining black history at one level symbolized by Lerone Bennett Jr.'s visions—a noticeable body of scholarship has critically and creatively defined black history. By the 1990s, black women's history institution builder Darlene Clark Hine effectively publicized a philosophy of black history that centered the experiences of black women. In the twenty-first century, Manning Marable has offered an especially insightful and relevant interpretation of what black history means and can become.

The first professionally trained black historian, W. E. B. Du Bois, theorized black history in a variety of ways that both further refined the ideas of amateur African American historians in the antebellum era and also influenced black historians who came of age after him. An ideological forerunner of the modern black studies movement, Du Bois injected historical analyses into his scholarship to explain the contemporary status of black America. This is exemplified in *The Philadelphia Negro* (1899). In his famous *The Souls of Black Folk* (1903), Du Bois articulated his widely cited and frequently manipulated "double-consciousness" theory. He reasoned that African Americans possessed a sense of "two-ness—an American, a Negro; two souls, two thoughts, two unreconciled strivings; two warring ideals in one dark body, whose dogged strength alone keeps it from being torn asunder." In defining black history, Du Bois emphasized this sense of black America's cultural duality. "The history of the American Negro," he noted, "is the history of this strife,— this longing to attain self-conscious manhood, to merge his double self into a better and truer self. In this merging he wishes neither of the older selves to be lost."[6]

Du Bois highlighted that African American history was a combination of African, African American, and American cultural elements and experiences and that blacks' Africanity shaped multiple dimensions of American life and history. He stressed that it was around black people that "the history of the land has centered for thrice a hundred years." Abandoning the objectivity exhibited in *The Suppression of the African Slave-Trade to the United States of America, 1638–1870* (1896), *The Philadelphia Negro* (1899), and his early Atlanta University studies, in *The Souls of Black Folk* Du Bois passionately celebrated the contributions of blacks to U.S. history:

> Actively we have woven ourselves with the very warp and woof of this nation,—we fought their battles, shared their sorrow, mingled our blood with theirs, and generation after generation have pleaded with a headstrong, careless people to despise not Justice, Mercy, and Truth, lest the nation be smitten with a curse. Our song, our toil, our cheer, and warning have been given to this nation in blood-brotherhood. Are not these gifts worth the giving? Is not this work and striving? *Would America have been America without her Negro people?*[7]

At the dawning of the twentieth century when Du Bois wrote "Of Our Spiritual Strivings," he was a cultural pluralist who envisioned an American society in which the African American would be a "co-worker in the kingdom of culture."[8] He viewed black history as representing a struggle for human rights, American citizenship, cultural recognition, and integration. When *The Souls of Black Folk* was published, the vast majority of African Americans had been "free" for only thirty-eight years. Thus, black history for Du Bois in 1903 was largely characterized by slavery, failed attempts at reconstructing U.S. race relations, a denial of basic civil rights, and overall struggle. For Du Bois, in American history, "the shadow of a deep disappointment rests upon the Negro people," in turn making it "doubly difficult to write of this period calmly."[9] In *The Souls of Black Folk,* Du Bois shared his view of the tragic side of black history. "Throughout history," he noted, "the powers of single black men flash here and there like falling stars, and die sometimes before the world has rightly gauged their brightness."[10] Du Bois's view of black history in *The Souls of Black Folk* is multilayered. He celebrated the beauty, perseverance, and influence of black culture; critiqued the openly anti-black nature of U.S. culture; showcased America's black heritage; and perceived black history as representing a dynamic interaction between African, American, and African American cultures.

Though he articulated and publicized his visions of the psychologically pragmatic and revisionist functions of black history throughout his career, Carter G. Woodson did not devote a great deal of his scholarship to directly defining black history in abstract and philosophical terms, and Du Bois was especially critical of Woodson for this. While he dubbed Woodson's *The Education of the Negro Prior to 1861* "the most significant book concerning the Negro race" published in 1915, he was outspoken in his October 1922 critique (published in *The Freeman*) of Woodson's *History of the Negro Church.* "Mr. Woodson is a monographist of the strict Harvard dryasdust school" who "has collected and carefully catalogued and pigeon-holed an enormous number of facts concerning American Negro history." Du Bois proclaimed that Woodson lacked knowledge of the deeper complexities and meanings of the black church and religion. "Of all this," Du Bois pronounced, "Mr. Woodson not only says nothing but understands nothing." Du Bois concluded his review: "Mr. Woodson's services as a fact-finder are invaluable. But let us call his findings fact, source-stuff, raw material, and not history." In essence, Du Bois wanted Woodson to probe more creatively into the complexity of the black church, delving into the unrecorded "inner spirit and motive of that marvelous faith and unreason which made a million black folk on the shores of exile dance and scream and shout the Sorrow Song."[11]

Despite Woodson's tendency to publish histories of "well-authenticated truths," in a 1928 pamphlet on Negro History Week he expanded upon many conventional ideas of history and briefly defined history. Woodson argued that "there is no such thing as Negro history . . . in the sense of isolated contributions." He proposed that all peoples in the United States contributed significantly to the nation's development. "History, then, is a record of the progress of mankind rather than of racial or national achievement," Woodson noted.[12] He was opposed to history as "the record of the successes and disappointments of those who engage in contentions for power" and as a "register of the crimes and misfortunes of mankind."[13] While he shared many of Du

Bois's sentiments, Woodson did not characterize black history in the manner that Du Bois did in *The Souls of Black Folk*. Woodson's view of history was fundamentally pragmatic and directly connected to the present.

Woodson emphasized that history was a necessary ingredient to a people's self-knowledge and collective identity. One of his most famous sayings, shared by Marcus Garvey and appreciated by many Black Power activists, was: "If a race has no history, if it has no worth-while tradition, it becomes a negligible factor in the thought of the world, and it stands in danger of being exterminated."[14] Woodson perceived black history as being an essential part of American history. In a 1927 Negro History Week circular, he asserted that "we should emphasize not Negro History, but the Negro in history. What we need is not a history of selected races or nations, but the history of the world void of national bias, race hate, and religious prejudice. There should be no indulgence in undue eulogy of the Negro. The case of the Negro is well taken care of when it is shown how he has influenced the development of civilization."[15]

Woodson routinely stressed that the purpose of black history was not to focus on how blacks had been victimized, but instead was to demonstrate how blacks influenced U.S. and world history. Woodson shared black American, white American, and European nineteenth-century historians' "fetishism of facts."[16] In promoting black history, Woodson argued that "the aim has been to emphasize important facts in the belief that facts properly set forth will speak for themselves."[17] As it was for Du Bois, black history for Woodson was American history; the two were inseparable. This idea has been long lasting, gaining prominence in the 1980s with historians like Nathan Huggins, who advocated "a new synthesis, a new American history." For Huggins, U.S. history "cannot be told as a story of black history and white history." He argued: "It must be told as one. While that idea is simple enough—a truism indeed—too few of us accept the radical implications of it. We do not put it into our thinking, our writing, our courses. That idea, nevertheless, is a key to any new, successful narrative of American history."[18]

Throughout the pages of the *Negro History Bulletin* during the late 1930s and the 1940s, Woodson articulated his vision of how history could serve mankind. Although he wrote many polemics, Woodson never really altered his fundamental belief that history entailed the objective chronicling of the "facts." While he certainly did emphasize black achievements and at times employed history as some form of propaganda, he insisted to *Bulletin* readers that "real history requires the elimination of self. . . . Facts properly set forth will tell their own story."[19]

During Woodson's times, a few of his protégés and coworkers offered philosophical inquiries into what black history constituted. In the widely read *The New Negro* (1925), for example, pioneering black bibliophile Arthur A. Schomburg shared Woodson's sentiments and defined black history as being functional to black peoples' struggle to recover from the detrimental effects of slavery. "The American Negro must remake his past in order to make his future," Schomburg asserted, "History must restore what slavery took away, for it is the social damage of slavery that the present generations must repair and offset." Schomburg argued that black history was revisionist in nature, a record that challenged Americans to rewrite "many important paragraphs of our common American history."[20]

During the peak of the Great Depression, in a 1935 essay titled "The Reconstruction of History," historian and Woodson disciple Charles Wesley explored conceptualizations of history from the writings of Herodotus through the early 1900s. Wesley defined history as "the study of the development of men and things throughout the ages." Echoing Woodson, he maintained that history needed to be all encompassing, acknowledging the contributions of all people throughout the world. "History is not the study of men and women of one race or color and the neglect and omission of the men and women of another race or color. It is neither the glorification of white people nor black people, but it is the story of the people irrespective of race or color. It should deal with people in all times and places and should present the contributions of all the people to civilization," Wesley concluded, "When a part of a people has been neglected or given subordinate places, history in order to be truthful must be reconstructed."[21] At the same time, foreshadowing modern Afrocentric thinkers' pleas, he called for the writing of history to be reconstructed to place Africa at the center and to give African Americans a central place in world history as agents of their own destiny.

Several years after Wesley's article appeared, L. D. Reddick published an important essay in the *Journal of Negro History* that assessed the collective scholarly endeavors of generations of black historians whom he subdivided into "two divisions, *before* Woodson and *after* Woodson." In essence, Reddick called upon black historians to embrace a more complex "social philosophy" of black history. He unapologetically critiqued black historians for their narrow foci, "traditional" approaches, preoccupation with slavery, overarching "liberalism," amateurism, simplicity, and superficial analyses. He beseeched his colleagues to abandon the naïveté of the early chroniclers of black history and to adopt more nuanced and wide-reaching interpretations of the black experience. He defined "Negro history" as having a distinct "purpose which is built upon a faith" and argued that the writing of history had never really been totally objective. He agreed with Croce that history was "contemporary thought about the past."[22]

Reddick defined the purpose of black history as being threefold: "to discover and record the role of African peoples in world as well as in the more restricted histories-as-actuality," to educate "a majority population" about blacks' historical contributions, and to instill within blacks race pride. For Reddick, black history not only sought to contribute to the growth of knowledge, but it was a byproduct of the black scholar's attempts to highlight blacks' roles in "human achievement." Like others before him, Reddick acknowledged the relationship between the past, present, and future, noting that "the whole movement is an evidence of the emerging self-consciousness of a minority group and is, in part, its view of the present, even future, in the light of the statement of the past." In 1937 Reddick envisioned black history in a modern manner that Robin D. G. Kelley would later postulate with his theory of "Black history from way, way below."[23]

> We are concerned, at least we should be, that those writing today, especially the younger men, shall not fall into the errors of their literary fathers. Since point-of-view is inescapable, it is, therefore, essential that the frame of reference should be large, generous, and socially intelligent; that the development of Negro life be seen in connection with those of the general pattern, of other racial, minority and laboring groups. Even in observing the black men themselves, the historian may become more penetrating if he turns away a little more from the articulate professional classes to the welfare, feelings and thoughts of the common folk—the domestic servants, the tenant farmers, the dark men on the city streets.[24]

In his controversial essay "'Social Determination' in the Writings of Negro Scholars" (1944), William T. Fontaine directly critiqued how Reddick and other black historians envisioned, in his estimation, the purpose of black history. Fontaine was equally critical of other leading black scholars active during the early 1930s and through the early 1940s, especially E. Franklin Frazier and Ernest E. Just. According to Fontaine, the thought and actions of professionally trained black scholars "have become interwoven with 'defense mechanisms,'" and the "knowledge of the Negro scholar, in the larger number of cases, is a counterknowledge propagated from an immediate 'defense' perspective, it is a particularized knowledge reflecting the angle of vision from which it has been generated." Fontaine called upon black scholars to recognize how "existential factors" in U.S. race relations affected their scholarship, to critically engage the mentality of the "opposite group," and to recognize that in creating their knowledge they embrace an "interchange of attitudes" with white scholarly publics.[25]

Fontaine argued that leading black historians, including Woodson, Du Bois, Wesley, and Reddick, embraced as a priority an environmentalist perspective and philosophy of history that "enables ascription of the shortcomings of Negroes to external handicaps" and "counterattacks the arguments of those who point to innate incapacity." While he did not explicitly outline his own philosophy of history, he did applaud Reddick's "criticism of the Negro historian" and poignantly highlighted the limitations of bodies of knowledge like history. "All knowledge," he observed, "contains a measure of perspective. Every generation is limited, first, by the necessarily incomplete development of knowledge up to that time; second, by the plastic nature of mind itself; and, third, by the inseparable connection of feelings, emotions, moods, interests, and beliefs with the so-called purely logical processes of thought. In the activity of knowing, no pure reason or transcendental self remains poised in passionless objectivity while recording an external world in itself." Though not active in the community of professional African American historians, philosopher Fontaine was a unique black scholar of his era in that he questioned the widely accepted practice and strategy of conscripting scholarship in the battle for black advancement and the notion of "black history as a weapon in the fight for racial equality."[26]

Definitions of Black History: World War II through the Black Power Era

In the early 1940s, novelist Richard Wright described black history in a manner that would have certainly troubled Fontaine. In his *12 Million Voices*, Wright defined black history by comparing it to whites' historical experiences and by highlighting the elements of struggle in the African American past. "The many historical phases which whites have traversed voluntarily and gradually during the course of Western civilization we black folk have traversed through swift compulsion," Wright proclaimed. "Brutal, bloody, crowded with suffering and abrupt transitions, the lives of us black folk represent the most magical and meaningful picture of human experience in the Western world. . . . We black folk, our history and our present being, are a mirror of all the manifold experiences of America. . . . If America has forgotten her past, then let her look into the mirror of our consciousness . . . for our memories go back."[27] Wright's radical tone resembled that which characterized many black cultural nationalists' writings during the Black Power era. Unbound by the sometimes restricting mores, standards, and quest for objectivity of the U.S. historical profession, Wright's characterization of black history was very emotional, African American centered, and militant in tone when compared with John Hope Franklin's notion of black history as expressed years later in his 1947 classic *From Slavery to Freedom: A History of Negro Americans.* However, several years earlier in 1944, the same year that Fontaine's critique of black historians and historiography appeared, Franklin did publish a passionate essay in *Phylon,* "History—Weapon of War and Peace," in which he sought to answer the long debated question "What *is* the field and function of history?"

In the midst of World War II, Franklin argued that it was an ideal time "to find some specific function for the historical process in the shaping of human destiny." Franklin was disturbed by the fact that throughout the world, history had been used as a "weapon in waging war" and in the promotion of nationalism and notions of racial superiority. He offered his own ideal notion of how history should function. He called upon students of history to use the field as a "constructive" force. "As a social discipline," Franklin reflected, "the historical process should be forged into a mighty weapon for the preservation of peace." He believed that "the study of history demands the use of our best developed faculties of fairness and impartiality," that history should be ideally written with "dispassion, impartiality, and cautious judgment," that it needed to be "the truth, the whole truth," and that in post–World War II America, history could be used as an essential tool of social reform, as "a means of guiding man toward a better life."[28] Franklin advocated an objective philosophy of history that would remain consistent during the remainder of this career.

Franklin was explicit about this approach in his important 1948 essay in the *Journal of Negro Education,* "Whither Reconstruction Historiography?" Franklin surmised: "Every serious historian seeks to re-create the period in which he writes. He must be conscious, however, of the complexity of any event or set of circumstances and of the danger of focusing attention on certain events to the exclusion of others that might have some significant bearing. . . . There is, moreover, a grave danger of the author's injecting his point of view or of mis-constructing the period when he is not satisfied with permitting the characters to speak for themselves and feels called upon to explain and, perhaps, to extend their feelings." Franklin underscored, "Not only should the historian's conclusions be based on adequate and reliable evidence, but they should also reflect a judiciousness in keeping with the temperament of one disciplined in objectivity and preciseness."[29] At the same time, in a few instances he did argue that history should be used to help reform American thought and behavior, and though he did not mention black history by name in his 1944 *Phylon* essay, his conception of history could have very easily been applied to black history.

Franklin defined black history by paying close attention to its symbiotic relationship with U.S. history in general. As he articulated in *From Slavery to Freedom,* he believed that black history needed to acknowledge the "discreet balance between recognizing the deeds of outstanding persons and depicting the fortunes of the great mass of Negroes." Franklin added that "the history of the Negro in America is essentially the story of strivings of the nameless millions who have sought adjustment in a new and sometimes hostile world." Because he was seeking to integrate black history into mainstream U.S. historical discourse, Franklin did not dwell upon the tragedies of black history; instead, he highlighted African Americans' efforts to "accommodate . . . to the dominant culture."[30]

In the early 1950s, Herbert Aptheker published *A Documentary History of the Negro People in the United States* in two volumes, one of the most important collections of primary sources of black history for those scholars coming of age during the civil rights and Black Power eras. Aptheker is one of the few white historians to offer concrete definitions of black history. During the late 1930s and early 1940s, Aptheker published several pamphlets on black resistance from the antebellum era through the Civil War. He celebrated blacks' "deeds of unsurpassed heroism and titanic efforts." In his pamphlet on slave revolts that laid the foundation for his 1943 classic, *American Negro Slave Revolts,* Aptheker maintained that the history of slavery could be used to help inspire black self-pride as well as interracial unity. He deduced sweeping connections between the past and the present, interpreting black history to suit his goal of uniting blacks and whites:

> American slavery was a barbarous tyranny. . . . Its history, however, is not merely one of impoverishment, deprivation, and oppression. For imbedded in the record of American slavery is the inspiring story of the persistent and courageous efforts of the Negroes (aided, not infrequently, by poor whites) to regain their heritage of liberty and equality, to regain their right to the elemental demands of human beings. . . . An awareness of its history should give the modern Negro added confidence and courage in his heroic present-day battle for complete and perfect equality with all other American citizens. And it should make those other Americans eager and proud to grasp the hand of the Negro and march forward with him against their common oppressors—against those industrial and financial overlords and the plantation oligarchs who today stand in the way of liberty, equality, and prosperity.
>
> That unity between the white and Negro masses was necessary to overthrow nineteenth-century slavery. That same unity is necessary now to defeat twentieth-century slavery—to defeat fascism.[31]

In the late 1940s, Aptheker reiterated his belief in the need to use black history as a tool of liberation. In an article titled "Negro History: Arsenal for Liberation," a Negro History Week tribute in *New Masses,* Aptheker declared that black history was an essential ingredient of U.S. history and that it could "serve as a weapon of incalculable power in our present critical period when each man must stand up and be counted."[32] In reviewing Aptheker's *Toward Negro Freedom* (1956), Benjamin Quarles accurately described Aptheker's perspective of black history: "The most distinguishing mark of Aptheker's writings is their thoroughgoing Marxist orientation. Very much of one opinion, Aptheker sees everything through red-colored glasses. To Aptheker Negro history is of a piece with all human history, which is the 'struggle for freedom against an oppressing class.' In Aptheker's hands Negro history becomes a fill-in for a picture whose delineations have already been outlined by Marx and Engels."[33]

In introducing the first volume of *A Documentary History of the Negro People in the United States,* Aptheker characterized black history as being a history of oppressed yet resilient people. Black history, Aptheker asserted, "demonstrates that no matter what the despoilers of humanity may do— enslave, segregate, torture, lynch—they cannot destroy the people's will to freedom, their urge towards equality, justice and dignity. . . . To work in this history, to see the defiance of slaves, the courage of martyrs, the resistance of the plain people, and to study the great human documents they left behind is a most rewarding experience." As Reddick and Franklin envisioned, Aptheker viewed black history as being the history of how the masses lived. Despite Harold Cruse's openly harsh indictment of his motivations, Aptheker was relatively unique in that he was among the very few white historians who embraced a black nationalist-like interpretation of black history. Harry Washington Greene certainly thought so, including him in his 1948 study *Holders of Doctorates among American Negroes: An Educational Study of Negroes Who Have Earned Doctoral Degrees in Course, 1876–1943.*[34] Similarly, Robin D. G. Kelley, who himself discovered that Aptheker was not black more than several years after first reading *American Negro Slave Revolts* as a high school student, labeled Aptheker an honorary "black historian" based upon his commitment to understanding and overturning racial and economic oppression.[35]

A decade after first publishing *From Slavery to Freedom,* John Hope Franklin expanded upon his conceptualization of black history in an article published in the *Journal of Negro History,* titled "The New Negro History" (1957). Echoing Carl Becker's "Everyman His Own Historian," Franklin argued that "in discussing the history of a people one must distinguish between what has *actually* happened and what those who have written the history have *said* has happened. So far as the *actual* history of the American Negro is concerned, there is nothing particularly new about it. It is an exciting story, a remarkable history. It is the story of slavery and freedom, humanity and inhumanity, democracy and its denial. It is tragedy and triumph, suffering and compassion, sadness and joy."[36] In this article, Franklin acknowledged the element of struggle characterizing black history. Franklin suggested that the *interpretation* of what actually occurred in black history must be explored side by side with what actually *happened,* especially since the actualities of black history had been so much distorted in order to justify the subordination of African Americans. The overall tone of Franklin's article is optimistic. Writing during the modern civil rights movement, Franklin was perhaps hopeful about the growth of black history, commenting that there was a "striking resemblance" between what historians wrote about black history and the history that "actually happened."[37]

In 1958 historian Earl E. Thorpe published the first major study on the black historical enterprise, *Negro Historians in the United States,* in which he briefly defined black history as "not simply a biography of great men and the chronicling of noble achievements," but as "a record, viewed in the light of conditioning circumstances, of the race's achievements and failures, dreams and lack of dreams." Thorpe added that "Negro history is largely social history. And running throughout the dark gloomy picture which it usually depicts is a small note of optimism, of faith in a coming new day."[38] By labeling black history social history, as did Reddick and Aptheker, Thorpe argued that it was largely the history of the black working class and masses.

Scholars' definitions of black history were certainly influenced by the escalation of the modern civil rights movement. In the early 1960s, for instance, Samuel Du Bois Cook contended that black history, its "grim and grinding realities," could be best understood within a "framework of tragedy." Cook argued that "the tragic conception of Negro history" is "an interpretation which seeks to grasp the full dimensions and naked depths of the systematic, persistent, and institutionalized negation of the Negro's meanings and values on grounds of ethical desirability and necessity." Cook claimed that blacks, especially during the era of slavery, were creatures and objects "of action," not participants, that they were excluded from the "historical process." He downplayed and even ignored black agency and implied that black history was characterized by victimhood and victimization. When viewed in the context of how most blacks characterized black history, Cook's approach was refreshing. Perhaps Cook highlighted the "tragic dimension" of black history because so many of his predecessors had portrayed a much more optimistic, less harsh version of black history in hopes of integrating blacks into white America. He argued that the "tragic conception of Negro history" had three main virtues: it helped blacks better understand their contemporary struggles, it helped them appreciate the achievements of blacks in the past, and it could help blacks better understand their status in U.S. history.[39]

Perhaps more than any other scholarly discipline, history became an important tool of psychological and cultural empowerment and liberation for young black activists during the Black Power era. Black Power movement historian William Van Deburg has suggested that black intellectuals coming of age between 1965 and 1975, especially poets, playwrights, musicians, and novelists, used black history as a "wellspring of group strength and staying power" that could help them create "the black nation" in the future. Malcolm X, "archetype, reference point, and spiritual advisor in absentia" for Black Power activists, believed adamantly that history was central to the black struggle.[40] The son of a Garveyite, Malcolm X rediscovered the power of history while imprisoned in the Norfolk Prison Colony in Massachusetts. Black history was an essential ingredient to his transformation from a convicted criminal to a conscious critical thinker. While in prison he studied history "intensively," reading the historical scholarship of Du Bois, Woodson, and J. A. Rogers, among others.[41]

After he was released from prison in 1952, Malcolm incorporated history into his ideology and program. While he was the minister of the very popular and important Nation of Islam Temple Number 7 in Harlem, New York (also known as the Muhammad Temple of Islam and Muhammad's Mosque No. 7), Malcolm routinely lectured to his followers about the importance of black history. In a speech during the early 1960s, "Black Man's History," he envisioned history as being an important factor in black liberation.

> The honorable Elijah Muhammad teaches us that of all the things that the black man, or any man for that matter, can study, history is best qualified to reward all research. You have to have a knowledge of history no matter what you are going to do; anything that you undertake you have to have a knowledge of history in order to be successful in it. The thing that has made the so-called Negro in America fail, more than any other thing, is your, my, lack of knowledge concerning history. We know less about history than anything else. . . .We have . . . experts in every field, but seldom can you find one among us who is an expert on the history of the black man. And because of his lack of knowledge concerning the history of the black man, no matter how much he excels in other sciences, he's always confined, he's always neglected to the same low rung of the ladder that the dumbest of our people are relegated to. And all of this stems from his lack of knowledge concerning history.[42]

Malcolm maintained his respect for and faith in black history after he split from Elijah Muhammad and the Nation of Islam. In a speech to members of the Organization of Afro-American Unity in January 1965, Malcolm argued that blacks lacked knowledge of their history, which contributed directly to their oppression. Like others before him, he defined black history in direct relation to the present. "When you deal with the past, you're dealing with history, you're dealing actually with the origin of a thing. When you know the origin, you know the cause. If you don't know the cause, you don't know the reason, you're just cut off, you're left standing in mid-air," Malcolm continued to break down history in laymen's terms to his followers, "It is so important for you and me to spend time today learning something about the past so that we can better understand the present, analyze it, and then do something about it."[43] For Malcolm, ever since he had become a member of the Nation of Islam, black history had to be, above all else, practical and aid in the psychological black struggle for liberation. Perhaps more than any other leader, after his death Malcolm shaped the worldviews of black activists during the Black Power era. He became "a Black Power paradigm," "the embodiment of a timeless black rage."[44]

Many black historians echoed Malcolm's tone during the Black Power era, defining black history in direct relationship with the struggle for black liberation and cultural autonomy. Seasoned professional black historians like Benjamin Quarles and John Hope Franklin who had established themselves as objective historians published essays in which they adopted more passionate and emotional tones that resonated with a more popular and militant black clientele. Black nationalist scholars John Henrik Clarke and Harold Cruse continued to advocate philosophies of black history closely linked with a desire to liberate black Americans and aid in the struggle of nation building. The younger generation of budding black historians during the late 1960s and early 1970s, such as Vincent Harding and Sterling Stuckey, articulated Malcolm's ideas in more scholarly terms. *Negro Digest,* published from 1942 until 1950 and from 1962 until 1969, and then from 1970 until 1976 as *Black World,* served as an important outlet for black historians to share their philosophies of black history. Beginning in the 1960s, *Negro Digest* routinely published an "annual history issue." The magazine's motto, "Knowledge is the Key to a Better Tomorrow," reflected the pragmatic vision of black history articulated by Woodson and his Black Power era protégés.

In February 1966, John Hope Franklin offered some philosophical thoughts on the meaning of history to *Negro Digest* readers. He stressed that history was not static and unchanging and that each generation wrote history based on their distinct realities. He believed that how a people approached their past reflected "the way it will approach the future." Franklin suggested that black history was the product of historians who were molded by various historical experiences. "The changes that each generation experiences provide new ways of looking at the past," Franklin said, cognizant of the pivotal social transformations ushered in during the 1960s. "Nothing better illustrates the way that experience guides the writing of history than the manner in which the history of the Negro has been viewed and written."[45]

Echoing Franklin and Malcolm, Harold Cruse suggested in *The Crisis of the Negro Intellectual* (1967) that black activists, creative artists, and intellectuals of the civil rights and Black Power eras failed to critically study the thoughts, actions, successes, and failures of their early-twentieth-century predecessors, especially those active during "the nadir" and the Harlem renaissance, in order to construct new historically grounded ideologies and programs. Cruse repeatedly chastised those blacks coming of age in the 1960s as being "anti-historical," for failing to "see the historical connections." He defined black history in several instances. Cruse reiterated Du Bois, Ralph Bunche, and others and in the process downplayed the theory of black history as social history in commenting that "American Negro history is basically a history of the conflict between integrationist and nationalist forces in politics, economics, and culture, no matter what leaders are involved and what slogans are used."[46] For Cruse, knowledge of history was essential for blacks coming of age during the Black Power era. "The farther the Negro gets from his historical antecedents in time, the more tenuous become his conceptual ties, the emptier his social conceptions, the more superficial his visions. His one great and present hope is to know and understand his Afro-American history in the United States more profoundly. Failing that, and failing to create a new synthesis and a social theory of action, he will suffer the historical fate described by the philosopher who warned that 'Those who cannot remember the past are condemned to repeat it.'"[47]

Vincent Harding's most noted publication is *There Is a River: The Black Struggle for Freedom in America* (1981). But a decade before this work appeared, he published an essay in *Negro Digest* and a brief pamphlet in which he laid out his early philosophies of black history. Harding opened *Negro Digest*'s 1968 black history issue with an article titled "The Uses of the Afro-American Past." He adamantly supported the early black history movement philosophy that "Any American history that ignores the central role of black people as actors and foils on this maddening stage is a falsified and misleading history." He believed that blacks' knowledge of history was "absolutely indispensable" in helping them place their lives in perspective. In an unapologetic tone that certainly resonated with Black Power era activists, Harding proclaimed that "the Afro-American past must remind black people that we are children of the humiliated and the oppressed, that our fathers were colonized and exploited subjects, and that the ghettos we have recently left are still too often filled with the stench of poverty and despair." Harding called upon blacks to use their history as a social force. He declared that blacks should routinely remember their ancestors and create a future based on how they in their times sacrificed for future generations. Like Woodson, he told blacks that if they forgot and did not live up to the contributions of their ancestors, they would "deserve nothing but the scorn of men and the judgments of the gods."[48]

In his pamphlet *Beyond Chaos: Black History and the Search for the New Land* (1970), Harding proclaimed that black history sought to recognize blacks' contributions to American culture in an objective manner, yet with emotion, "writing history through tears." Harding did not share the optimism of many of his predecessors. Like Samuel Du Bois Cook, he emphasized the more tragic component of black history; yet unlike Cook, he argued that his ancestors' past could be used to help redefine American history. Rejecting notions of "great man" history, Harding avowed that black history focused on "exposure, disclosure, on reinterpretation of the entire American past." Black history in Harding's view was an ideal counter master narrative that could deconstruct American history, suggesting "the American past upon which so much hope has been built never really existed, and probably never will." Harding believed that black history needed to expose the suffering of black people accurately without glossing over the harsh realities. He reasoned that it was time to abandon John Hope Franklin's goal of integrating into American society. Black history, he said, is "the hard and unromantic reading of the experiences of black people in America. It is the groans, the tears, the chains, the songs, the prayers, the institutions." "It is," Harding professed, "a recording of the hope, even if we no longer participate in them. It is seeing not only what we have done, but what has been done to us."[49] Harding the pragmatist insisted that black history be used to expose blacks to the realities that they have encountered and would experience in America.

John Henrik Clarke was a regular contributor to *Negro Digest* and *Black World*. Though intrigued most by African history, he occasionally theorized African American history. In "The Meaning of Black History," Clarke, a student of Arthur Schomburg, viewed African American history as being a key factor in helping blacks rebuild the black community and in instilling pride within black people—a psychological necessity for survival, he reasoned. "To some extent, Black history is a restoration project," Clarke said. "The role of history and the history teacher in this restoration project is to give Black people a sense of pride in their past and memories that they can love and respect. The fulfillment will be in the total restoration of the manhood and nationhood of Black people, wherever they live on earth." Echoing Malcolm X, with whom he worked in Harlem, Clarke maintained that black history revealed to blacks "where they have been where they are and what they still want to be." Black history in Clarke's view was a prerequisite for a healthy black identity. He summoned scholar-activists like himself to research black history and "weld it into an instrument of our liberation."[50]

Nearly three decades ago, Sterling Stuckey authored one of the most critical analyses to date of the role of black historians. He also provided an intriguing definition of black history. During the middle of the Black Power era, Stuckey indicted professionally trained black historians and scholars for not producing innovative scholarship that, in his mind, adequately challenged racist historiography while embracing an African American–centered approach. In his classic essay "Through the Prism of Folklore," Stuckey argued that folklore was an essential source for reconstructing the history of slavery from the perspective of the slaves themselves. He chastised most black historians for "reflecting their training in white institutions of higher learning," for ignoring "the realities as projected" in slave folklore. Stuckey asserted that the failure of black and white historians to seriously address slave folklore reflected their inability to make black history what it really was in his mind, the "values and life styles of the supposedly inarticulate" black masses.[51]

Beyond serving as a window into the consciousness of enslaved blacks and the black masses, Stuckey also maintained that black history needed to serve as "a search-light flashing over the terrain of the American night, illumining hidden, horrible truths." For Stuckey, black history was a window into the "white institutional and personality development" that perpetuated racism and black oppression. In order to attack and dismantle American racism, Stuckey reasoned that it was necessary to carefully revisit and genuinely understand its deep historical roots. Embracing black history's function as a political tool, Stuckey shared Du Bois's vision that "Art and Propaganda be one." "Black history recognizes the indivisibility of history and politics: As history has been used in the West to degrade people of color, black history must seek dignity for mankind," Stuckey noted. He was openly pessimistic about his contemporaries' abilities to embrace his approach to black history. Based on the middle-class black intellectual community's overall responses to Du Bois and Paul Robeson while they were being prosecuted for their Communist leanings during the Cold War era, Stuckey deromanticized black historiography and challenged his colleagues: "We cannot with absolute certitude state that this generation of black historians will have the integrity to tell the full story."[52]

During the Black Power era, a few white historians offered intriguing

definitions of black history. In a 1969 essay assessing how "major interpretive works of American history" published from the early twentieth century
through the modern civil rights movement treated African Americans, I. A.
Newby, one of the few white historians from the South to recognize blacks'
contributions to U.S. history before it became a fad field, offered a definition of black history that acknowledged a dual function of black history by
highlighting what it entailed for blacks and whites. "Properly construed,"
Newby surmised, "Negro history encompasses two principal subjects: what
blacks have done in America, and what whites have done to them. The former
encompasses the activities, aspirations, and achievements of the race, the
positive side of its history; the latter concerns white racism, the nature and
extent of racial discrimination, the patterns of exploitation and repression.
The two sides are equally important." Echoing Woodson, Newby believed that
black history could instill within blacks a "secure sense of personal identity,
self-confidence, and racial pride" while helping whites overcome their "overriding superiority complex" and discover how black history challenges the
master narrative of U.S. history.[53]

Around the same time that Harding, Clarke, and Stuckey posited their
visions and interpretations of black history, Earl E. Thorpe revised his *Negro
Historians in the United States* (1958), publishing *Black Historians: A Critique*
(1971). Probably inspired by the Black Power era, Thorpe elaborated on his
earlier study stressing the component of struggle in the black experience.
"Black history is American history with the accent and emphasis on the
point of view, attitude, and spirit of Afro-Americans, as well as on the events
in which they have been either the actors or the objects of action." Thorpe
added, "Black history is that American history which, until the 1960s, was
viewed by white America with contempt and disdain or ignored altogether,
just as black people themselves were viewed and treated. Men tend either
to deny or force out of consciousness the evil that they do. Much of black
history, then, is the story of the cruelties and inhumanities which a powerful
white majority has inflicted on a defenseless black minority."[54] Thorpe posited
that the "central theme of black history is the quest of Afro-Americans for
freedom, equality, and manhood."[55]

Definitions of Black History, the 1970s–1990s

In the immediate aftermath of the Black Power era, discussions concerning
the question *What is black history?* continued to be of some concern among
black scholars and historians. A look at two very different views highlights
the diversity of opinion that persisted. In the closing of the 1970s, poet and

longtime activist Haki R. Madhubuti captured many of the sentiments of black nationalists' interpretations of black history's meaning and function. In an essay in *Enemies: The Clash of Races* (1978), Madhubuti echoed Stuckey, arguing that whites had traditionally used history as an "effective weapon" of war to conquer African Americans. He envisioned black history (the "sum total" of black people) as being "a fighting history—a war history document-ing our struggle against white domination." Like other advocates of social history before him, Madhubuti maintained that black history was dominated by the lives of the black masses. "History is produced from the gut of the people . . . the history of a people is the survival and development record of that people. It tells of their accomplishments and defeats, of their ups and downs," Madhubuti added, "One of the greatest accomplishments of a people is to produce their own history."[56] This cultural nationalist and renown poet chastised blacks for not taking control of their history and, in turn, allow-ing whites to control a significant part of their identity. Black history for Madhubuti was, in essence, the key to self-knowledge.

In the immediate post–Black Power era, Benjamin Quarles, longtime professor of history at Morgan State University, offered a much different view of what black history meant. As a well-known and respected historian, he published "Black History's Diversified Clientele," in which he explored how, during the early and mid-1970s, black history was being used and in-terpreted in distinctly different ways by four groups of people: the black masses, "black revolutionary nationalists," professional black academicians, and whites in general. Although Quarles did not really directly propose his own authentic philosophy of black history, his essay is valuable because he acknowledged that black history has been interpreted by different "publics" in various ways.[57]

During the 1980s, many key definitions about black history emerged, cor-responding with the substantial growth in African American historiography and the black historical profession. In his popular book *There Is a River: The Black Struggle for Freedom in America* (1981), Vincent Harding eloquently likened black history to a river. He asserted:

> We may sense that the river of black struggle is people, but it is also the hope, the movement, the transformative power that humans create and that create them, us, and makes them, us, new persons. So we black people are the river; the river is us. The river is in us, created by us, flowing out of us, surrounding us, re-creating us and this entire nation. I refer to the American nation without hesitation, for the black river in the United States has always taken on more than blackness. The dynamics and justice of its movement have continually gathered others to itself, have persistently filled other men and women with

the force of its vision, its indomitable hope. And at its best the river of our struggle has moved consistently toward the ocean of humankind's most courageous hopes for freedom in integrity, forever seeking . . . "the right to develop our whole being."[58]

Several years after *There Is a River* was published, in the *Journal of American History* August Meier critiqued Harding, Mary Frances Berry, and John W. Blassingame for the so-called "pessimistic air" of their scholarship. Meier contended that the "militant" and "radical" tone of these black historians abandoned the idealistic "hopefulness and optimism" championed by John Hope Franklin and Benjamin Quarles.[59] Meier was perhaps unprepared to deal with a younger generation of black historians active in post–civil rights era America who, unlike Franklin and Quarles, disregarded hyperobjectivity and wrote with a great deal of emotion, passion, and anger. William H. Harris concurred with Harding that black history needed to showcase the multiple forms of oppression overcome by black people. In defense of Berry, Blassingame, and Harding, Harris concluded that the pessimism expressed by Meier and his colleagues is "easily understood when one does perceive our time from the perspective of the black experience. It is a pessimism that I share as a historian and a sentiment that I share as a historian."[60]

Black studies entered predominantly white colleges and universities during the Black Power era, but the 1980s "marked a period of formal standardization and institutionalization of African American Studies."[61] While black studies is a "multidiscipline," history has been especially vital to this educational reform movement. In his classic introductory text first published in 1982, *Introduction to Black Studies,* Maulana Karenga outlined the value of "the seven core subject areas" of black studies, emphasizing the unique role of history. In discussing the "undeniable relevance" of black studies, Karenga stressed the necessity of history as a vital core subject area. "Black Studies then begins with rigorous research and critical intellectual production in the key social science, history, which lays the basis for and informs all others and which will affirm the truth of the Black experience and negate the racist myths which have surrounded it." Karenga further underscored the significance of history, defining it in relation to black studies. For Karenga, "Black studies also begins with Black History because it is relevant, even indispensable to the introduction and development of all the other subject areas. Black History places them in perspective, establishes their origins and development, and thus, aids in critical discussion and understanding of them. Moreover, each of the other subject areas of Black Studies teaches its own particular history which in turn is a part of general Black History. Black History, then, offers not only a broad framework for critically viewing and understanding Black people, but also a necessary background perspective for critical insights into other subject areas of Black Studies."[62]

By the early 1980s, Lerone Bennett Jr. had clearly established himself as a leading African American historian who, like Woodson, committed his life to popularizing black history. In 1954, a year after becoming associate editor for *Jet*, Bennett became the associate editor for *Ebony*. Several years later, he was named the magazine's first senior editor, and by 1987 he was promoted to executive editor of *Ebony*. Bennett almost single-handedly popularized black history among the many *Ebony* and *Jet* readers. *Ebony*, founded in 1945, routinely featured a history section in its issues from the 1960s through the 1970s and 1980s. According to Benjamin Quarles, "the popularization of black history in the mass-circulation monthly, *Ebony*, particularly the writings of its senior editor, Lerone Bennett, Jr., left a deep imprint on hundreds of thousands of readers hitherto unresponsive to the call of the past."[63] Beginning in the 1970s, Bennett published more than a few articles under the heading "Great Moments in Black History." From the 1960s through the present, Bennett has published countless passionate, simple, and thought-provoking historical articles in *Ebony*. Between 1981 and 1985, Bennett published three major articles in *Ebony* that creatively probed into the deeper meanings of black history.[64]

In a provocative essay, "Listen to the Blood: The Meaning of Black History," a speech that he originally delivered in 1980 at the annual meeting of the Association for the Study of Afro-American Life and History, Bennett discussed several different ways that blacks have interpreted, and should view in the future, the meaning of black history. Many blacks, Bennett posited, interpreted black history as being dictated by God in "mysterious ways" and believed that history "moved at the behest of other forces—charms, curses, and so forth." He suggested that blacks have often viewed history as a spiritual concept bound to their daily lives, actions, and beliefs. Bennett also remarked that during the modern civil rights movement, the "God-controlled" notion of black history gained popularity. As a scholarly field of study, Bennett underscored that black history needed to be viewed within the broader scope of world history, and that it was "a history of the insider outsiders. And it must be interpreted . . . both in terms of its particularity and its universality." He contended that black history shared certain commonalities with others' histories throughout the world, but at the same time black history was distinctly different and unique.[65]

Bennett asserted that black history was "real," something much deeper than "a story in a book or a career or a monograph in a scholarly journal," that black history was relevant to the daily lives of African Americans. He told black people: "You *are* that history. And there is nothing you can do in history that will free you of the historical responsibility of being born at a certain time, in a certain place, with a certain skin color. . . . You cannot, no matter what you do, escape the meaning history gave you and that history demands of you." Bennett avowed that African Americans living in the present owed a great debt to those who laid the foundations for their existence. "We are responsible," Bennett proclaimed, "totally responsible, not only for ourselves but for the whole of the Black experience. For it is only through us that the dreams of the past can be fulfilled. It is only through us that the first slave can reach the finish line."[66] Bennett's ideal conception of black history would have required African Americans of his times to sacrifice.

In another article, "Why Black History is Important to You," Bennett defined history in an all-encompassing manner. "History is everything; it is everywhere. It is an all-pervading atmosphere, an ambiance, a milieu. History to us is what water is to fish. . . . History is knowledge, identity, and power. History is knowledge because it is a practical perspective and a practical orientation. It orders and organizes our world and valorizes our projects." Bennett sought to convince *Ebony* readers that history was much more important than most people probably thought it was. He acknowledged that black history had multiple expressions, appearing as an ideology, a scholarly discipline, and a source of pride and energy. Bennett insisted that black history needed to be functional and pragmatic. Blacks, in his opinion, needed to "base their vision of the future on the Black past and . . . must justify their calls by a historical analysis of the Black experience." Bennett went a step further, underscoring that "no one interested in mobilizing Black people can escape the necessity of thinking historically." He lamented that many viewed black history as "an intellectual ghetto" and "a minor-league pastime" and declared that it was an essential part of U.S. history. Echoing Harding's and Stuckey's ideas from the Black Power era, he proposed that black history constituted a "total critique" of what most Americans—whites—perceived as being standard U.S. history. Black history, he noted, challenged the uncritical vision of America as being the "land of the free." Bennett also believed that there was a revealing universality to black history, that it was similar to the histories of many people throughout the world and was "the history of man taken to the nth degree."[67]

One of the last major articles Bennett seems to have published in *Ebony* that directly probes the deeper meanings of black history appeared in 1985. In "Voices of the Past Speak to the Present," an essay that was reprinted in several issues of *Ebony* in the 1990s, Bennett summarized his strong belief that black history needed to be functional, pragmatic, and this-worldly in orientation. Black history, he eloquently maintained, "is a challenge and a call. . . . To understand Black history today is to understand that something or somebody in that history is calling your name. For in and through Black history, the voices of the past speak to us personally, calling us by name, asking us what we have done, what we are doing and what are we prepared to do to ensure that the slaves and activists and martyrs did not dream and die in vain. . . . Black history is a perpetual conversation in which men and women speak to one another across the centuries, correcting one another, echoing one another, blending together into a mighty chorus which contrasts and combines different themes." Foreshadowing Manning Marable, Bennett deemed black history a "living history," a series of ongoing interactions between various generations of blacks, living and deceased. He emphasized that African Americans must approach black history "actively and not passively." He said: "We must become, as we read and celebrate, slaves and sharecroppers, victims and martyrs, . . . and rebels. We must relate these images to the challenges and opportunities of our own lives, or we shall learn nothing and remember nothing."[68] Bennett's belief that blacks need to "actively" get involved in history is reminiscent of Woodson, who charged black children with the responsibility reenacting scenes from black history in plays and pageants during Negro History Week celebrations.

In the 1980s, several historians of the African American struggle for education offered useful conceptualizations of black history's meaning. In the mid-1980s, historian V. P. Franklin provided a definition of black history that focused on blacks' "predominant cultural values." He proposed that slavery, more than any other collective experience in black history, shaped blacks' post-emancipation worldview and history. The "common experience of slavery" for Franklin represented "the foundation for the 'cultural value system' that was handed down from the Africans to their American-born offspring, the Afro-Americans." Franklin maintained that "since more than one generation of Afro-Americans was victimized by enslavement in the United States, certain values remained relevant for one generation to the next and indeed became 'core values' of the Afro-American experience." Franklin identified the main "core values" of black history as being a striving toward freedom, resistance, a quest for education, and self-determination.[69] Such a thematic approach is useful and must be adjusted to suit the specific periods under investigation. In 1988, in his thoughtful historiography of the African American educational experience, Ronald E. Butchart defined black history's function with the pragmatism of earlier generations of black historians: "If history is to have value beyond a literary form of collecting antiques, it must provide a guide to action. For those struggling against oppression and for justice, history must appraise the past to suggest political, social, and economic strategies for the present and future. Like schooling, history, too, is inescapably political."[70]

In the 1980s and 1990s, Robert L. Harris Jr. presented several intriguing definitions of black history. In an important article titled "Coming of Age: The Transformation of Afro-American Historiography," Harris not only noted that black history needed to be interpreted "within the context of American history," but added that it needed to be analyzed within the context of Afro-diasporan history. Simply put, "events on the African continent and in the African Diaspora have profoundly affected Afro-American thought and action."[71] In a brief, informative pamphlet first published in 1985 and then re-released in 1992, Harris construed African American history as "the study of the thought and actions of people of African ancestry in the United States over time and place." He explained that we study African American history in order to "understand the position that black people have occupied in American society, their efforts to cope with their status, and their successes and failures in pursuing full equality."[72] While Harris's definitions are straightforward, he did not really provide a philosophical discussion of the deeper meanings of black history.

Darlene Clark Hine, who made her most significant contributions to black women's history in her capacity as a John A. Hannah Professor of History at Michigan State University, has been largely responsible for helping institutionalize black women's history during the last several decades. Building upon the ideas raised by her predecessors and colleagues during the 1970s and 1980s, in the 1990s she defined black women's history on several occasions, thus further complicating previous definitions of black history that largely ignored issues of gender and the perspectives of black women.

In the editor's preface of *Black Women in America: An Historical Encyclopedia* (1993), Hine depicted black women's history as a discipline that needed to be directly related to the contemporary conditions facing black women. "We cannot accurately comprehend either our hidden potential or the full range of problems that besiege us until we know about the successful struggles that generations of foremothers waged against virtually insurmountable obstacles," she continued. "We can, and will, chart a coherent future and win essential opportunities with a clear understanding of the past in all its pain and glory."[73]

Echoing generations of black historians before her and black women scholars like Toni Cade, Michelle Wallace, Angela Davis, Rosalyn Terborg-Penn, and Sharon Harley, Hine openly linked the past to the present in defining black women's history.[74] "History has its own power and Black women more than ever before need its truths to challenge hateful assumptions, negative stereotypes, myths, lies, and distortions about our own role in the progress of time. Black women need to know the contradictions and ironies that our unique status presents. . . . Yet it is not enough only to know about the injustices and exploitation Black women endured. . . . As we garner the inspiration contained in past and present Black women's lives, we acquire the power to take history further and the will to use the power of history to construct a better future."[75] Hine's statement resonates with the clear influence of Woodson, who advocated that black history be used to combat racism while inspiring blacks. In another instance, Hine contended that black women's history is instructive in helping us piece together the various processes of history making. "Black women's history," according to Hine, "compels the individual to come to grips more completely with all of the components of identity. Through the study of Black women it becomes increasingly obvious how historians shape, make, or construct history, and why we omit, ignore, and sometimes distort the lives of people on the margins."[76]

During the institutionalization phase of Black women's history of the 1990s—in part in response to mainstream feminists' failure to theorize the intricate relationships between race, power, gender, sexuality, class, and history—Evelyn Brooks Higginbotham called for more theoretical definitions of African American women's history in her groundbreaking 1992 essay, "African American Women's History and the Metalanguage of Race." Higginbotham called upon her colleagues to embrace a "three-pronged approach to the history of African-American women" that borrowed from a variety of scholarly vantage points. She concluded that African American women's history was complex: "Black women of different economic and regional backgrounds, of different skin tones and sexual orientations, have found themselves in conflict over interpretation of symbols and norms, public behavior, coping strategies, and a variety of micropolitical acts of resistance to structures of domination. . . . We must problematize much more of what we take for granted. We must bring to light and to coherence the one and the many that we always were in history and still actually are today."[77]

* * *

Definitions of Black History in the New Millennium

At the dawning of the new millennium, historian W. D. Wright published two studies that critically inquire into African American history and historiography, *Critical Reflections on Black History* (2002) and *Black History and Black Identity: A Call for a New Historiography* (2002). Wright puts forward several definitions of black history in these think pieces. He surmised, "As a philosophical, perceptual, and historiographical understanding, Black history should be understood as Black history that focuses on Black people, their identity, their culture, their social life, their psychology, and the way they have used these ethnic, group, and personal attributes to make history in America and to contribute to histories, countries, and peoples elsewhere on the globe."[78] In another instance, echoing Du Bois's "double-consciousness" theory, Wright stresses that black history has "two dimensions: a Black dimension and an American dimension." For him, both "tracks" must be acknowledged because they both influenced "the functioning, development, and reality of the other. . . . Black history, as a history, has never been an either-or history, where Black people did this but not that."[79] Wright's contributionist idea that black history must be approached as a part of American history is certainly not new, but it is important as we proceed into the twenty-first century, especially because (since the Black Power era) university courses in black history have all too often been taught separate from mainstream U.S. history. Isolating the African American experience gives it the attention that it deserves, yet at the same time it allows for professors of U.S. history—the vast majority of whom are white—to give lip service to aspects of black history, usually in the form of token leaders or select incidents here and there, without really highlighting the centrality of African Americans to life, history, and culture in the United States. While it would be very easy to defend placing black America at the center of U.S. history, very few U.S. historians teach U.S. history from such a revealing vantage point. Like Robert L. Harris, Wright also maintains that black history "in a whole and deeper manner" needs to be linked to African history.

Since 2000, at least half a dozen major textbooks have been published on the African American historical experience. While helpful and necessary, these studies are grounded in the narrative tradition and do not explicitly theorize or define black history.[80] Yet, in one of the more recent general surveys of African American experience, *Fire from the Soul: A History of the African American Struggle* (2003), Donald Spivey delineates black history as being directly related to the present. Black history for Spivey is an essential key for understanding the present battle against racism. "How can appropriate programs be implemented to combat racism if the roots of the dilemma are not understood? They cannot," Spivey asserts. "Solutions flow from understanding history. The past is our source of enlightenment and wisdom. . . . What we know for sure is that failure to embrace that past will yield a problematic outcome in the present and future."[81] Without really providing a philosophical inquiry into the deeper meaning of black history, Spivey advocates an openly pragmatic vision of black history. His pragmatism echoes the sentiments of many black historians from the Black Power era. He also shares their pessimistic critique of the future, remarking "the historical barometer is a stern warning of perilous waters ahead."[82] Spivey's message is especially relevant to the hip-hop generation, who face a struggle for equality that is essentially hard to define and decipher.

Reminiscent of L. D. Reddick's and John Hope Franklin's pleas for "new" interpretations of black history in 1937 and 1957 respectively, Manning Marable has recently articulated "the construction of a new black history from the vantage point of the evolution of black consciousness over time," a refashioning of black history that "is inextricably linked to the political practices, or *praxis,* of transforming the present and future" and that reduces "the distance between the past, the present, and the future to effectively reconstruct . . . authentic narratives." The founder of Columbia University's Center for Contemporary Black History, Marable outlines a philosophy of black history that is essentially pragmatic, political, and directly bound to black America's present and future struggles for equality and liberation. For Marable, the historical culture of black resistance can serve as a "practical [example] of how a new generation of African Americans and other minorities might challenge racism today. Preserving the past," Marable stresses, "creates a living legacy that can help shape the future."[83]

In "Living Black History: Black Consciousness, Place, and America's Master Narrative," an essay in *Living Black History: How Reimagining the African-American Past Can Remake America's Racial Future,* originally delivered as a lecture at Harvard University in 2004, Marable prioritizes history in framing black America's struggle for political empowerment and reforming white America's views of their country's past, especially the "common history" they share with African Americans. For Marable, "living history"—a concept first introduced to him by C. L. R. James as well as terminology employed differently by Lerone Bennett Jr. in 1985—seeks to reconstruct African American history with "a multidisciplinary methodology employing the tools of oral history, photography, film, ethnography, and multimedia digital technology." Marable contends that "we all 'live history' every day. But history is more than the construction of collective experiences, or the knowledge drawn from carefully catalogued artifacts from the past. History is also the architecture of a people's memory, framed by our shared rituals, traditions, and notions of common sense." Marable equates "living history" with an "authentic history of black people" that, like the Afrocentrism defined by Molefi Kete Asante, centers African Americans and their experiences from their own perspectives; draws from revealing nontraditional primary source documentary troves; challenges myths of and pseudoscientific scholarship espousing black inferiority; and critically unearths and analyzes the history of black oppression and resistance.[84]

Black history, in Marable's estimation, serves as a scholarly corrective mechanism in revising the whitestream "master narrative of American history," a record of the past that systematically ignores historic racism, especially the tradition of the violent oppression of black people. Like scholars who have researched the teaching and learning of African American history, and Benjamin Quarles, who recognized black history's "diversified clientele," Marable asserts that black America and white America view black history in distinctly different ways. While the "great masses of white Americans" tend to shy away from acknowledging and confronting centuries of overt and covert antiblack behavior in the United States, African Americans recognize that black history "is indelibly part of the fabric of our collective destiny. Indeed this alternative understanding of history . . . is the most important quality that makes African Americans as a people different from other Americans." In Marable's view, blacks' repositories of black historical knowledge "have practical and powerful consequences in shaping civic behavior and social consciousness." Marable's philosophy of black history is refreshing. While clearly similar to the approaches of many black historians active during the early black history movement from approximately 1915 until the death of Woodson in 1950, as well as black historians and scholars who came of age during the Black Power era, Marable's theory of black history possesses a sense of newness. It was crafted based upon twenty-first-century realities and technological advancements as well as on the unknown future of black America, U.S. democratic ideals, and U.S. race relations.[85]

Since the dawning of the twentieth century, many scholars, historians, and intellectuals have formulated thoughtful philosophies and definitions of black history that were influenced by their personal views of the role of history in American life and culture, their predecessors' musings, the historical contexts in which they existed, and their visions for the future. While the philosophy of black history remains an undertheorized area of black historiography and the debates surrounding what black history means and can potentially entail have been minimal, the collective reflections of philosophers of black history are instructive and deserve consideration as we continue to grapple with the question *What is black history?* From the founding of Negro History Week in 1926 until Lerone Bennett Jr.'s conceptualizations of black history during the 1980s, black history has been fairly consistently conceived as what Marable deemed "a critical force for change."[86] Building upon previous historical thought, Manning Marable's recently proposed theory of "living history" is promising for future conceptualizations of black history. The study and teaching of African American history in all levels of American educational institutions, from the classrooms of elementary schools to the ivory towers of the academy, indeed has the potential to help improve, reform, democratize, and enrich American culture and society. Defining what black history entails, encompasses, and can become, moreover, is central to this educational and cultural reform movement.

2. Approaches to Teaching and Learning African American History

Instruction with respect to the life and history of the Negro requires probably more preparation than any other phase of social science for the simple reason that no other problems have been so grossly misinterpreted and so generally misunderstood. To undertake to give instruction in this field in which one is not prepared, then, would be a most expensive error for which future generations must pay in suffering from other misunderstandings like the many which handicap us today.

—Carter G. Woodson, "Annual Report of the Director," 1929

African American history should no longer be relegated to the discussion of the enslaved and the civil rights movement. . . . We need to train students to carry on the work of researching, writing and presenting black history to the general public, in our classrooms and in historic-preservation settings. . . . Black history urges the development of innovative and creative ways of dissemination. There need to be more forums to allow greater participation of both scholarly and nonacademic audiences in order to enhance our mutual enjoyment of black history. . . . There is an ongoing responsibility of black history scholars to share this important knowledge with black people in particular and the American public in general in as many venues as possible. . . . The black past opens an important window onto the epic of America.

—Darlene Clark Hine, "Challenges in Teaching Afro-American History," 1977

Following the pivotal black student protests of the civil rights era and Black Power movement, mainstream, predominantly white universities began offering basic and foundational courses related to the African American experience often under the umbrella of black studies. It was during and after the "blistering years" of the black studies movement from the late 1960s until the early 1970s that the multilayered African American experience (past, present, and future) became a not-to-be-overlooked topic in many college and university curricula throughout the United States. History has always been a main "core subject area" of black studies, and it was also one of the first major disciplines in which African American scholars created autonomous intellectual traditions and institutions, most notably the early black history movement and the Association of the Study of Negro Life and History that existed side-by-side with white America's various exclusionary academic infrastructures during the era of Jim Crow segregation. By the later years of the Black Power era, the mainstream American historical profession arguably began no longer to view African American people "as an out-group with a blank past." In 1974, Benjamin Quarles remarked: "If white historians still think of themselves as the custodians of the word and the gatekeepers of the citadel, they are no longer set on viewing the Negro as a stranger, if not a barbarian at the gates. They now deal more circumspectly with blacks, hoping to avoid what logicians call the 'fallacy of initial predication.'"[1] Several years following the 1983 "state of the art" conference on the study and teaching of African American history at Purdue University, Darlene Clark Hine echoed what more than a few historians like Quarles had observed in the 1970s and optimistically commented: "Today Afro-American history is a respected and legitimate field of American history." Presently, African American history represents one of the most dynamic subfields of U.S. historical inquiry and higher education, and courses in African American history are among the most popular courses at leading universities.[2]

At the same time, scholarship on the teaching and learning of African American history, an important dimension of the black historical enterprise, is an undertheorized area of black historical discourse. Leading scholarship on history teaching and learning, most notably the illuminating study *Knowing, Teaching, and Learning History: National and International Perspectives,* has failed to address African American history. The first major anthology on teaching African American history by professionally trained scholars and historians in colleges and universities, *Teaching the American Civil Rights Movement: Freedom's Bittersweet Song,* was published in 2002. Though focusing on the modern civil rights movement, the essays in this collection—several of which were written by productive hip-hop generation black historians—are insightful and refreshing. More studies of this nature are needed. As data from the report of the American Historical Association's Committee on Graduate Students suggest, lack of preparation for teaching is a serious concern for history and other graduate students. American culture and society and black history—its course and the scholarship on it—has undergone a host of pivotal transformations since the so-called mainstreaming of African American history several decades ago that require university professors of African American history to reconsider, reframe, and critically reflect upon their approaches to teaching as well as the increasingly diverse learning processes of their students. As Nell Irvin Painter has recently underscored, "Contrary to what many people assume, history exists in two time frames: the past and the present. . . . As new issues emerge, new questions surface, and the past yields new answers. For this reason, African-American history written a generation ago no longer gives today's readers all the answers they seek. Not only have things happened in the intervening years, but also we ask different questions of the past."[3] The observations of educational theorists Mary Taylor Huber and Pat Hutchings made so passionately in 2005 are equally as instructive: "The scholarship of teaching and learning is an imperative for higher education today, not a choice" because "teaching today is harder than it used to be."[4] Sam Wineburg's introductory sentiments in *Historical Thinking and Other Unnatural Acts: Charting the Future of Teaching the Past* (2001) are also informative: "The strategy of labeling, rather than trying to understand, students' historical knowledge has lead to arid discussions of pedagogy. . . . But the role of history as a tool for changing how we think, for promoting a literacy not of names and dates but of discernment, judgment, and caution, does not receive prime billing in the public sphere."[5]

Focusing on the historical evolution of the scholarship on the teaching of African American history in higher education, this chapter grapples with the following inquiries. What is African American history's educational value? What are some useful goals for teaching African American history to today's university students? How have scholars theorized the teaching of African American history since the early twentieth century? How can history professors today help their students—mainly diverse groups of hip-hop generation and millennial learners—intimately understand African American history?

An investigation into the teaching of African American history must begin with a concrete conceptualization of this phenomenon that has been theorized and described by many generations in different ways. Notwithstanding the various philosophical interpretations of black history identified in chapter 1, as a field of study black history is the interpretation, application, and rigorous study of the black past with all its complexity. The knowledge of African American history evolves and changes as new historical interpretations, paradigms, and ideas are generated.

Since its earliest phases, the history of African Americans has been characterized by an enduring struggle for fundamental civil and human rights, justice, equality, and liberation. Vincent Harding captured the essence of this enduring quest with his classic "river metaphor." The African American historical experience is also characterized by a unique sense of human resilience, with its "capacity to rebound from a major setback or tragedy," constituting "more than stoicism or a return to the status quo; it involves going beyond healing and recovery."[6] The teacher of African American history faces the challenge of maintaining a delicate balance between themes of victimization and oppression, and perseverance and resistance, constantly acknowledging and highlighting African American agency and subtle forms of resistance without trivializing the multitude of tragedies and setbacks that African Americans have encountered for centuries. In order truly to understand and contextualize blacks' post-emancipation progress, achievements, and non-static culture of resistance, the harsh oppression that generations of African Americans have experienced from the era of the slave trade through the period of Jim Crow segregation and beyond must be broken down and taught. The successes of major black leaders during "the nadir," for instance, must be placed within the context of lynching, among other antiblack practices of the period. When teaching about lynching, I lecture from the foundational secondary sources and assign, among other sources, the NAACP's *Thirty Years of Lynching in the United States, 1889–1918* (April 1919); Ida B. Wells's antilynching scholarship; and Ginzburg's *100 Years of Lynching* (1962). I also show and discuss with them the graphic images from *Without Sanctuary: Lynching Photography in America* (2000).

The African American experience is, of course, not monolithic. It is composed of many diverse experiences and should be taught and learned as such. African Americans' day-to-day lives at different time periods were contingent upon many factors, such as region; religious orientation; intraracial dynamics; gender and sex; class; legal and extralegal forms of oppression; as well as broader social, political, economic, and cultural transformations; change over time; and blacks' relationships with other Americans. African American history has many subfields determined by eras, topics, and themes. African American history is inevitably a part of America's past and consists of the total experience of black people in the United States. At the same time, throughout history many phenomena in Africa, the vast diaspora, and the world have affected black Americans in meaningful ways, and vice versa. African Americans are culturally an African people and, as Tsehloane Keto and Molefi Kete Asante have emphasized, represent "a specific discrete African ethnicity."[7] Acknowledging a genetic, cultural, and spiritual connection with Africa and Africanisms, we should teach African American history as a history of an

African people. While African American history is an established distinct subfield in American history, and black people have unique experiences therein, African Americanists must avoid simply teaching African American history as that of a "self-contained," "insulated," historical "group in isolation from the others."[8] African Americanists should teach about their subjects as they intersect with other groups in the United States and compare with other peoples throughout the world.

The African American experience, African Americans' lives in the formal United States, has lasted from 1789 until the present, 2010. For teaching purposes, this experience of 221 years can be subdivided into the three broad, major phases: phase 1, *Enslavement and Quasi Freedom, 1789–1865*, presently represents 34.4 percent of the total African American experience; phase 2, *The Struggle for Citizenship and Fundamental Civil and Human Rights, 1865–1965*, 45.2 percent; and phase 3, *Post–Civil Rights Era Trends, 1965–2010*, 20.4 percent.

During phase 1 of the African American experience, from the ratification of the U.S. Constitution in 1789 until 1865 when the 13th Amendment was ratified and slavery abolished, the vast majority of African Americans were slaves. The first federal census of 1790 indicated that there were 697,897 enslaved blacks and 59,557 free blacks. In 1820, there were 1,538,125 enslaved blacks and 233,504 free blacks; and in 1860 there were 3,953,760 enslaved blacks and about 488,000 free blacks. As a significant group of scholars has demonstrated, free blacks in the North and South often lived their lives as "quasi free" peoples and "slaves without masters."[9] During phase 1, the African American experience was shaped most profoundly by slavery. Not only was slavery arguably the most important, defining characteristic of pre-Reconstruction U.S. history, but surviving, resisting, and abolishing slavery comprised the main themes of black life during phase 1.

The one hundred years from emancipation in 1865 until the Voting Rights Act of 1965—phase 2 of the African American experience and close to half of the total African American experience—was marked by African Americans' struggles for basic civil and human rights. Phase 2 consists of a multitude of important periods and transformations, including Reconstruction (1865–77); "the nadir" (according to Rayford W. Logan the low point of black life from 1877 through the early 1920s); the Great Migration; World Wars I and II and the Korean War; the Great Depression; the era of Jim Crow segregation from the *Plessy v. Ferguson* case in 1896 until *Brown v. Board of Education, Topeka, Kansas* in 1954; the initial phases of the Cold War; and the modern civil rights movement (roughly 1954–65). Though slavery was formally abolished at the outset of phase 2, for the next one hundred years the vast majority of African Americans lived their lives as second-class citizens whose freedoms were limited by de jure and de facto segregation. As Douglas A. Blackmon has recently argued in *Slavery by Another Name: The Re-Enslavement of Black Americans from the Civil War to World War II* (2008), "a form of American slavery persisted into the twentieth century" that was "embraced by the U.S. economic system and aided at all levels of government."[10] For more than a decade since the 1980s, scholars tended to define the civil rights movement as the period from the mid-1950s until the mid-1960s. More recently, scholars have extended the civil rights movement to include the period from the mid-nineteenth century until the mid-twentieth century. Darlene Clark Hine has identified the period from 1890 until 1950 as embodying the "origins of the civil rights movement." She has asserted: "Understanding the proto–civil rights movement is fundamental to the reconstruction of the origins of the classic civil rights movement of the late 1950s and 1960s." Extending Hine's theory, Glenda Gilmore, in *Defying Dixie: The Radical Roots of Civil Rights, 1919–1950* (2008), contends that groups of black radicals during the 1920s, 1930s, and 1940s paved the way for the activism that exploded during the classic civil rights movement.[11]

Despite the continuing oppression of African Americans, the permanence of institutional racism, and the continued economic, political, and social underdevelopment of many African Americans nationwide revealed in books like *The Covenant* (2006) and the National Urban League's annual *State of Black America,* during phase 3 of the African American experience (1965 until the present or whatever the present is in the future), African Americans have attained and been granted *most,* but by no means all, of their basic civil rights. At this point, the vast majority of the African American experience in the United States, about 80 percent of the total experience, has been lived in some form of overt struggle for basic equal rights and justice. The African American historical experience that I have outlined here must be revised every year, reflecting the increase in time elapsed from the passage of the Voting Rights Act in 1965 marking the end of the second legislative Reconstruction and phase 2. The fate of African Americans in the future is unsure. Nonetheless, it will not be until about 2140, more than a century hence, that at least 50 percent of the total African American experience will have been spent in a post–civil rights era—theoretically, a period devoid of the widespread and overt denial of African Americans' fundamental civil and human rights. Students should be challenged to view each phase of the African American experience as it relates to the other phases and the broader experience as a whole.

The Value of African American History in Education

African American history's educational value can be discerned in numerous ways, and its political nature as an educative device operates at various levels. Even though they did not explicitly refer to African American history in their study *Knowing, Teaching, and Learning History: National and International Perspectives,* Peter N. Stearns, Peter C. Seixas, and Samuel S. Wineberg depicted the political dimension of history in a manner that is solidly applicable to the historically and politically motivated application, study, and teaching of African American history. They suggest: "History, qua school subject, has a hard time avoiding present political purposes. Given the inherent moral implications of any historical narrative, insofar as school history engages with and shapes a collective memory, it is inherently political, whether the agenda is focused on national progress, the struggle for human rights, global awareness, ethnic identity, or something else."[12]

African American history helps revise, complicate, and diversify "standard" U.S. historical narratives. For many white millennial learners, African American history serves as a useful introduction to African American culture. Exposure to African American history can help counter U.S. popular culture's routine misrepresentations of blackness, thereby potentially diminishing whites' stereotypes and misunderstandings of African Americans. African American history can help today's black college and university students, especially members of the millennial hip-hop generation (those blacks born from the early to mid-1980s until the early 1990s), better understand their particular location within the enduring African American struggle for advancement, instilling within them a sense of social responsibility, historical and cultural identity, and historicity. Exposure to African American history can challenge them to critically contemplate their status and compare their contributions with those of other generations of young black people during and before the civil rights era and Black Power movement.

Products of an unprecedented state of multimedia technology and internet information, millennials tend to be ahistorical. For many, "the half-life of information is short" and "results and actions are considered more important than the accumulation of facts."[13] Moreover, despite hip hop's recognizable historicism, in *The Hip Hop Generation: Young Blacks and the Crisis of African American Culture* Bakari Kitwana has convincingly argued that the hip-hop generation has abandoned important elements of historical and cultural values. A significant number of today's college and university students have presentist worldviews, often overlooking the intimate connections between the past and the present. The monumental problems facing African Americans today are many: continuing social and political inequality, U.S. institutional racism, health issues (especially HIV/AIDS, diabetes, sickle cell anemia, and obesity), fatherlessness and unhealthy male-female relationships, male incarceration rates, poor college and university retention rates, unemployment, and poverty. The recent productions of CNN Specials, "CNN Presents: Black in America," which premiered July 23–24, 2008, and "Black in America 2" (July 2009), affirmed and exposed these numerous problems so much that they ultimately portrayed black people as a doomed, pathological group. This presentation failed by not providing even a basic historical and environmentalist perspective to contextualize blacks' present collective status. The African American experience historicizes these dilemmas, directly linking them to deeply rooted evolutionary processes. A careful study of African American history demonstrates that the contemporary problems facing blacks are the byproducts of various pasts and incidences, are influenced by contemporary developments and interpretive models, and are inevitably related to future trends.

Several studies published since 2000 are especially useful in demonstrating to millennial learners the connection between black America's past and present, including W. Michael Byrd and Linda A. Clayton's two-volume *An American Health Dilemma* (2000, 2002); Randall Robinson's *The Debt: What America Owes to Blacks* (2000); Philip F. Rubio's *A History of Affirmative Action, 1619–2000* (2001); Raymond A. Winbush's *Should America Pay? Slavery and the Raging Debate on Reparations* (2003); Ira Katznelson's *When Affirmation Action Was White: An Untold History of Racial Inequality in Twentieth-Century America* (2005); Manning Marable's *Living Black History: How Reimagining the African-American Past Can Remake America's Future* (2006); William C. Rhoden's *Forty Million Dollar Slaves: The Rise, Fall, and Redemption of the Black Athlete* (2007); and Harriet A. Washington, *Medical Apartheid: The Dark History of Medical Experimentation on Black Americans from Colonial Times to the Present* (2008). Many contemporary issues and incidents can serve as insightful teaching opportunities for African American history, such as the reinvestigations into the murder of Emmett Till and the killing of other martyrs of the civil rights era; the murder trial and conviction of Edgar Ray Killen; the University of Michigan's precedent-setting affirmative action cases and the subsequent Supreme Court's decisions; the Senate's June 2005 apology for lynchings; the July 30, 2008, House of Representatives' apology for slavery and Jim Crow segregation; the tragedies of Hurricane Katrina; the Jena 6 case; numerous racial profiling and police brutality cases; startling black-male prison population statistics; the rare posthumous pardoning of Jack Johnson by Congress; and the state of hip-hop culture and rap music.

Goals for Teaching African American History to College Students

History teachers and professors certainly have individual goals and purposes for teaching African American history. One could say that they also have a challenging responsibility and ideally should help their students to

* Historicize the African American experience while developing what Peter Seixas has called a "multiperspectival historical truth" for their times
* Acquire knowledge and understanding of African American history based on analyses of the existing historiography, multiple interpretations, conflicting accounts, and primary sources
* Recognize African Americans' various contributions in the creation of the United States culture and history in relationship to other groups of American peoples
* Place African American history within diasporic and international historical contexts
* Decipher how African Americans have historically responded to legal and extralegal forms of racial- , class- , and gender-motivated oppression
* Determine what historical factors make African Americans a unique group despite their intraracial diversity and commonalities with other American peoples
* Imagine—from Afrocentric, authentically descriptive, and explicitly non-presentist perspectives—what life was like for African Americans during the different historical periods under consideration
* Construct their own insightful and practical systems for explaining, comprehending, and operationalizing African American history

The teaching of African American history in colleges and universities poses many challenges and, not surprisingly, has been an issue of importance for African American scholars and historians since the late nineteenth and early twentieth centuries. While the American Historical Association's Committee of Seven assessed the teaching of history in U.S. schools in 1899, sophisticated discussions about the teaching and study of African American history were initiated by black intellectuals, including countless late-nineteenth- and early-twentieth-century educators, early black historians such as George Washington Williams, W. E. B. Du Bois, and Carter G. Woodson, and other scholars at historically black colleges and universities (HBCUs). During the era of Jim Crow segregation, many black historians and scholars at HBCUs actively taught African American history and certainly developed pedagogical ideologies and strategies: George Edmund Haynes at Fisk University; Benjamin Brawley at several colleges and universities; Carter G. Woodson,

Rayford W. Logan, Elsie M. Lewis, Charles H. Wesley, Walter Dyson, and Marion Thompson Wright, among others, at Howard University; Earl E. Thorpe at Southern University; Lorenzo Johnston Greene and William Sherman Savage at Lincoln University, Missouri; James Hugo Johnston and Luther Porter Jackson at Virginia State College; Benjamin Quarles at Morgan State University; Helen G. Edmonds at North Carolina Central University; L. D. Reddick at Dillard University; Merl R. Eppse at Tennessee State University; Alrutheus A. Taylor at Fisk University; and John Hope Franklin at St. Augustine's College, North Carolina College for Negroes, and Howard University. August Meier was among the few white scholars to teach black history at an HBCU during the mid- to late 1940s.[14]

In response to the black student protests of the 1960s and 1970s, predominantly white universities scrambled to initiate courses in African American history. Prior to the civil rights movement, the Black Power era, and the "blistering years" of the black studies movement, the teaching of African American history at predominantly white universities was rare. In 1919, Woodson was optimistic in observing that Ohio State University, the University of Nebraska, the University of Oklahoma, the University of Chicago, the University of Missouri, and Harvard University offered courses pertaining to the so-called "Negro Problem." At the same time, he acknowledged the near-unanimous white academic racism of his times. In the 1930s, Philip Foner introduced African American history at City College of New York (CCNY), and in 1937 Max Yeargan, the first African American to teach at CCNY (part-time), taught "what was probably the first formal black history course in the curriculum of a predominantly white college." At the end of World War II, "there were scarcely twenty black historians with PhDs engaged in or available for college teaching positions" and the first full-time African American historian to teach at a predominantly white university was John Hope Franklin. In 1956, he was hired to serve as the chairman of Brooklyn College's history department.[15]

In the late nineteenth century, several self-trained black historians published books that addressed the teaching of African American history. In 1891, amateur historian, lawyer, and teacher Edward Augustus Johnson published the first textbook on black history, *School History of the Negro Race in America from 1691 to 1890,* largely as a tool for schoolteachers to help inspire black children. In 1897, Philadelphia native John Stephens Durham published his brief (yet insightful, according to William Toll) *To Teach the Negro History (A Suggestion),* and during the 1890s he lectured on teaching black history at Hampton Institute, Tuskegee Institute, and other HBCUs.[16] Nevertheless, published scholarship on the teaching of African American history began as a distinct topic of interest in the 1920s and has flowered in two major phases: the 1920s until the eve of the modern civil rights movement, and during the "blistering years" of black studies. From the 1980s until about 2000, a small collection of studies on the teaching of African American history were produced. Beyond a handful of articles in the *History Teacher, School Review, Journal of Black Studies,* and *Social Education,* many scholarly articles on the teaching of African American history have appeared in the *Journal of Negro Education* and the *Journal of Negro History,* now called the *Journal of African American History.* Most of these articles, moreover, have tended to focus on teaching African American history at the secondary-school level.[17] The historical scholarship on teaching mainstream U.S. history predates that on African American history and since the early 1990s has "come into being" as a field.[18] Although provocative, this body of scholarship has collectively failed to directly acknowledge the teaching of African American history, even including the most recent comprehensive study.

Discussions about the teaching of African American history were common at early meetings of the Association for the Study of Negro Life and History (ASNLH). For instance, at the annual ASNLH conferences during the early black history movement, teachers and scholars—often black women—routinely discussed teaching African American history in secondary schools and black colleges and universities. After founding Negro History Week in 1926, Carter G. Woodson routinely philosophized about the importance of teaching African American history at all educational levels. Beginning with *The Negro in Our History* (1922), Woodson produced a distinct genre of scholarship to specifically aid in the teaching of African American history. In his 1929 "Annual Report of the Director," Woodson stressed the importance of teaching African American history: "Instruction with respect to the life and history of the Negro requires probably more preparation than any other phase of social science for the simple reason that no other problems have been so grossly misinterpreted and so generally misunderstood. To undertake to give instruction in this field in which one is not prepared, then, would be a most expensive error for which future generations must pay in suffering from other misunderstandings like the many which handicap us today."[19]

During the 1930s and 1940s, the work of the ASNLH focused on encouraging black youth to study black history. Woodson and the ASNLH even rewarded young blacks who studied their past by offering children various opportunities to win black history awards. Founded in 1937, the *Negro History Bulletin* essentially served as a pragmatic teaching tool for African American teachers. As indicated by Woodson's sentiments above, he believed that successfully teaching black history required "more preparation than any other phase of social science." Between the early 1920s and the early 1950s, a handful of articles focusing on the teaching of African American history were published in the *Journal of Negro History*. Echoing Woodson, in "The Teaching of Negro History" (1923), J. W. Bell insisted that the teaching of African American history "will serve the two-fold purpose of informing the white man and inspiring the Negro." About a decade later, in another article, J. A. Bailey maintained that the African American history teacher should "take as his aim the dissemination of the truth . . . with the idea of opening the minds of the class to the possibilities of the future."[20]

In 1940, Samuel E. Warren, a professor at Prairie View State College, shared with *Journal* readers an innovative class that he conceptualized on "the historical development of Negro labor in the United States." Referring to the most recent publications on black labor by Sterling D. Spero and Abram L. Harris, Charles Wesley, Lorenzo J. Greene, Du Bois, and Horace R. Cayton and George S. Mitchell, Warren outlined a multidisciplinary course for black colleges and universities that brought together a wide cross section of the community. "Instructor, students, workers employed nearby and available labor leaders, government officials, representatives of foundations, and pressure groups— these would be engaged cooperatively in offering the course. They would have different approaches—orthodox, unorthodox and heterodox—emanating from some basic theory or philosophy of life."[21] Certainly idealistic for its time, Warren's wide-reaching approach would be worth revisiting today.

In 1951, two articles on teaching African American history appeared in the *Journal of Negro History*. In the first, "The Teaching of Negro History in Secondary Schools," William M. Brewer called on history teachers to be organized, dispassionate, and dedicated to "the stubborn facts of history."[22] His practical "methods of teaching Negro history" included using biographies, analyzing African Americans in business and the professions, and drawing upon visual arts, family records, African American magazines and newspapers, and socio-drama. The second, R. O. Johnson's insightful article "Teaching Negro History to Adults," proposed that African American history teachers focus on the "nature of the learners" when determining "the guiding principles for the selection of content" and called for "dramatic" yet "educative" teaching methods that were relevant to adult learners' realities. Drawing from popular culture, he suggested, for instance, using Ethel Waters's life as a point of departure into investigating broader trends in African American history. A pragmatist, Johnson also encouraged teachers of African American history to use the mass media, existing adult education programs, and engaging, readable materials.[23]

Collectively, the published pre–black studies movement scholarship on the teaching of African American history was limited, largely free from debates, and reflected the fundamental ideologies of the formative years of the African American historical profession. Warren's 1940 essay on teaching black labor history and Johnson's 1951 essay on teaching African American history to adult learners were perhaps the most innovative pre–civil rights era and Black Power movement assessments on teaching African American history. Their ideas of tailoring the teaching of African American history to the black community and a particular group of learners are especially applicable when considering the millennial hip-hop generation.

While there may be a lack of published scholarship on teaching African American history from the early 1950s until the late 1960s, with the Black Power era, the black studies movement, and the gradual institutionalization of African American history and studies in the late 1960s and the 1970s, scholarship on teaching African American history flowered. Mirroring the sudden upsurge of African American historiography and black studies scholarship, many articles were produced on teaching African American history in higher education between 1969 and 1979. Interestingly, many of these articles were written by scholars who made marginal contributions to African American historiography.

The treatment of African American history in the quarterly journal *The History Teacher,* an important scholarly outlet for historians' discourse on teaching founded in 1966, is a testimony to the mainstream U.S. academy's response to black studies activists' passionate demands for the study of African American history. Between 1969 and 1980, eight articles on African American history appeared in the journal, five of which briefly reviewed teaching resources.[24] The remaining three articles probed more deeply into the actual processes, strategies, and challenges of teaching African American history. For instance, Michael W. Whalon and Davis D. Joyce imparted their experiences of teaching a well-received "experimental course" in African American history at the University of Tulsa during the peak of the Black Power era. With only three black students in their class, Whalon and Joyce placed a priority on African Americans' perspectives. "As whites teaching Black History," they recalled, "we thought it essential to permit the black experience to speak for itself as much as possible. One way we attempted to do this was through black speakers and films."[25] Similarly, Dominic Candeloro published an intriguing essay on his experiences of teaching African American history at the Ohio State University, Lima campus. As an "experience in cooperative historical research and writing" and oral history, he required his students to research the history of blacks in Lima. Candeloro celebrated the fact that his class "brought inexperienced white students into contact for the first time with numerous black figures in the community."[26]

As many mainstream colleges and universities raced and struggled to initiate black studies programs, institutes, and courses, more than a few significant articles were published on the teaching of black studies and black history. One of the more critical articles on the teaching of African American history, published during the outbreak of Black Power in the academy, was Melvin Drimmer's "Teaching Black History in America: What Are the Problems?" A history professor at Spelman College, Drimmer argued that two different curricula were needed to teach African American history, "one for black and one for white students" because "blacks and whites bring various levels of awareness and knowledge to the basic course." Drimmer maintained that "white students must be brought along slower, realizing—and I do not mean to be patronizing—that they are culturally deprived. To whites every little thing must be explained and proved." Drimmer suggested that universities hire white professors to teach white students African American history and black professors to teach black students. He argued that knowledgeable black high school teachers be used as resources and that there be the development of "a dozen or more centers for the teaching and study of black history" at institutions with intact African studies centers as well as at black colleges.[27]

Drimmer proclaimed that African American history was a consciousness-raising device for white and black students and should be taught in a manner that recognized the suffering that characterizes the African American experience so that whites in particular will "not forget what it has meant to be a black man in white America." He also stressed that the teaching of African American history be integrated into the teaching of the American experience so that a totally new, "revolutionary" approach and narrative is produced. "What is needed most," Drimmer highlighted, "is not to segregate black history from the basic American history programs, but to build the Black vision and experience so into the American experience that a completely new version of American history emerges. This is . . . the revolutionary potential of black history." Drimmer's historical integrationist argument and ideal, initiated first most explicitly by Woodson, remains to be achieved.[28]

In 1968, Yale University hosted a historic symposium on black studies where a diverse group of professional scholars, intellectuals, and activists discussed higher educational institutions' responsibilities to reevaluate the role of African American life and culture in their curricula. Edwin S. Redkey presented a paper titled "On Teaching and Learning Black History," wherein he argued that African American history could not only enlighten white students but could also serve as a device for teaching other disciplines and subjects. Redkey structured his paper as a critical response to popular ambivalence and objections "to the idea of teaching the Black experience in schools." Among other teaching strategies, Redkey encouraged history educators to consider African American history within the contexts of colonialism and nationalism in order to teach the African American experience within a comparative framework with other ethnic groups.[29]

In 1969, *Social Education,* the official journal of the National Council for the Social Studies, devoted its April issue to the teaching of African American history. Contributors Nathan Hare and Louis R. Harlan offered some thought-provoking insights. Hare, founder of the seminal black studies movement at San Francisco State College in the late 1960s, maintained that in order to fulfill its "therapeutic value," African American history must be taught from "the Black perspective" that is relevant to black community health and the creation of a "new America." Hare's ultimate goal was unapologetically activist-centered. "The teacher of Black history and culture," he pronounced, "must be an agent for transforming history and culture, making the student . . . a part of that transmission and ultimate transformation." For Hare, African American history needed to strengthen black students' commitment to their communities at local and national levels. It should be no surprise that he supported creative and pragmatic teaching methodologies, such as community-based fieldwork assignments. Like Woodson and, decades later, Manning Marable, Hare also advocated that African American history teachers tap into African American holidays, historical sites, pageants, and oral histories so that "the student experiences some of the fabric of the history and culture as he learns it."[30]

In direct contrast to Hare, Louis Harlan, a self-proclaimed "old-fashioned integrationist" white professional historian, opened his article by disagreeing with those black cultural nationalists who sought to enlist "Black history in the cause of racial revolution." Harlan offered five major interpretive themes for teaching African American history: white racism, a non-progressive character, historical cyclicalism, cultural history, and urbanization. Harlan concurred with his black cultural nationalist adversaries on at least one key pedagogical tool: the autobiographies and other writings of African American spokespersons. Yet, out of touch with the visions of youthful black studies leaders, Harlan, like other moderate commentators on the teaching of African American history, was clearly uncomfortable with novice and professional black historian-activists' militant rhetoric and their quest to employ African American history as a viable vehicle for black advancement and psychological liberation. By deeming African American history a nonprogressive history stamped by racial oppression, Harlan also ignored the central theme of per-severance in African American history, a concept that needs to be explained to students.[31]

Challenging the racism and opportunism of white scholars, as well as the nationalistic tones and agendas prevalent during the black studies move-ment, moderate consensus builder John W. Blassingame argued in his essay "Black Studies and the Role of the Historian" that African American history be taught by rigorously trained historians in the field, black and white—objectivity being paramount. Blassingame prioritized delving into the con-troversial debate surrounding who should and could effectively teach African American history. Objectivity, scholarly precision, and an ideal "search for the truth" were paramount in his view. White historians, he noted, must strive for cross-cultural and multidisciplinary understanding and acknowledge new methods of retrieving knowledge. According to Blassingame, black historians, who were called on by black university students for their insiders' views and who were in great demand during the scramble to hire African American teachers, had to avoid the pitfalls of myth-making and seeking to "obtain a hearing for the have nots."[32]

At the end of the 1970s, B. Lee Cooper published a practical essay in the *Journal of Negro Education* about using black popular music as an effective medium for generating "reflection by young blacks on issues of historical significance" within their communal realities. Essentially, Cooper outlined how the lives and music of R&B, soul, and blues artists, "major lyrical spokes-persons," could "provide significant insights into the past, present, and future." Especially intriguing is Cooper's charting of how prevailing themes, concepts, and issues of contemporary African American history were expressed by black musical artists. Cooper repeatedly made a direct plea to historians to be creative in acknowledging black musicians' place within African American oral history. "It is my opinion that without the introduction of such innova-tive instructional techniques," Cooper wrote, "the majority of students will continue to question the validity of Black history in their lives." Cooper also provided his readers with a bibliography of scholarship on black music as well as a "core album collection." Cooper's approach is very relevant today, since hip-hop and R&B music are central to millennial black students' lives.[33]

Despite several important publications during the Black Power era, since the 1980s scholarship on the teaching of African American history at the university level has been scant. The "state of the art" conference on African American history at Purdue University in 1983 did, however, offer some valu-able insights into teaching African American history; as well, several essays in *The State of Afro-American History: Past, Present, Future* (1986) probe into the value and philosophies of teaching. For example, based on syllabi that she received from six different universities, Bettye J. Gardner suggested that many history professors ignored the black past's complexity, the role of black women, and vital primary sources. At the same time, she acknowledged those professors whose course descriptions were exemplary. "The teaching of Afro-American history," Gardner exclaimed, "is serious business."[34]

In 1992, Robert L. Harris Jr. published *Teaching African-American History.* For those expecting a methodological manual on how to teach African American history, the title of Harris' study may be a bit misleading. This pamphlet essentially summarizes the broad trends in African American history from black Americans' African origins through the modern civil rights movement. However, Harris did offer a very useful outline, noting that the "transitions from 'Africa to America,' 'Slavery to Freedom,' 'Countryside to City,' and 'Segregation to Civil Rights' provide a conceptual framework for organizing the Afro-American experience thematically and chronologically and for incorporating it in the trajectory of American history." Harris's chart for African American history is also pragmatic, highlighting what he identified as the four major transitions: the overriding changing process, the turning point, the watershed years, and the transformation of the majority of African Americans.[35]

A byproduct of a 1998 NEH teaching institute at the W. E. B. Du Bois Institute for Afro-American Research at Howard University, *Teaching the American Civil Rights Movement* (2002) includes more than a dozen thought-provoking essays based on a multidisciplinary group of scholars' challenging yet rewarding experiences teaching African American history, particularly the modern civil rights movement, to diverse groups of college and university students. These scholars reflect upon and share their practical and insightful teaching strategies, course syllabi, lecture outlines, and sample assignments. They discuss the value of a host of innovative ways to teach African American history, stressing the importance of "pre-teaching" (contextualization); gender, race, and class analyses; music and fiction as windows into the African American experience; oral history and interviews; personal narratives and autobiographies; acknowledging the diverse backgrounds and worldviews of their students in order to develop student-centered teaching methods; stressing the intimate relationship between the civil rights movement and the Black Power era (in other words, revising normative periodizations of African American history); and recognizing "lesser-known" figures and alternatives to the widely recognized strategies of nonviolent direct action. Rhonda Y. Williams's student performance projects, exercises in "expressive culture and history," are particularly applicable to hip-hop generation millennial learners. "Performance projects," Williams contends, "do the pedagogical work of forcing students to take the responsibility for their learning while simultaneously reorienting the general lore that history is a boring, passive enterprise. Through the performance piece, history and other disciplines can become active, and for many, more engaging."[36]

Two of the most recent articles on teaching dimensions of African American history in colleges and universities have been published by female scholars in the *Journal of American History* and the *Journal of Women's History*. In 2000, Beverly Bunch-Lyons shared her experiences teaching black women's history using novels and literature from the 1700s until the 1990s, including works by Phillis Wheatley, Octavia Butler, Jessie Redmon Fauset, Alice Walker, Toni Morrison, Gayl Jones, Elaine Brown, Sister Souljah, Terry McMillan, and Noliwe M. Rooks. Based on her experiences, Bunch-Lyons concluded that the works by these writers "proved to be an extremely useful tool for teaching the history of black women in the United States." For Bunch-Lyons, this approach allowed for application of "a nontraditional teaching methodology in history that challenges notions of the discipline."[37] Historians can certainly enlist numerous novels in teaching black history.

More recently, in 2007 Daina Ramey Berry wrote an essay on teaching Deborah Gray White's popular *Ar'n't I A Woman? Female Slaves in the Plantation South* (first published in 1985). Drawing from her experiences teaching black women's history at Michigan State University, Berry points out the usefulness of White's study as "an instructive tool" for teaching "the history of slavery from a gendered perspective." Berry recalls how White's study "pushed" her students "to consider the lives of enslaved females" and laid the foundations for papers that discussed a range of provocative issues, including "labor and marriage; enslaved children, runaways, and truants; rape and domestic abuse." Berry also discussed the range of primary sources that she introduced to her upper-division undergraduate students. Essays like Berry's are important in helping history professors, especially junior faculty, think more deeply about teaching African American women's history.[38]

The significant interest in generating scholarship on the teaching of history among a coterie of Americanists during the 1990s does not seem to have been shared by African Americanists. It is worth noting that scholarship on the teaching of African American history surfaced during two important periods: the early black history movement and the black studies movement during the late 1960s until the early 1970s. Woodson was the preeminent figure of the former era, and he and the ASNLH saw great value in teaching African American history. The *Journal of Negro Education,* an important outlet for scholarship on teaching African American history, was also founded during this critical period in 1932. The published scholarship on teaching

African American history during the middle of the Black Power movement was largely influenced by the fact that "Black Studies programs began in undergraduate instruction."[39] The post–Black Power era lack of scholarship on teaching black history does not mean, however, that teaching was not important in the African American historical enterprise. It has always been central to the profession, especially before the integration of African American history at mainstream, predominantly white universities. It must also be acknowledged that the scholarship on teaching and learning (SOTL) has been a subfield for only several decades.

Teaching African American History to Today's College Students

There are many possible creative approaches to teaching African American history in higher education today, many of which are derived from the monumental advancements in information and multimedia technology. My brief suggestions for teaching an introductory survey on African American history are based on what Brookfield has identified as the "four complementary lenses" of the "critically reflective practice": one's own personal experience ("autobiography as a learner"), the existing scholarship on teaching and learning African American history ("theoretical literature"), conversations with experts in the African American historical profession ("colleagues' experiences"), and interaction with students (the "learner's eyes").[40]

In 2008, the *Journal of Blacks in Higher Education* noted that "the stereotypical view of the African-American college student rushing into black studies majors is totally false." Based on data from the Department of Education, in 2006 less than 0.8 percent of all bachelor's degrees awarded to blacks were in black studies, and for the same year 1.2 percent of blacks earning bachelor's degrees were history majors. In 2006, less than 0.3 percent of all master's degrees awarded to blacks were in black studies and 0.2 percent of blacks earning master's degrees did so in the field of history. However, in 2006, 25.4 percent of all bachelor's degrees and 30.4 percent of all master's degrees awarded to blacks were in business management.[41] Viewed in economic terms, it is no surprise that very few black students nationwide pursue B.A. and M.A. degrees in African American studies and history. Instead of chastising the millennial hip-hop generation for their lack of historicity and their apparent disconnect from African American studies and history, professors of history should develop new and refreshing strategies for stimulating their students' interest in African American history. How can professors teach

African American history so that it attracts greater attention from today's millennial learners, especially African Americans? What are some effective teaching approaches and strategies for today's African American college and university students? What should we know about their (borrowing from Sam Wineburg) "historical cognition?"

Professors should actively make African American history relevant to the lives of African American students. This requires that they understand their students' culture. Beyond reading the recent scholarship on the hip-hop generation and millennial learners, the most effective way to understand black students is through intimate interaction. Without compromising the social distance between the professor and the student, the African American history professor should attend black students' events as much as possible. Among other discoveries, it will become clear that hip-hop culture, fraternity and sorority life, the black church, and of course various social events (parties, fashion shows, cultural programs) are among the salient features of African American millennial student culture. At a minimum, professors, especially those not teaching at HBCUs, should peruse recent issues of the *Journal of Blacks in Higher Education* for its coverage of black college and university student life. Many scholars, including essayists in recent volumes of the *Journal of Negro Education* such as Gordon L. Berry, Joe R. Feagin, Hernán Vera, Nikitah Imani, Jawanza Kunjufu, and Deborah Davis have offered useful insight into the challenges facing black college and university students.

Hip-hop culture is historically grounded and can serve as an ideal teaching tool, the basis for a "culturally relevant pedagogy."[42] Hip hop consists of many elements and pillars: DJ-ing (deejaying), MC-ing (emceeing), graffiti art, rapping, clothing, visual art, dialect and language, food, accessories, and style. Hip hop is essentially a way of life, a culture. "Hip-hop is where our students live—the music they listen to, their traditions, the language they speak, the clothes they wear, the way they interact in the streets."[43] There are many ways that African American history professors can tap into and appropriate the various components and symbols of hip hop to teach effectively. As Derrick P. Alridge has suggested, "teachers should become familiar with Hip Hop culture as a social movement. By doing so, teachers can show their students how hip-hop can be interpreted within the larger context of the black freedom struggle."[44]

While Blake Harrison and Alexander Rappaport's *Hip-Hop U.S. History: The New and Innovative Approach to Learning American History* (2006) was designed for elementary and high school students, they raise some valuable insights about using rap, an essential pillar of hip hop, to teach history. "It is up to us to put these stories and facts in a form that makes them feel immediate, and there is nothing more engaging or immediate than hip-hop music." Harrison and Rappaport accentuate, "Flocabulary produces educational hip-hop music to teach and engage students of all backgrounds. We truly believe that hip-hop music, when combined with a positive message and academic content, is an amazingly powerful learning tool."[45]

The artistic expressions of many of today's hip-hop emcees, most notably Nas, dead prez, Common, Talib Kweli, and Mos Def, can also serve as useful historical, pedagogical mechanisms. These major lyrical spokespersons and other artists delve into African American history in some of their tracks. Hip hop has been in many ways shaped by history and since its "golden age" has actively sampled from the past.[46] Furthermore, by nature, historians of the African American experience are similar to emcees. Pioneering hip hop scholar Tricia Rose has defined the role of the emcee in the black community in a manner that is strikingly similar to the role of the black historian.[47] Historians of African American culture and emcees both tell stories about the past, present, and future. Historians of the black experience and emcees are both modern day "griots." Historians of the African American experience have the potential to be academic emcees, approaching the historian's craft with the passion, energy, and competitiveness characterizing hip hop. Younger African American historians can also appropriate the rhetorical conditions, rhythms, and styling of exemplary emcees. This will increase their popularity among the millennial hip-hop generation who appreciate information presented to them with passion, energy, realism, and humor, as their favorite emcees and entertainers do. While historians of the African American past do not need to rely on the same language that hip hop artists do, it can be advantageous, as linguist and African American language expert Geneva Smitherman has argued, to be familiar with hip-hop language, style, and attire. And as Molefi Kete Asante has argued, "visual styling" in mannerisms and attire are vital parts of the African American, Afrocentric rhetorical tradition. "The genius of the speaker determines the quality of the visual styling."[48] Many African American historians born before and during the civil rights era may view this approach as being unnecessary and counterproductive to the academic rigor and seriousness of the traditional historian's craft. Nonetheless, research indicates that learner-centered teaching is effective.

The hip-hop generation, like today's U.S. youth culture in general, is very much visually oriented. We have access to countless photographs and images as well as numerous excellent African American history documentaries, especially those produced by California Newsreel and PBS. There are also a host of contemporary and recently released Hollywood films that can serve as useful windows into African American history. Any of the myriad films in the most recent edition of Donald Bogle's classic *Toms, Coons, Mulattoes, Mammies, and Bucks: An Interpretive History of Blacks in American Films* could be used as fruitful points of departure into a wide range of themes, events, turning points, and important and even more "ordinary" figures in black America's past. Spike Lee's *Malcolm X* (1992), *Four Little Girls* (1997), *Bamboozled* (2000), *Jim Brown: All American* (2003), and *Miracle at St. Anna* (2008) are excellent films for delving into dimensions of pre–Black Power era African American history. Among the most recent Hollywood films that re-visit important periods and incidents of African American history are *Miracle at St. Anna* and *The Great Debaters* (2007). Directed by Denzel Washington and inspired by a true story, *The Great Debaters* film chronicles the life of scholar-activist Melvin B. Tolson and his debate team at a small rural black college in Texas during the Great Depression. The early years of C.O.R.E. co-founder James L. Farmer Jr. are also depicted in the film. There are many powerful scenes in this film (including a lynching) that help visual learners better comprehend the nuances of pre–civil rights era African American history. Lee's *Miracle at St. Anna* depicts many of the realities faced by black male soldiers during World War II. There is an especially powerful scene in this film in which black soldiers in uniform are denied service in a white Jim Crow diner. Lee's historical imagination and recreation of black resistance is empowering for young black viewers.

More than anything else, the millennial hip-hop generation has been significantly influenced and shaped by today's unprecedented information technology, especially the internet. Professors of African American history must acknowledge that their students rely on the internet. You Tube can be a very useful source for visual footage and audio recordings of African American historic figures and events. James B. Stewart has recently suggested that various digitized internet resources should be used more creatively in college and university Africana studies courses. Stewart posited that such an approach is necessary in the new millennium because "the learning styles of traditional-age college students today are generally more tactile and visu-ally oriented than earlier generations." Equally important, Stewart argued that since Africana studies courses "disproportionately attract students from digitally-underserved populations," using the internet in such classes can help increase many black students' knowledge of digital technology, an essential tool for twenty-first-century students.[49] Such an approach makes sense. In 2005, for instance, it was estimated that about 40 percent of blacks, compared to about 67 percent of whites, had access to the internet in their homes. More-over, "black children are roughly 35 percent less likely to have a computer at home and have Internet access than white children."[50] Abdul Alkalimat's

The African American Experience in Cyberspace: A Resource Guide to the Best Web Sites on Black Culture and History (2003) is a very helpful starting point for introducing students to those useful internet sources on African American history and culture. In his most recent study, Manning Marable has offered an approach to African American history that is very relevant to various groups of millennial learners, "a method of historical investigation" that deduces "the distance between the past, the present, and the future to effectively reconstruct these authentic narratives."[51]

Educational theorist James A. Banks has argued that knowledge of the African American past could and "should make a unique contribution to the development of students' decision-making and social action skills" and that African American history is in essence applied history.[52] After exposing their students to African American history, professors should develop assignments that challenge students to develop solutions to the multitude of historically rooted dilemmas still affecting African Americans nationwide. At minimum, students of the African American experience should be challenged to speculate the future of African Americans based on the historical record, distant and more contemporary. As Bakari Kitwana and Todd Boyd have adamantly argued, there is a great cultural divide between the hip-hop generation and their elders socialized by the civil rights era.[53]

Professors of African American history can help diminish this rift while increasing the hip-hop generation's historicism. For instance, oral history assignments that require students to interview elder African Americans for information about the Great Depression, the eras of World War II and the Cold War, and the civil rights and Black Power movements not only stimulate cross-generational dialogues, but also serve as insightful, first-hand windows into and primary sources for these various periods. As educational theorist Thad Sitton argued several decades ago, exercises in African American "community-specific history," public history, and oral history can allow black students to tap into "a living history that is all around them and from which they personally derive."[54]

James W. Loewen, Sam Wineberg, and others have adamantly addressed the limitations of using textbooks to teach U.S. history.[55] At the same time, if correctly supplemented, textbooks can help professors of U.S. history provide their students with a basic framework and narrative, however elementary. Peter Kolchin has identified the challenges of teaching U.S. history to college and university students with textbooks. "As the number of textbooks has proliferated, it has become more difficult to assess their relative quality. Students seem to dislike them all. . . . Although tempted to dispense with a textbook altogether and to rely only on the primary documents that I also assign, I feel that students need one—and that *I* too need one, so that I can be selective and interpretive in lecture without worrying that the students are missing important parts of the national narrative."[56]

Scholars, historians, and educational reformers have been concerned with the treatment of African Americans in U.S. history textbooks since the first half of the twentieth century. Woodson published *The Negro in Our History* because mainstream U.S. history textbooks ignored and misrepresented African Americans. In the preface of the first edition of his *The Negro in the Making of America* (1965), Benjamin Quarles observed that many textbooks were "silent on the Negro." Since *The Negro in Our History* was first published in 1922, numerous leading historians have published sweeping narratives of the African American experience. Building upon the critiques of L. D. Reddick, W. E. B. Du Bois, Edna M. Colson, and Marie Carpenter during the 1930s and 1940s, in 1986 James D. Anderson published an insightful essay that critically explored how six major secondary school history textbooks published between 1977 and 1981 portrayed African Americans. He concluded that the "overall portrayal of the black experience" in these textbooks was "misleading, superficial, and even racist, not so much in an overt manner as during the pre-1960s, but certainly in an institutionalized sense."[57] Similarly, hip-hop generation black educational historian Derrick P. Alridge has recently critiqued how the "master narratives" in leading mainstream U.S. history textbooks have limited high school students' exposure to "one of America's most heroic icons, Martin Luther King, Jr."[58]

John Hope Franklin's *From Slavery to Freedom* (first published in 1947) remains one of the most widely read and best-selling textbooks for university courses in African American history and "has been by far the most influential, not least in forcing 'establishment' colleges and universities to take African-American history seriously as an intellectual endeavor." Celebrating the fiftieth anniversary of Franklin's classic, in the late 1990s the *Journal of Blacks in Higher Education* and the *Journal of Negro History* published dozens of leading historians' tributes to *From Slavery to Freedom*.[59] In 2009, Franklin and Evelyn B. Higginbotham published the ninth and most recent edition of *From Slavery to Freedom*. Since 2000, five major textbooks suitable for college and university students have been published on the African American experience: Robin D. G. Kelley and Earl Lewis's *To Make Our World Anew: A History of African Americans* (2000); Joe William Trotter Jr.'s *The African American Experience* (2000); Darlene Clark Hine, William C. Hine, and Stanley Harrold's *The African American Odyssey* (first published in December of 1999 and most recently updated in 2009); Clayborne Carson, Emma J. Lapsansky-Werner, and Gary B. Nash's *African American Lives: The*

Struggle for Freedom (2005); and most recently Nell Irvin Painter's *Creating Black Americans: African-American History and Its Meanings, 1619 to the Present* (2006). Concurring with Kolchin's reflections on textbooks, I review these books focusing on their usefulness in the college and university African American history survey.

To Make Our World Anew represents, as one reviewer noted, "the first new interpretation of African American history for the twenty-first century."[60] Subdivided into ten chapters covering the vast period from the early sixteenth century through the 1990s, this study is not a traditional, mundane textbook, but rather a chronologically organized anthology of the African American experience —"truly a collective endeavor" in the editors' words— featuring the contributions of eleven leading scholars in various subfields in African American history. *To Make Our World Anew* differs from previously published studies of its genre not only in terms of its structure, but in its embracing of the social and cultural history of women and working-class peoples. Equally significant, the authors also place black America within broader diasporic and international contexts. "For if this book demonstrates anything," Kelley and Lewis write, "it is that African Americans saw themselves as both Americans and part of a larger, international black diaspora. *To Make Our World Anew* tells the story of the nation but places the struggles and achievements of black people in a larger international framework."[61] The last three chapters are especially excellent in exposing students to the underresearched African American experience since the Great Depression. Equally noteworthy, each chapter is written in sophisticated yet simple language.

A year after Kelley and Lewis's work appeared, Joe William Trotter Jr. published *The African American Experience.* Structured like a typical U.S. college and university history textbook, Trotter's study begins with ancient Egypt and independent, precolonial African societies and ends with black life during the 1990s. Central to Trotter's analysis is acknowledging the diversity within the black community. "This book," writes Trotter, "shows how African Americans developed their own notions of work, family, culture, and power and forged their own community. The black poor, working-class, and business and professional people created a broad range of multiclass institutions." Building upon "research in African American social, working-class, and women's history," Trotter's text "probes both class and gender conflicts within the black community."[62] Included in *The African American Experience* are revealing photos in color as well as black and white, a comprehensive chronology and bibliography covering each of the book's six parts, population statistics, and important primary documents.

First released around the same time as Kelley and Lewis's study, Darlene

Clark Hine, William C. Hine, and Stanley Harrold's *The African-American Odyssey* has been updated four times. In 2009, a "special edition" of this study was completed. This is quite remarkable since the eighth edition of Franklin's *From Slavery to Freedom* was released more than fifty years after it was first published. Popular among many college and university professors as well as being the official textbook adopted by Philadelphia's public schools, this textbook is exemplary. Spanning the period from ancient Africa through the 1990s, the authors view this work as being a first. "This survey is the first comprehensive college textbook of the African American experience," drawing "on recent research to present black history in a clear and direct manner, with a broad social, cultural, and political framework." Like the works of Kelley, Lewis, and Trotter, *The African American Odyssey* addresses the contributions of various classes and groups of African Americans. To a much greater extent than previous texts, Hine, Hine, and Harrold detail the contributions of black women "as active builders of black culture."[63] The documents that appear in Trotter's text also appear in the appendix of *The African- American Odyssey*. More important, *The African-American Odyssey* has numerous special features, including many timelines, unique photos, useful internet websites, an audio CD of African American oral tradition, as well as many pragmatic supplementing instructional materials. Though written for high school and college and university students, this textbook is also an invaluable tool for novice professors of the African American experience. Simply put, it provides its readers with a very solid, clearly articulated, and logically organized narrative.

In 2004, Clayborne Carson, Emma J. Lapsansky-Werner, and Gary B. Nash published *African American Lives: The Struggle for Freedom*. One of the numerous historians to review the book before its debut, I find this study to be useful. It departs from its predecessors by engaging "the reader in viewing history through the lens of many biographies and through the perspectives of people who lived those struggles." In embracing such an approach, the authors position "African American lives at the center of the narrative and as the basis of analysis." In this study, the lives of individual African Americans serve as the "pivot points that provide a window on the historical changes of their generation." They focus on "the experience of people rather than forces."[64] While showcasing the activism of major black leaders, they also use the lives of "ordinary" black people as representations of the worldviews of the black working-class masses. While the text's "First Person" shaded areas are revealing, and while introducing each chapter with a biographical sketch is engaging, *African American Lives* probably will not supersede *The African-American Odyssey*.

The most recent major textbook on the African American experience is Nell Irvin Painter's *Creating Black Americans: African-American History and Its Meaning, 1619 to the Present* (2006). Painter distinguishes her study from previous black history narratives by using "black artists' images" that directly relate to African American history to accompany the "historical narrative." Deeming that artists act as historians not bound by professional historians' rules, Painter argues that "black visual artists have forged a magnificent account of the creation of a people."[65] Painter's approach is new and innovative, departing significantly from that of earlier African American history textbooks. The seemingly countless visual images and brief descriptions of the artists' works are refreshing, adding to the effectiveness of the overarching narrative. This book would be excellent for African American art history courses.

In order to be commercially and intellectually successful, the next major textbook on African American history must add something significant to the five studies that have been published in the twenty-first century. Robin D. G. Kelley, Tera Hunter, and Earl Lewis are completing a general survey of African American history to be published by Norton. It faces the challenge of transcending some solid, previously published millennial black history narratives.

Another potentially effective educational tool for college and university students are African American historic sites and museums. As revealed by a perusal of *Profiles of Black Museums* (1988), *Historic Black Landmarks: A Traveler's Guide* (1991), *African American Historic Places* (1994), *Black Heritage Sites: An African American Odyssey and Finder's Guide* (1996), *Landmarks of African American History* (2005), and the National Park Service's listing of its many African American sites, there are abundant opportunities throughout the nation for engaging in hands-on learning with college and university students. There are many African American museums that professors can use as useful teaching devices. I concur with John E. Fleming's assessment that "African American museums grow directly from the culture and history of African Americans," are "modern-day keepers of the culture," and can help present "for the current generation those values and visions that sustained the African-American community throughout the eras of slavery and segregation." Indeed, "museums are a wonderful place to learn" and "can help by giving us a sense of history that allows us to call upon our own experiences to interpret the past and to use that knowledge to shape and influence the future."[66]

As a professor of history and African American and African Studies at Michigan State University, I have been fortunate to have access to two very important museums of African American history: the Jim Crow Museum of

Racist Memorabilia at Ferris State University in Big Rapids, Michigan, and the Charles H. Wright Museum of African American History in Detroit, Michigan, which is currently (until Washington, D.C.'s National Museum of African American History and Culture is completed in 2015) the "world's largest institution dedicated to exploring the African American experience." Over the last ten years, I have persuaded, often with the enticement of extra credit, several hundreds of students to visit these museums, especially the latter. Students have consistently viewed their visits as being important in helping them better contextualize the African American experience. Excerpts from their reflections testify to the effectiveness of Detroit's Museum of African American History:

> The exhibition is like watching an IMAX cinema 3D, this exhibition grabs the audience from the beginning to its end. It is like being in a theater where different scenarios are portrayed on stages, hitting you in the depth of your soul. I have never endured such a feeling in an exposition; nobody can be indifferent from such "entertainment."

> Learning about history is usually made up of a lot of reading and sitting through boring lecture after lecture. Since everything happened so long ago you can only read about what happened and try to picture what it was like through pictures and descriptive accounts by people that were living at the time. However, for the first time I actually felt more like I was part of history when I visited the Museum of African American History. Being white it's hard to imagine what it was like for African Americans and everything they had to go through. When walking through the "And Still We Rise" exhibit you feel as if you are black and are actually living the experiences that you're learning about.

> Having been through the museum, it 100% expanded my knowledge of African American history and culture. Again, we talked in class and saw pictures but nothing compares to actually seeing first hand what the African Americans went through to get where they are today.

> The museum helped me understand African American history because I am a visual learner. The exhibition allowed me to be a part of the experience. I had the opportunity to travel from Africa to Detroit in a couple of hours.

> Throughout the entire museum I felt as if I was living a part of our valuable history. It is one thing to read it in books and see it in pictures, but to see life size visuals and walk through their hard times made this experience really come to life. . . . The museum really helped further my understanding by giving me better knowledge about what challenges African Americans had to over come.

> When I think of the exhibit, and how amazing it was, I feel that it should be mandatory for students to check this out for class. . . . I have never felt so emo-

tional or remorseful as I did when I went to the museum. Going to the museum gives deep feelings, feelings that the classroom lecture can only begin to touch. . . . The class would not be the same without my visit to the museum.

After years of torture and humiliation, African Americans can finally stand proud and have others experience slightly what they encountered years ago. It was not until this past Sunday that my view on life during the early 1900s changed. . . . Textbooks, videos, and other teaching aspects do not quite give the experience that is portrayed in the Charles H. Wright Museum of African American History.

The blossoming of scholarship on teaching African American history during and after the 1960s and 1970s occurred hand in hand with the mainstream academy's sudden interest in African American history. Some of the studies were provocative, while others appear to have been capitalizing on the post–civil rights era novelty of African American history in the mainstream U.S. academy. The post–Black Power era decline in scholarship on the teaching of African American history warrants further investigation and perhaps represents part of a broader characteristic within the U.S. academy that prioritizes "the research ideal" over teaching.[67] During the 1990s, a noticeable group of Americanists reinvigorated the scholarship on teaching and learning. Despite the historically rooted and ever-present value of teaching, revisionism, and activism in the African American historical enterprise, African Americanists have not made many noticeable contributions, in terms of publications, to the important field of historical scholarship on teaching and learning. Today, there is clearly room for more rigorous scholarship on the philosophies, methodologies, and techniques of teaching African American history at the university level. Teaching black history is also part of a larger multicultural educational movement in higher education, dating back to the early-twentieth-century Intercultural Education Movement that has grown enormously and sought to consider more seriously the multiple groups that compose American culture. Future studies in the teaching of African American history could certainly benefit from considering these approaches and movements as well as the scholarship of more scholars of education. One thing remains clear: the teaching of African American history is a reform project that has the potential to help positively transform millennial learners, the millennial hip-hop generation, U.S. race relations, as well as American culture.

3. *Carter G. Woodson's Appeal*, Black History, and Black Radical Thought

> Africans were the first to smelt iron and to use it as the great leverage of civilization by which the world has been enabled to accomplish its wonders in modern times. When the Greeks, the Romans, and the Mesopotamians were still in the stone age, these progressive people had learned to make implements of iron and solve the problem of easily earning a subsistence and to control the forces of nature. . . . The whole history of the white race has been cruelty in the extreme, justified by its claim to be the sole representative of God in remaking the world and shaping the destinies of nations. . . . Violating the law is the prerogative of the white. . . . In spite of these facts as to superior qualities of the Negro, the average white man is of the opinion that the Negro has a feeling of inferiority in his presence. Nothing can be so far from the truth.
>
> —Carter G. Woodson, "The Case of the Negro"

Black history institution-builder Carter G. Woodson (1875–1950) is most widely recognized in American—specifically African American—academic and popular cultures for his many pioneering and enduring accomplishments, including founding the Association for the Study of African American Life and History (ASNLH) in 1915, the *Journal of Negro History* (now the *Journal of African American History*) in 1916, Associated Publishers in 1922, and the *Negro History Bulletin* in 1937; authoring numerous books, journal articles, newspaper columns, and book reviews; mentoring generations of African American scholars and historians; and creating "Negro History Week" in 1926 that, in the immediate post–Black Power era, developed into what we celebrate today as Black History Month, a concrete, modern manifestation of the successful, though at times commercial, popularization of African American history.[1] Woodson's most famous and widely read book is *The Mis-Education of the Negro* (1933). It has served as a consciousness-raising road map for generations of young black thinkers, especially scores of Black

Power–era activists and Afrocentric social critics, and even hip-hop gen-
erationers, as epitomized by hip-hop "nation-conscious" emcee and soulful
R & B singer Lauryn Hill's debut and Grammy Award–winning album *The
Miseducation of Lauryn Hill* (1998). More than any other book that he wrote,
The Mis-Education of the Negro has for many become synonymous with
Woodson's philosophy and legacy.

It is not surprising that this work is Woodson's most popular book. Not
only is it a polemic, but it speaks to pressing issues facing black America
today with the same keenness and insight that it did to its original targeted
readership. Recently, the popularity of this book entered hip-hop culture in an
interesting manner. In February 2008, Nike commemorated and capitalized
on Woodson's contributions and *The Mis-Education of the Negro* by releasing
at special events in New York and Los Angeles "Dr. Carter G. Woodson Black
History Month Air Force Ones." An online shoe company (Nice Kicks) has
described the commemorative footwear: "The shoes have such incredible
details and touches that represent African American history and culture.
The canvas on the rear panel was chosen and treated to represent mud cloth
that is unique to each pair. The shoes also have special wooden laces debays
engraved with BHM 08 as well as wooden lace tips. Inspirational words from
Dr. Carter G. Woodson can be found on the insole and special packaging."
Indeed, in the insole of these Black History Month Air Force Ones one reads,
in all capital letters, a citation derived from *The Mis-Education of the Negro*:
"The easiest way to control a people is to deny them a history. Another is to
falsify history that demeans one's past. Therefore minimizing present achievement." On the inside of the box, there is a brief tribute to Woodson. Though
not made available to the public at large, these kicks were reviewed well by
hip-hop generationers.[2]

Though not as influential as *The Mis-Education of the Negro*, Woodson's
"lost-now-found" manuscript, "The Case of the Negro," written in 1921, is
an important document of early-twentieth-century African American intellectual history. While providing a revealing window into Woodson's expressions of early radical thought and rhetoric, it also helps us better understand
the wide spectrum of black scholars' interpretations of blacks' post–World
War I status and a changing American society during the early 1920s. As an
intellectual, Woodson, in "The Case of the Negro," validates Cedric J. Robinson's assertion: "Among the vitalizing tools of the radical intelligentsia, of
course the most crucial was words. Words were their means of placement
and signification, the implements for discovery and revelation. With words
they might and did construct new meanings, new alternatives, new realities
for themselves and others."[3] This newly discovered collection of essays clearly

places Woodson within a trajectory of black intellectual radicalism or black radical thought.

In order to determine whether or not (or the degree to which) an African American intellectual's ideas, actions, rhetoric, style, or approaches are radical in nature (in other words, nontraditional and nonconventional, extreme, challenging to the mainstream, counternormative, sweeping, and/or threatening to white American political, economic, and cultural systems), one must contextualize radicalism, especially by understanding the particular historical context in which the specific intellectual lives or lived. When examining the writings and thought of professionally trained African American scholars of the early twentieth century like Woodson (PhD, Harvard University, 1912), we must acknowledge that these black intellectuals, whose dissertations and doctoral degrees were approved by universities and departments that embraced racist policies and notions of black inferiority in varying degrees, faced the challenges of balancing their radicalism with scientific scholarship and objectivity as well as with their self-imposed social responsibility (as well as that imposed by historical context) of representing and defending the masses of their people. Unlike the self-proclaimed black intellectual radicalism of the late twentieth century that Adolph Reed Jr. openly critiques in *Class Notes: Posing as Politics and Other Thoughts on the American Scene* (2000), most black academics with radical views during most of the twentieth century, especially before the modern civil rights movement, did not openly enjoy the intellectual and scholarly liberties of being able to freely engage in radical discourse in mainstream U.S. academic cultural spaces.[4] While black scholars with radical and nonconventional leanings during the era of Jim Crow segregation could and did opt to publish their corrective scholarship and ideas with radical and black-owned presses (as Woodson did with his Associated Publishers), in making these choices they encountered the possibility of being ostracized, marginalized, underfunded, scrutinized, and essentially written off as being merely propagandists and dissidents by the racialist whitestream U.S. academic gatekeepers.

According to one of his leading biographers, Woodson arguably "became more radical as he grew older," especially by the 1930s. His radicalism evolved over time, changing with his personal transformations that were inevitably linked to the broader changes in the U.S. historical landscape, black America's post-Reconstruction development, and the growth of the ASNLH. As a member of the Washington, DC, branch of the NAACP in 1915, he dubbed himself a "radical" and challenged his colleagues to embrace black economic nationalism by boycotting antiblack businesses. He spoke out against lynching, openly admired radicals like A. Philip Randolph and Chandler Owen (hailing Randolph as a "twentieth-century prophet" in 1920), and joined the radical organization the Friends of Negro Freedom in 1920.[5] At the same time, during the early and foundation-building years of the ASNLH, from approximately 1915 until he severed ties from white philanthropists during the early 1930s, Woodson focused much of his energies on laying the foundations for the scientific study of black culture and the popularization of black history. His early expressions of radicalism before the 1930s were therefore often couched within his conservative scholarly approach to reconstructing blacks' past and articulated privately to his co-workers at ASNLH meetings and functions.

Woodson did indeed act as a radical black intellectual, scholar, and spokesperson of the U.S. progressive-era historical profession as well as the early black historical enterprise. This is epitomized in the radical, uncensored rhetoric and philosophies expressed in his 1921 collection of essays, "The Case of the Negro," which he decided not to publish during his lifetime. Woodson was very much like many other important twentieth-century black leaders who have been acknowledged for their radical approaches to critiquing the treatment of blacks by white society, achieving black liberation, and describing blacks' status in the United States, despite their conservatism.[6] Like many black professionally trained scholars of his generation, Woodson expressed his radicalism in nuanced, multilayered, and often seemingly contradictory ways. In "The Case of the Negro," Woodson challenged the conventional racism and Eurocentrism of the U.S. academy, popular culture, and historical profession; called for drastic changes and reforms in the social order of American society; chastised white America for its collective mistreatment of blacks; and critiqued the normative and widespread worldviews of black middle-class and elite leadership.

As his sentiments cited at the opening of this chapter reveal, the tone of Woodson's observations and rhetoric was often bold, iconoclastic, and unapologetic. While generations of professionally trained and amateur black scholars and historians before him shared and articulated Woodson's candid critiques of white America and his celebration of black Americans' and Africans' cultural contributions, his unique status as one of the two African Americans to have earned a PhD in history by the early 1920s add complexity to the radical nature of his sentiments. When Woodson wrote "The Case of the Negro," the U.S. historical profession, grappling with the enduring "objectivity question," was clearly dominated by racist overtones.[7] In order to earn their doctorates at white institutions, the few African American doctorate-holders during the early 1920s had to strategically embrace objectivity, especially when confronting historical and contemporary issues related to race relations and African American culture. Woodson's radicalism was, in turn, often masked and expressed in spheres separate from his academic scholarship. At the same time, he also meshed a scientific approach to research with a radical rhetoric and flavor. Rooted in a sweeping analysis of the African American historical experience, "The Case of the Negro" showcases dimensions of Woodson's early radical rhetoric and disposition.

In this chapter, I explore chronologically how a multigenerational, insightful group of scholars and black leaders has defined what being a black radical means and what black radicalism means. Couching "The Case of the Negro" within a broad framework of what black radical thought can possibly entail, I specifically discuss the work as an expression of Woodson's early radicalism, as a byproduct of the dawning of the Harlem renaissance, and as a part of the vindicationist tradition of African American intellectual thought or "heretical" black radical thought.[8] I also compare the ideas articulated in "The Case of the Negro" with those in *The Mis-Education of the Negro*. Using Woodson's "The Case of the Negro" as a case study, the ultimate goal of this chapter is to broaden conventional notions of what scholars have implied it means to be a radical black intellectual and professionally trained scholar.

"The Case of the Negro" Rediscovered

In 2005, while working on a project for the Association for the Study of African American Life and History, historian Daryl M. Scott discovered an unpublished manuscript, "The Case of the Negro," completed by Woodson in 1921. Recognizing the significance of this manuscript, in 2008 Scott decided to edit and publish it. Scott clarified his vision at the outset: "While I have added footnotes to illuminate obscure references and esoteric terminology, I have sought to produce a clear, readable text that will allow most readers to follow Woodson's social criticism without the intrusions of strikeouts, extensive editing symbols, and editorial comments."[9] Scott also changed the title of Woodson's manuscript to *Carter G. Woodson's Appeal* and provided an introduction. Though Scott's changing of the name of Woodson's work may be a bit controversial in the future, at a well-attended roundtable on *Woodson's Appeal* at the 2008 ASALH Annual Meeting, Evelyn B. Higginbotham welcomed the change because in her estimation Woodson did in fact evoke a rhetoric reminiscent of David Walker's 1829 *Appeal*. According to Scott, "Woodson did not desire to publish this book."[10] Scott offers a range of potential, intriguing reasons for this decision, including the manuscript's potentially limited commercial success, its critical stance toward black preachers, its often nonscientific flavor, and its critique of the white power structure, an entity that largely funded the ASNLH from its founding until the early 1930s.

I agree with Scott's various theories and would stress that Woodson's decision not to publish "The Case of the Negro" was probably greatly influenced by his decision to secure funding from the white power structure as manifested in the Carnegie and Laura Spelman Rockefeller Foundations. Woodson did not sever his ties with white philanthropy until a decade later in the 1930s during the Great Depression. "After 1933 no white foundations made substantial contributions to the association [the ASNLH]."[11] Woodson may have consciously and strategically decided to shield some of his radicalism from the general pubic, both black and white. "The Case of the Negro" reveals Woodson's radical vision during a period when it was risky to be an openly radical, professionally trained, black historian. Like his predecessors, contemporaries, and descendants as late as the modern civil rights era, Woodson faced the challenges of producing scientifically rigorous yet vindicationist and corrective scholarship. If he had openly embraced a boldly radical rhetoric and stance toward white academic and popular culture in the early 1920s, he would have risked delegitimizing the scholarly rigor of his work and the ASNLH's endeavors of establishing a scholarly foundation for the study of black history during the Progressive Era. Equally important, his radical critiques of the black community, especially of black ministers and leaders, could have further ostracized a pioneering scholar who was known for his iconoclastic and even mean-spirited nature. Woodson's early radical thought was a carefully calculated philosophy that must be analyzed as such. Unlike black radicals who were not concerned with working within the structures of the mainstream U.S. academy, Woodson attempted to balance two (at times) conflicting ideologies: one, an openly radical worldview that critiqued white racism and African Americans' faults and deficiencies; the other, the approach of an objective scholar and historian searching for "the truth" regarding African American history. Though his philosophy may appear contradictory or schizophrenic, it was a byproduct of the challenging times in which Woodson operated during the ASNLH's formative years that coincided with blatant antiblack thought and behavior in American society.

The theories as to why Woodson did not publish "The Case of the Negro" during his lifetime are many. He probably did not publish it at a later date because of its direct connection to the time that he wrote it; that is, his specific rebuttals to white scholarship and his assessments of the black community were contemporary ones. They possessed a sense of immediacy. Many of Woodson's assessments were rooted in his here and now. This does not mean that his critiques would not have been valid at a later date, but they would have had to have been modified and updated.

Why then did Woodson decide to write "The Case of the Negro" in the first place? What was he seeking to accomplish? What were his intentions and who were his targeted audiences? Perhaps Woodson wrote "The Case of the Negro" as a supplement to the cut-and-dried, scientific, fact-based history presented in *The Negro in Our History* (1922) published a year later, and his other earlier publications like *The Education of the Negro Prior to 1861* (1915) and *A Century of Negro Migration* (1918). When he was thinking about and writing "The Case of the Negro," Woodson was also working on completing *The Negro Church* (1921) and his most popular book, *The Negro in Our History.* As he explained in the fall of 1919, Woodson had essentially completed *The Negro in Our History* several years before it was actually published. One of the reasons this book was so popular is that it was the first major twentieth-century textbook for African American history that could be widely used in secondary education, colleges and universities, and black popular culture. *The Negro in Our History* is essentially a chronological account of the black experience in America that was written primarily for African Americans. While corrective in nature, it is largely a narrative of blacks' abilities to persevere.

At one level, "The Case of the Negro" may have served as Woodson's less scientific, less historical, less celebratory, and less chronological analysis of African American history and culture in the early 1920s. Equally important, while some progressive whites may have purchased and read *The Negro in Our History,* it was primarily aimed at instilling within blacks a sense of historical pride. Further, while he did regularly publish his bold, iconoclastic opinions in the "Notes" section of the *Journal of Negro History* before the 1920s, Woodson's early publications often possessed an objective, scientific flavor, as is demonstrated in his *Journal* articles and countless book reviews, as well as *The Education of the Negro Prior to 1861.* From the outbreak of World War I through the 1920s, Woodson sought to establish a respected, legitimate, and rigorous scholarly approach to the study of black life and history. When Woodson wrote "The Case of the Negro," the Association's primary goal was to collect records pertaining to African peoples and to disseminate the truth about African American history. By the early 1930s, Woodson began to address African American history and culture more publicly in the tone reflected in "The Case of the Negro." After he cut his ties from white philanthropists in the early 1930s, it appears that Woodson became more willing to openly publish his critiques of white America with a more radical flavor.

Woodson may have originally written "The Case of the Negro" as an alternative assessment of and critical complement to the factual information offered in *The Negro in Our History.* "The Case of the Negro" represents what Woodson was really thinking about white America's treatment of blacks and what he wanted to tell them while he was laying the scholarly foundations for the ASNLH and producing refined scientific scholarship. It is important to read "The Case of the Negro" in a comparative context, side by side with *The Negro in Our History* and Woodson's other early scientific scholarship. Two Woodsons of the early 1920s emerge: the scientific historian and professionally trained historian role model, and the radical social critic, outspoken race vindicationist, and activist.

Theorizing Black Radicalism

For scholars of U.S. history, Timothy Patrick McCarthy and John McMillian have offered an important definition of radicalism: "'Radical' has always been an elusive adjective—a contested and fluid concept that owes no allegiance to any particular movement, ideology, or period. Radicalism must always be understood, therefore, within specific historical contexts. It is also a painfully subjective concept: One person's radicalism is often another person's reform."[12] In his study on the modern civil rights movement, Herbert H. Haines made a similar observation: "Moderation and radicalism are troublesome, relative terms; they mean different things to different people." He added that "both terms may be applied to the same actors or organizations at different times."[13] This observation is true with regard to Woodson, who acted in conservative and radical ways at different points in his life and whose radicalism evolved over time.

In the historiography on the African American historical experience, radicalism has been associated with various groups, individuals, and social movements. By historians and other social scientists, it has been most widely associated with the architects of slave rebellions and revolts; certain abolitionists (most often those who advocated violence and immediatism); various black religious leaders and theologians; blacks in different periods who advocated violence and what were considered extreme measures as strategies of resistance and black liberation; and especially black communists, leftists, and socialists during the entire twentieth century as well as many different Black Power–era activists. Those organizations and social movements most explicitly linked to black radicalism by scholars include the African Blood Brotherhood, the Universal Negro Improvement Association, the Nation of Islam, the Black Panther Party, and a conglomeration of black feminist organizations such as the National Black Feminist Organization (NBFO), the Combahee River Collective, the Third World Women's Alliance, Black Women Organized for Action, and the National Alliance of Black Feminists from the 1960s through the 1970s. One of the most recent studies that discusses black radicalism, Glenda Gilmore's wide-reaching narrative

Defying Dixie: The Radical Roots of Civil Rights, 1919–1950 (2008), embodies
the equating of radicalism with black communists and socialists.[14] Among
those professionally trained blacks with PhDs during the era of Jim Crow
segregation to be dubbed radical include Rayford W. Logan, Abram Harris
Jr., E. Franklin Frazier, Ralph Bunche, and especially W. E. B. Du Bois.[15]

In assessing the state of African American history twenty-five years ago,
William H. Harris called for a more encompassing conceptualization of what
radicalism constituted in black history: "Scholars have long lamented the
'fact' that black people in America have been reluctant to become involved in
radical activities. Such comments come from too narrow a definition of what
radical means. By and large, scholars have associated radicalism with the ideas
of socialism and communism. But black people know quite well that it was
a radical act for Frederick Douglass or Henry Highland Garnett to take the
radical stands they did during the antebellum years. Indeed, in some parts of
the American South, well into the twentieth century, the very act of attempting
to go to the polls to vote was an act of radicalism."[16] In 1999, Herbert Aptheker
echoed Harris, declaring that "the basic character of African-American history and society is radical."[17] Harris's and Aptheker's comments, especially
Harris's, are useful in that they emphasize that we consider the historical
context when labeling an African American thinker, leader, or movement
radical. Presentism must of course be eliminated in our consideration of
black historical figures' radicalism or lack thereof. At the same time, Harris's
framework could potentially open the floodgates to labeling the majority of
black historical figures until the modern civil rights movement as being radical because countless African Americans directly confronted and challenged
the multifaceted racial oppression of their times.

While the term radical has been used to describe a vast and varied ethnography of black leadership, as a theoretical concept radicalism has not
been scrutinized and deconstructed in African American historiography.
It is beyond the scope of this chapter to provide a comprehensive review of
the historiography and scholarship concerning black radicalism. Instead,
I briefly delve into how, since the early twentieth century, some important
black leaders and insightful scholars have explicitly theorized what it means
to be a black radical and how these conceptualizations could be relevant to
Woodson's thought. Among the most explicit formulations of black radicalism is the classic *Black Marxism: The Making of the Black Radical Tradition*
(1983) by political scientist Cedric J. Robinson. Though he casts his net wide
and deep in conceptualizing the historical origins of this intellectual tradition, he focuses on W. E. B. Du Bois, C. L. R. James, and Richard Wright,
whose radicalism critiqued the limitations of Marxism within Afrodiasporic

contexts and envisioned alternative models. Before Robinson, scholars' and writers' usage of the term *radical* in reference to African American thinkers and leaders was often politically motivated, ahistorical, and juxtaposed against what the black status quo leadership advocated with their frequently labeled philosophies of "assimilationism," "integrationism," "accomodationism," and "compromise."

In his classic *The Souls of the Black Folk* (1903), Du Bois used the term radical in reference to one distinct group of African American leaders. "Today," Du Bois pronounced, "the two groups of Negroes, the one in the North, the other in the South, represent these divergent ethical tendencies, the first tending toward radicalism, the other toward hypocritical compromise."[18] Du Bois, the patriarch of the modern "protest tradition," was calling upon his contemporaries to embrace radicalism by challenging Booker T. Washington and by fighting for black higher education and blacks' civil, social, and political rights. Longtime Howard University professor Kelly Miller was also among the first scholars to use the term radical in direct reference to black thought and leadership. In his 1908 essay "Radicals and Conservatives," Miller defined what it meant to be a radical, turn-of-the-century black leader by, like Du Bois, juxtaposing it against what it meant to be conservative. For him, simply put, "a 'radical' clamors for amelioration of conditions through change." Using Frederick Douglass and Booker T. Washington as representatives of radical and conservative black leadership "tendencies" respectively, Miller concluded that there was value in both approaches and that most black leaders ranged "between these wide-apart views, appreciating the good and the limitations of both."[19] By no means did Miller or Du Bois offer detailed conceptualizations of what it meant to be radical in the context of black leadership approaches. They did, however, help lay the foundations for the usage of the term *radical* by modern historians and scholars of the African American experience.

Roughly a decade after Miller's "Radicals and Conservatives" appeared, revolutionary socialists, labor activists, and self-proclaimed radicals A. Philip Randolph and Chandler Owen offered perhaps the first major expansive definition of what it meant to be a radical black leader in their *The Messenger*, "the only magazine of scientific radicalism in the world published by Negroes."[20] In "The Negro—A Menace to Radicalism," Randolph and Owen proclaimed that "all radicals are opposed to the status quo; they desire change; but not mere change, but progressive change." The editors of *The Messenger* added that the "Negro radical" had two main tasks: to challenge capitalism and to "educate Negroes so that they may understand their class interests."[21] In the October 1919 volume of *The Messenger*, Randolph and Owen expanded on their discussion of black radicals by critically analyzing the approaches of nine black male contemporary leaders, most of whom they considered to be more liberal than radical. Even Du Bois, who modern scholars tend to treat as a personification of black radicalism and protest, was not a "full-fledged" black radical for Randolph and Owen. They included him in their assessment mainly because of his "vigorous and militant fight against Booker T. Washington." The most radical African American leader for them was George Frazier Miller, a minister who most modern scholars of the African American experience would probably not consider to be more radical than Du Bois. Yet, in their editorial "The Negro Radicals," Randolph and Owen did offer a straightforward conceptualization of black radicals. "Among all races there are Conservatives, Liberals and Radicals. The Negro is no exception to the rule. The term 'Radical,' however, is a relative term, and what may be regarded as radical among one group, may not be regarded as radical among another." They surmised, "Radicalism is like luxuries. It varies with time, place and circumstance. . . . One who has neither political nor industrial radicalism can hardly be called radical in the strictest sense of the word."[22] In other words, though they were open to discussing "alleged Radical Negroes," Randolph and Owen believed that authentic black radicals needed to possess certain qualities, especially a commitment to challenging capitalism, recognizing the value of a class analysis, and embracing socialism's fundamental principles.

Roughly two decades after Randolph's and Owen's musings appeared in *The Messenger,* political scientist Ralph Bunche addressed what it meant to be a "radical" black leader in his 1940 "A Brief and Tentative Analysis of Negro Leadership," part of the exhaustive research that Bunche did for Gunnar Myrdal's *An American Dilemma: The Negro Problem and Modern Democracy* (1944). Bunche offered many subcategories of black leadership, noting that "radical leaders" were among those "dynamic and aggressive" spokespersons who base their appeals "on the fighting attitude, on boldness, on the uncompromising stand."[23] Myrdal, whose *An American Dilemma* was arguably authored by leading black scholars of the 1940s, reiterated Bunche's descriptions of radical black leadership and thought in identifying the "two extreme policies of behavior" among black leaders as being "accommodation and protest." While Myrdal did refer to Woodson's black history movement as being "basically an expression of the Negro protest," he explicitly associated "radicalism" with the post–World War I activism of Chandler Owen, A. Philip Randolph, and blacks affiliated with communism.[24]

During the modern civil rights movement, August Meier expanded upon Bunche's and Myrdal's categorization of black leadership by drawing clear distinctions between black leaders during "the nadir" who were "conciliators"

and "agitators." For Meier, conservative black leaders from 1895 until 1915 supported Booker T. Washington; "put greatest emphasis on moral and economic
development"; and advocated "gradualism, conciliation, the middle-class
virtues, racial solidarity," and "self-help." Radical black leaders, on the other
hand, desired "immediate and complete integration"; were interested in the
labor movement; and "stressed agitation, political activism, and civil rights."[25]
What was missing from Meier's paradigm, a framework that enjoyed an uncritical acceptance for decades, is the recognition that many important black
leaders and intellectuals, including Woodson, meshed radical and conservative beliefs and vacillated between the two extremes during their careers, not
always in an evolutionary manner. Black radicalism is complex and could in
many ways be defined in a similar manner that August Meier, Elliott Rudwick, and also John Bracey Jr. and Wilson Jeremiah Moses, among others,
have theorized black nationalism. There are certain assumptions that surface
when considering what constitutes a black nationalist. Black nationalism
not only possesses many diverse perspectives, but a black leader could have
been a black nationalist and an integrationist/assimilationst simultaneously.
Similarly, a black leader could have been a radical and a conservative simultaneously. For example, within the black studies community and the African
American historical profession Booker T. Washington is usually recognized as
being the poster child for black conservatism. Yet particular components of
his program, namely his commitment to outreach educational activities, were
radical when viewed within the context of black leaders' relationships with
the masses of their people and black leaders' views of who should get access
to education during the late nineteenth and early twentieth centuries.[26]

   In *Black Marxism: The Making of the Black Radical Tradition*, Cedric J.
Robinson articulated one of the first exhaustive conceptualizations of black
radicalism. According to Robinson, black radicalism "is not a variant of
Western radicalism whose proponents happen to be Black. Rather, it is a
specifically African response to an oppression emergent from the immediate
determinants of European development in the modern era and framed by
orders of human exploitation woven into the interstices of European social
life from the inception of Western civilization." In discussing a "radical black
historiography," Robinson marginalized Woodson's contributions, noting
that he, along with George Washington Williams, achieved "a fragile construction, its integrity subject to challenge whenever capitalist indulgence,
the foundation upon which it rested, might be dissipate or be withdrawn."
For Robinson, Du Bois was the quintessential radical of Woodson's time
because he simultaneously critiqued U.S. culture, capitalism, and politics;
the Communist Party of the United States of America; the American So-

cialist Party; and black elite leadership. For Robinson, *Black Reconstruction* (1935), "the first ledger of radical Black historiography," was so important because Du Bois not only critiqued the "Black petit bourgeoisie," but also recognized that the "slave system and capitalism" was at the root of African Americans' oppression.[27] Though Woodson did not meet the criteria of Robinson's "Black Radical Tradition," he did nonetheless exhibit some radical thought patterns that fit within Robinson's paradigm of black radicalism. In "The Case of the Negro," Woodson explicitly made the connection between blacks' contemporary status and slavery. He maintained that slavery and the segregation that followed it were the basis of black America's problems and underdevelopment. Though not with the same detail and sophistication as Du Bois, Woodson also noted that blacks needed to scrutinize the economic structure and culture of the United States.

In the same year Robinson's study appeared, Gayraud Wilmore published the second edition of *Black Religion and Black Radicalism: An Interpretation of the Religious History of African Americans.* Though his discussion of radicalism is not as extensive as Robinson's, Wilmore provides some clear parameters for his usage of the concept. For Wilmore, with regard to black intellectual history, radicalism "had to do with the assumption that race and color are at the root of the problems of Western civilization and that the only lasting solution would require a transformation of human relationships that would amount to a national conversion involving the recognition of the dignity and equality of blacks." Wilmore's more specific definition of black radicalism is directly linked with black religion. There are "three characteristics of the radical tradition in black religion" according to Wilmore: "(1) the quest for the independence from white control; (2) the revalorization of the image of Africa; and (3) the acceptance of protest and agitation as theological prerequisites for black liberation and the liberation of all oppressed peoples."[28]

Since Robinson's *Black Marxism,* numerous scholars have used notions of black radicalism in describing black communists, leftists, socialists, and expressions of working-class and Black Power–era activism. Currently in African American historiography, radicalism is most often associated with black communists and Black Power activists.[29] In *Holding Aloft the Banner of Ethiopia: Caribbean Radicalism in Early Twentieth-Century America* (1998), Winston James defined radicalism broadly: it represents "the challenging of the status quo either on the basis of social class, race (or ethnicity), or a combination of the two." In using the term radical, he was referring to those "avowed anti-capitalists ('Socialists,' 'Communists,' adherents and practitioners of other variants of Marxism, and non-Marxist anti-capitalists such as anarcho-syndicalists) as well as adherents of varieties of Black Nationalism (emigrationists, pan-Africanists, Garveyites, black statehood supporters, or a combination of these). Included here, too, are those who have attempted to organically conjoin Marxism and Black Nationalism."[30]

Though he does not theorize black radicalism to the extent of Robinson, Robin D. G. Kelley has analyzed the radical views of a wide range of black activists. His early scholarship highlighted the contributions of black working-class and communist radicals.[31] More recently, in *Freedom Dreams: The Black Radical Imagination,* Kelley explored how a group of "renegade black intellectuals/activists/artists challenged and reshaped communism, surrealism, and radical feminism" in envisioning alternative worlds for the most underrepresented populations of their people. Because of these thinkers' radicalism, their "critical visions . . . were held at bay, if not completely marginalized." Relevant to Woodson's "The Case of the Negro," Kelley also noted how the radical ideas of black intellectuals were the byproducts of their interactions with "systems of oppression" and "political struggles."[32]

Since Kelley's *Freedom's Dreams,* several other scholars have conceptualized black radicalism. In *Black Heretics, Black Prophets: Radical Political Intellectuals,* Anthony Bogues focuses on two main strains of black radical thought, heretical and prophetic. Woodson would certainly fit ideally within Bogues's heretical tradition because this approach centers on race vindication, challenging the existing Eurocentric norms while seeking to create a viable alternative strategy. In *The Geography of Malcolm X: Black Radicalism and the Remaking of American Space,* James Tyner expands upon the ideas of Kelley and Bogues and theorizes black radicalism's relationship with geography, space, and Malcolm X's worldview. "Black radicalism likewise is about alternative geographies, social and spatial; black radicalism is about the remaking of spaces." Tyner continues, "The epistemology of black radicalism is thus predicated on a ground-level reality. Indeed, Black radical intellectual production oftentimes began with an engagement and dialogue with Western radical political ideas, and then moved on to a critique of these ideas as their incompleteness was revealed." Tyner's main argument is that "the objective of Malcolm X's black radicalism was the attainment of respect and equality within American society; this was to be accomplished through a remaking of American space."[33] More recently, borrowing from Winston James, Erik S. McDuffie has offered an encompassing definition of black radicalism. For him, black radicalism "includes Marxism, socialism, revolutionary nationalism, Pan-Africanism, anti-colonialism, and separatism."[34] This conceptualization is clearly stated, broad, opens the door to including countless leaders, and requires that each one of these "isms" be specifically defined.

Woodson's early radical thought was different from that of many of the

African American leaders, intellectuals, and activists who have been heralded for their radicalism in that his early radical ideologies were more moderate and contained, did not permeate the vast majority of his early writings, were often meshed with scientific objectivity, were not associated with communism or socialism, and, as was the case with "The Case of the Negro," were often hidden from the public transcript.

Woodson's Radical "New Negro"

While he has not been considered an elder ideological forerunner or states-man of the Harlem renaissance, as were Alain L. Locke, Charles S. Johnson, and W. E. B. Du Bois, Woodson was certainly influenced by the "New Negro" revolution, and the ASNLH was certainly among the most important cul-tural institutions of the Harlem renaissance.[35] It is clear that when Woodson penned "The Case of the Negro" he was caught up in the upsurge of black pride. Defending and celebrating African Americans' progress and "new" visions, a significant part of the tone of this work is optimistic, unlike *The Mis-Education of the Negro,* published more than a decade later during the peak of the Great Depression. Many examples reflect Woodson's optimism of the "New Negro" of the new decade.

Throughout "The Case of the Negro," Woodson praised what African Americans were doing "now," his "now" referring to the period from about 1919 until 1921. After briefly outlining blacks' struggles during slavery and emancipation as well as the contemporary challenges facing blacks, Wood-son (beginning in chapter 6, "What the Negro Is Learning") celebrated the "new ideas" that blacks were armed with. Woodson blamed slavery for many of blacks' contemporary problems and repeatedly compared blacks' early-twentieth-century status with their positions under the oppressive environ-ments of slavery, Reconstruction, and its immediate aftermath. In educational terms, Woodson noted that "thousands of Negroes today have a different attitude. Many now study law, medicine, or theology not to earn a living in their practice of a profession, but to make a contribution to knowledge in these fields. . . . The Negro is learning also to abandon imitation and blaze the way in unexplored fields."[36] As the contributors to Locke's *The New Negro* published four years after "The Case of the Negro" in 1925 would announce, Woodson proclaimed, "How different is the attitude of the Negro of today! Like other oppressed races the Negro is learning to strike back." "Fortunately now," Woodson observed, "there are few Negroes dependent upon some-body else to do their thinking."[37] Woodson pronounced that by 1921, blacks developed their ideas more independently; abandoned blindly following white-appointed, "so-called Negro leaders" and selfish "emotional mischief makers"; became more involved in "radical reform"; excelled in independent business ventures; understood the value of the press and organizations more; "appreciate[d] the value of the truth"; were more committed to the race; were superior to whites in many ways; and possessed and articulated a clear set of desires and goals for the future.[38]

In chapter 7, "Superior Qualities of the Negro," Woodson celebrated how blacks "boldly faced the ordeals of a hostile environment" and functioned as an unselfish, philanthropic mutual aid culture.[39] In chapter 8, "What the Negro Is Thinking," Woodson argued that blacks were beyond a doubt well informed about their status in America. His embracing of the "New Negro," however, was not universal, as demonstrated in his chastising of Jack Johnson, arguably one of the quintessential "New Negroes." The optimism that Woodson expressed in "The Case of the Negro" seems to have declined significantly by the time that he published *The Mis-Education of the Negro* in 1933. Along with the racial violence of the World War I era and the antiblack Woodrow Wilson years, the black cultural resurgence of the Harlem renaissance probably influenced Woodson to write "The Case of the Negro."

Defending "the Race"

"The Case of the Negro" is an ideal example of what V. P. Franklin has identified as the "race vindication" tradition in African American thought. In "The Case of the Negro," Woodson repeatedly challenged the existing racist historical discourse that sought to uphold the mental and cultural inferiority of African peoples.[40] Woodson's vindicationist approach also included a bold critique of whites and an open declaration of black superiority as embodied in the title of one of his chapters, "Superior Qualities of the Negro."

In the first four chapters of "The Case of the Negro," as he did routinely in countless book reviews in the *Journal of Negro History,* Woodson directly discredited the racist scholarship of people he called "pseudo-scientists," "so-called scholars," "slanderers," and "blind unscientific investigators." After dubbing the "European race" one of "secondary origins," Woodson rejected European notions of African primitiveness and "racial inferiority," stressing that such ideas had "no scientific foundation."[41] In defending African peoples and cultures against racist Eurocentric thought, Woodson adopted an Afrocentric perspective reminiscent of Du Bois in Du Bois's concise 1915 history of the African diaspora, *The Negro.* Woodson highlighted the Africanity and blackness of ancient Egypt and Africa; celebrated the cultural artifacts and civilizations of Ghana, Songhai, Mali, Dahomey, and Timbuctoo; and declared that Ra Nehesi and Nefertari were "full blooded Negroes" and that Ethiopia was "a highly civilized Negro land." In analyzing Woodson's published scholarship on Africa, Maghan Keita has argued that "Woodson had presaged the arguments of Afrocentrists, in particular the adherents of the 'Nile Valley School,' and the concepts associated with Cheikh Anta Diop's *Nations negres et culture* and *Anteriorite des civilizations negres.*" He "remained a champion of the history of African peoples."[42] In constructing his counter arguments, Woodson drew largely upon European and white American scholarship that undermined popular notions of black inferiority.[43] In this sense, he conjoined white revisionist scholarship with black corrective history. In 1921, Woodson concluded that scholars had not yet engaged in "intensive" studies "of the institutions of the peoples of the interior of Africa."[44]

In defending black America's African origins, Woodson belittled white America's European background and claimed that blacks were superior. "The earliest and lowest population of Europe were an extremely long-headed type of the stone age," Woodson noted, and "after the partial occupation of western Europe by a dolichocephalic Africanoid type in the stone age, an invasion by a broad-headed race from Asia followed."[45] He declared that Europeans descended from peoples of an "undeveloped state."[46] Woodson's comments echo the sentiments articulated by the radical (in the words of Joel Schor) Henry Highland Garnet. In his speech, "The Past and the Present Condition and the Destiny of the Colored Race" (1848), Garnet the amateur historian declared that Africans' "worthy deeds . . . were inscribed by fame upon the pages of ancient history." The "ancient Egyptians," Garnet continued, "were black, and had woolly hair. . . . When these representatives of our race were filling the world with amazement, the ancestors of the now proud and boasting Anglo-Saxons were amongst the most degraded in the human family. They abode in caves underground, either naked or covered with the skins of wild beasts. Night was made hideous by their wild shouts, and day was darkened by the smoke which arose from bloody altars, upon which they offered human sacrifice."[47]

Woodson credited African scholars who produced alternative narratives to European-authored racialist scholarship, calling upon his readers to revisit and consult the lives, contributions, and ideas of largely ignored African thinkers like Miguel Kapranzine, J. E. J. Captein, A. W. Awo, Francis Williams, and Adjai Crowther. When defending the African American masses, Woodson charted the progress that had been made by African Americans in the sixty years since emancipation. As he would continue to do in later years, he drew from U.S. census reports and other primary source records to demonstrate African Americans' transformations and progress from slave

labor to wage earning, property and home ownership, and successful professional and business enterprises "under adverse circumstances." Woodson
warned his readers about relying on the "misinformation found in most
books concerning the Negro."[48]

"The Case of the Negro" is reminiscent of earlier race vindication work by
Du Bois, Anna Julia Cooper, Ida B. Wells, the American Negro Academy, and
many other black intellectuals who were active during "the nadir" in that it
directly targeted an educated white audience. "The Case of the Negro," simply
put, spoke truth to power.[49] Woodson boldly asserted: "The whole history of
the white race has been cruelty in the extreme, justified by its claim to be the
sole representative of God in remaking the world and shaping the destinies
of nations."[50] Like Ida B. Wells, who openly challenged white men who raped
black women and lynched black men for supposedly raping white women
during "the nadir," Woodson spoke out against the "incursions of lustful
white men" on black women.[51] Though he offered biting critiques of black
ministers and leaders and he chastised the black masses for their faults, in
"The Case of the Negro" Woodson focused his energies on discrediting white
scholars' and the general white population's negative perceptions, treatment,
and portrayals of black America. Rejecting notions of black "shiftlessness,"
he clarified and celebrated what African Americans accomplished as laborers
"to a standard of high efficiency" under the yoke of slavery and during its
immediate aftermath.

Flipping the script, he proclaimed how blacks, the architects of a thriving
culture of survival and resistance, possessed many significant "superior"
qualities compared with their white counterparts. Chapter 7 of "The Case
of the Negro," "Superior Qualities of the Negro," is intriguing, inasmuch as
many of the claims to black superiority that Woodson makes could be considered stereotypical characteristics attributed to blacks by whites. Woodson,
however, casts these attributes as being positive dimensions of black behavior.
Woodson opens this chapter by declaring: "Nothing exhibits more forcefully
the Negro's superiority than his cheerfulness. Dark as the hour has at times
seemed, the Negro has never lost hope." Woodson added that blacks are superior to whites because of their "unusual gratitude," forgiveness, philanthropic
spirit, patience "in the midst of hostile men," law-abiding nature, loyalty and
patriotism, and morality. He highlighted blacks' superiority in religious terms
as well. "The blacks are superior to whites in that they are more religious."
Woodson underscored that if blacks did not possess a concrete sense of "the
Biblical doctrine," they would have probably responded to the "racial conflict"
in extreme ways. For Woodson, blacks were "the most law-abiding people

known to history," whites failed to acknowledge this, and blacks were keenly aware of their superiority.[52] "The attitude of many Negroes is that they are superior in many respects to the whites who are lording it over them in such an inhuman way." Woodson continued, "They feel that they are like the innocent captives of the Greek wars impressed into the service of the barbarians of Sparta. They dare not irritate the lion when the head of the innocent is in his mouth, but they do not feel that in character and moral fibre the beast is superior to his victim."[53]

In chapter 9, "What the Negro Is Thinking," Woodson empowers the black masses by telling white America how blacks viewed whites in bold terms. Foreshadowing Malcolm X's plain talk, Woodson avowed that "few Negroes consider more than one white man out of a thousand anything but a hypocrite." Woodson continued, "It is difficult for a white man except by repetition of good deeds to convince the Negro that he is friendly to the race." Woodson was open in his critiques of U.S. presidents' policies toward blacks, declaring that blacks were skeptical of "inconsiderate and narrow-minded prejudiced charlatans like William Howard Taft and Woodrow Wilson" and "the false political philosophy behind the whole system of government arranged against the man of color." Woodson told whites that blacks understood white America's racist policies and therefore had "little faith in the so-called Christian civilization." Woodson concluded this chapter by explaining black patriotism while blacks were being blatantly mistreated. Like Frederick Douglass and others before him who took pride in black contributionism, Woodson contended that blacks were attached "to the native soil" and despised "the gangrene jealous and clannish, autocratic Republicans and Democrats who are the same impediment to the triumph of democracy as the Junkers were to the liberation of the peoples of Germany."[54]

In the closing chapter, "What the Negro Wants," Woodson—foreshadowing Rayford W. Logan's *What the Negro Wants* (1944) and the Black Panther Party's practical 10-Point Program (1966)—spelled out for whites what his "New Negro" strove for and demanded. In essence, Woodson told those whites who were killing, disenfranchising, dehumanizing, stereotyping, and denying blacks their basic human rights that blacks simply wanted to be treated as U.S. citizens and human beings. Prefiguring Martin Luther King Jr.'s famous 1963 "I Have Dream" oration, Woodson concluded "The Case of the Negro" by saying, "Let every Negro be considered not according to his color but according to what he has done or is doing for the good of his family, community, and his country."[55] Though his black colleagues could have been challenged to rethink their positions in the black struggle by several essays in "The Case of the Negro," the bulk of the manuscript was aimed at critically deconstructing and rendering insignificant how whites viewed and portrayed black history and culture, and Woodson assumed a radical rhetoric in doing so.

Laying the Foundations for
The Mis-Education of the Negro

In some ways, "The Case of the Negro" foreshadowed what Woodson would spell out in *The Mis-Education of the Negro* twelve years later, wherein he focused his attention on arguing to what extent some "highly miseducated Negroes" had misled, exploited, and hampered the livelihood of the black masses and how these destructive behaviors could be abandoned or corrected. Woodson directly critiqued educated black leadership for failing to genuinely uplift the race, for being unoriginal, and for seeking assimilation into white society. On the other hand, in "The Case of the Negro" Woodson argued that, in 1921, blacks were not seeking white approval or assimilation. "The Negro has no desire to be everything the white man is or to do everything he does."[56] In *The Mis-Education of the Negro,* Woodson makes the opposite argument, claiming that educated blacks "do what they are told" and were victims to "slavish imitation."[57]

At the same time, by critiquing black leadership and by pointing out the flaws in black life in "The Case of the Negro," Woodson articulated arguments that resurfaced in *The Mis-Education of the Negro.* Woodson demonstrated this mainly in chapter 5, "The Debit Side of the Ledger." In discussing the "faults" of black people, he highlighted problems related to health and hygiene, religious practices and philosophies that were otherworldly and too emotionally charged, and irrelevant political ideologies. Woodson stressed that these problems were in no way "inherent in the Negro" and that many of them could be traced back to slavery and segregation. Woodson also argued that the problems facing the black community were also prevalent in white society.[58]

As he did in various venues throughout his life and in *The Mis-Education of the Negro,* in "The Case of the Negro" Woodson indicted the black preacher. Preachers, in Woodson's words, "often used their position of influence as a means to exploit the virtue of their women and the pockets of their parishioners. It is very difficult," he continued, "to find a minister who has not been branded as being a little crooked in handling the finances of his church or in connection with the women of his congregation."[59] Though he did provide a counternarrative to this critique by mentioning the positive uplift work of a few preachers, Woodson's critiques of the failures of the black church and ministers are clear and harsh. His commentaries on the black church in "The Case of the Negro" were probably more critical extrapolations from his *The Negro Church* published in 1921. Woodson remained committed to this idea in *The Mis-Education of the Negro.* In both "The Case of the Negro" and *The Mis-Education of the Negro,* Woodson echoed Booker T. Washington's pragmatism that critiqued the abstract theories of "the intellectuals." In "The Case of the Negro" Woodson also echoed Washington's 1895 conservative "Atlanta Compromise" political philosophy: "Negroes should direct their attention to larger problems of life which when properly solved will take care of the Negroes' political and civil rights."[60] In this sense, Woodson's "The Case of the Negro" possessed both radical and conservative ideologies of black advancement. While there are important similarities between "The Case of the Negro" and *The Mis-Education of the Negro* (namely, that both are collections of essays that mesh historical thinking with straightforward contemporary critiques of blacks' collective status), the latter is much more a critique of black leadership than the former: "The Case of the Negro" is largely a vindicationist work and part of heretical black radical thought directed at ideologically disempowering white academic and popular brands of racism.

* * *

Since the beginning of the twentieth century, the usage of the term radical in reference to black leaders, intellectuals, and social movements has evolved. While for obvious and understandable reasons certain groups of black leaders—mainly communists, socialists, and revolutionary nationalists—have been referred to as being radical, and many scholars' views of black radicalism have been molded by the theories of Cedric Robinson, among others, there is no real consensus as to what it means to be black and radical. Since Robinson's dense *Black Marxism,* scholars have continued to reconfigure theories of black radicalism or black radical thought. Despite the fact that he decided not to publish "The Case of the Negro," this collection of essays is further evidence of Woodson's pre–Great Depression radicalism. In 1899, more than two decades before Woodson wrote "The Case of the Negro," one of his historical role models and the father of black conservatism, Booker T. Washington, published an essay under the exact title in the *Atlantic Monthly.* While Washington did intimate that it was unjust if "the Negro be deprived of any privilege guaranteed him by the Constitution of the United States," the tone of Washington's article was far from radical. He reiterated his 1895 oration (the Atlanta Compromise speech); affirmed his commitment to industrial education, interracial cooperation, and self-help; and chastised his black radical counterparts, dubbing them "a certain class of impatient extremists among the Negroes in the North."[61] In 1921, Woodson was one of these impatient "extremists." Simply put, he was fed up with white America's mistreatment of his people.

Unconcerned with objectivity, a strict chronicling of the African American experience, or the opinions of his potential black and white readership, in his "The Case of the Negro" Woodson diverged from his role model and boldly defended his people from prevalent academic and popular racist thought; candidly deconstructed white American racism; called for drastic social change in U.S. race relations; outlined in no uncertain terms what black America was thinking, demanding, and striving for; and critiqued the black middle class along with elite leadership. Multidimensional in nature, "The Case of the Negro" must be added to the growing collection of early-twentieth-century black radical writings and rhetoric. Equally important, "The Case of the Negro" demonstrates how black scholars' unpublished works are essential to understanding the scope, variety, and evolution of their worldviews. As a leading black public intellectual and scholar of his time whose organization depended significantly upon white philanthropy for more than the first decade of its existence, Woodson carefully calculated when and how to publicize his radicalism.

4. "Ample Proof of This May Be Found"
Early Black Women Historians

> Despite the increased stature of lay historians and women doing
> history work, in the pre–civil rights era, only a few black women
> joined Anna Julia Cooper and Marion Thompson Wright in the
> ranks of the academically trained professional historians. To the
> miniscule pool came Merze Tate, Lula Johnson, Margaret Nelson
> Rowley, Elsie Lewis, Susie Owens Lee, Helen Edmonds, and
> Lorraine Williams. To say the least, their professional lives were
> not easy; they had all of the problems of black male historians
> and more.
>
> —Deborah Gray White, *Telling Histories: Black Women
>   Historians in the Ivory Tower*

In introducing her best-known novel and monumental contribution to what
Henry Louis Gates Jr. has labeled "the Afro-American woman's literary tradition," the prolific and multi-talented Pauline Hopkins (1859–1930) essentially
dubbed (the fictional) *Contending Forces: A Romance Illustrative of Negro
Life North and South* (1900) a historical study, declaring "that the incidents
portrayed in the early chapters of the book actually occurred. Ample proof
of this may be found in the archives of the courthouse at Newberne, N.C.,
and at the national seat of the government, Washington D.C."[1] While the
struggles of black women historians against sexism, racism, and classism
during the era of Jim Crow segregation can be easily deciphered, the testi-
monies of the scholars featured in Deborah Gray White's *Telling Histories*
(2008) reveal that black women historians, the "spiritual descendants" of the
intellectuals and scholars examined in this chapter, continued to encounter
racism and sexism in the mainstream academy decades after the modern civil
rights movement.[2] Black women historians, especially before the civil rights
movement, had to, as Pauline Hopkins did, provide "ample proof" of their
credentials in order to avoid being underappreciated by the male-centered
black historical profession and dismissed by the larger American academic

and popular culture that predominantly viewed them as being unfit for the historian's craft.

From the 1890s through the first half of the twentieth century, black women historians overcame a different set of barriers than their male counterparts in earning their doctorates, publishing, securing employment, receiving professorial promotions, and gaining respect in the academy. In 1925, at age sixty-six, Anna Julia Cooper became the first African American woman to earn a doctorate in history (University of Paris, Sorbonne). More than a decade after Cooper's historic accomplishment, Marion Thompson Wright became the first African American woman to earn a PhD in history in the United States (Columbia University, 1940). The significant lapse in time between Du Bois's earning his doctorate in history (Harvard University, 1895) and Cooper and Wright receiving theirs is neither surprising nor difficult to explain. Historically, black women have faced significant opposition on various fronts in pursuing and attaining education, especially at colleges and universities. During what Rayford Logan deemed "the nadir" of black life—the formative years for black intellectuals in William Banks's estimation—black women were widely and often systematically excluded from participating in mainstream U.S. and African American academic culture.[3] From the 1880s through the 1950s, as Stephanie Shaw has demonstrated, black women professionals were carefully socialized to work in the "feminized professions—as social workers, librarians, nurses, and teachers."[4]

During these times especially, black women in the historical profession and academe as a whole faced multiple forms of oppression, including sexism and racism, and in many cases class discrimination. In response to this environment, Paula Giddings has suggested that black female intellectuals have historically possessed a distinct desire to persevere. "Since education is the key to the more attractive occupations, black women intellectuals have possessed a certain history of striving for education beyond what their gender or their color seemed to prescribe," Giddings observed. "Black men have not had the same motivation, historically, because they had a greater range of options."[5] Clearly, African American women as a group have historically struggled to acquire an education and join the ranks of professionally trained scholars in white and black communities.[6] During the era of segregation, they reacted to the pervasive exclusionary policies of the broader white society by promoting an ideology and strategy of self-help while also responding to the stifling gender conventions within black communities. Deborah Gray White has recently explained black women's "late entry into the historical profession" and the challenges facing "could-be black women historians." White surmises:

The late entry of African American women into the historical profession is not, therefore, beyond our comprehension. Educated black women were socialized to be race women, to "pay forward" to the race the advantages they had received from higher education. As lay historians, many put African American and African American women's history to work for that purpose. Had they made it their profession, however, they would have met a world that was closed, if not hostile, to them and blind to the hurdles they had to jump. Just as important, however, was the paradox presented by their own history. Educated African American women believed they had to overcome their history before they could do their history. Yet the nature of the history they sought to overcome was so embarrassing and demeaning that it kept them from engaging that history in all but the most indirect manner. It was not by choice, therefore, but by necessity that we came late to the historical profession.[7]

During the proto–civil rights movement, a diverse group of revisionist African American female historians created a range of coping strategies, survival mechanisms, and alternative ways to approaching and writing history. While fewer than ten black women earned doctorates in history before the mid-1950s, thereby gaining access in some form to academic sanctioning, many black women intellectuals published historical scholarship without extensive academic credentials or the approval of mainstream academe. Other black women, such as Dorothy Burnett Porter Wesley (1905–1995), a self-proclaimed "bibliomaniac" and longtime chief curator for the Moorland-Spingarn Research Center, as well as black women librarians, functioned as key resource personnel. Before Anna Julia Cooper or Marion Thompson Wright, many black women without doctoral degrees published noteworthy historical scholarship and engaged in the historian's craft. They created their own authentic ideological "parallel institutions."[8] The Association of Black Women Historians (ABWH), founded in the immediate post–Black Power era,[9] was the first formal organization for black women historians.

Still the leading organization for black women historians, the ABWH has functioned, in Francille Rusan Wilson's words, as a "professional home for black women who are historians, and the central location of support of historical research on black women." Darlene Clark Hine added, "The ABWH became the institutional infrastructure of the black women's history movement just as the Association for the Study of Negro Life and History . . . served as the organizational foundation of the Black History Movement."[10] Since the creation of the ABWH, black women historians, many of who contributed to the black women's history and studies movements, have become directors of programs and chairs of departments and have earned national and international fame. Following in the footsteps of Mary Frances Berry, Darlene

Clark Hine and Nell Irvin Painter marked several important milestones in black women's history: each has served as president of both the Organization of American Historians and the Southern Historical Association.

It is important to properly contextualize the achievements of black women historians following the civil rights movement and the founding of the ABWH. These black women historians are "spiritual descendants" of a group of under-acknowledged black female intellectuals. During the era of segregation, black women historians, though not bound together by a single organization or institution, often shared common causes, approaches, and ideologies that ran parallel to those discursive spaces and perspectives existing in male-centered white and black communities.

The history of black women historians during the era of segregation, especially during the Progressive Era, constitutes a dynamic narrative, challenging us to revisit the lives and works of lesser-known black women scholars, reconceptualize conventional definitions of what makes one a historian, and rediscover valuable scholarly insights. This chapter explores the unique history of a diverse group of pioneering black women historians, professional and self-taught, from the 1890s through the mid-1950s, a history that has been largely ignored by the few historians who have chronicled the lives and works of black historians since the late 1950s.

Categorizing and Conceptualizing Black Women Historians

Historians have conceptualized black historians in two major ways. In their exhaustive 1986 study, August Meier and Elliott Rudwick considered only "professionally trained historians, the products of the system of university graduate education that matured by the beginning of the twentieth century." They limited their study to doctorates with "a record of significant publication."[11] On the other hand, Carter G. Woodson, Earl E. Thorpe, Benjamin Quarles, John Hope Franklin, Wilson Jeremiah Moses, Maghan Keita, John Ernest, Julie Des Jardins, Ralph L. Crowder, and Stephen G. Hall broadened their criteria by democratizing the profession to embrace formally trained and self-taught historians.[12] These scholars' research concurred with Moses's assertion that the black historical enterprise should include "the historical understanding of literate persons outside the academy."[13] This category of black historians is especially helpful when analyzing and subdividing black women historians during the era of segregation. In this chapter, I analyze the contributions of four main groups of black women historians: Progressive Era novelists; self-taught and self-proclaimed historians or "historians without portfolio" from the 1890s through the 1930s; accomplished and professionally trained scholars who, though not formally trained in history, published historical scholarship or engaged in rigorous historical research; and professionally trained historians with doctorates.

Many black women writers of the Progressive Era employed their novels in multifaceted, complex ways. Claudia Tate has convincingly argued that post-Reconstruction "black domestic melodramas" written by African American women were "symbolically embedded" with "cultural meaning, values, expectations, and rituals of African Americans of that era." More important, Tate explored "how black women authors of the post-Reconstruction era used domestic novels, as did other politically excluded writers, as entry points into the 'literary and intellectual world and as a means of access to social and political events from which [they as black women were] . . . largely excluded."[14] Tate's theory can be applied to black women as writers of history as well. Black women novelists, namely Frances Ellen Watkins Harper and Pauline Hopkins, wrote "female-centered," seemingly unthreatening, "domestic novels" which critically addressed controversial issues and events in U.S. history, such as slavery, the Civil War, and Reconstruction. "Without an historicized interpretive model, the black domestic novels seem maudlin, inconsequential, even vacuous," Tate has concluded.[15] In post-Reconstruction America, black women intellectuals who sought to write conventional historical texts may have faced more resistance than they did as novelists. They tapped into a literary genre perhaps more accessible to them as black women. In line with their pragmatic worldview, they also probably reasoned that novels had a much broader appeal than history texts among black and white middle-class readers. Harper and Hopkins, two of the most influential black women writers at the turn of the century, challenge us to broaden traditional definitions of historians.

According to Earl E. Thorpe, from the late 1890s until the civil rights movement, there existed a significant group of black "historians without portfolio," a "group of non-professional persons . . . who have a fondness for the discipline of history, feeling that their life experiences peculiarly fit them for chronicling some historical events."[16] More than a dozen self-taught and self-proclaimed black women historians fit within Thorpe's designation. They produced insightful, accessible, and practical historical scholarship. This diverse group included schoolteachers, clubwomen, social reformers, and journalists. Though not formally trained, they challenged the widely accepted notion that a woman's place was in the domestic sphere, and their scholarship was often innovative, polemical, and vindicationist in nature. Julie

Des Jardins has posited that they relied "more heavily on oral tradition, commemorative strategies, interdisciplinary methods, pedagogical techniques, and grassroots mobilization to shape the contours of race and memory and their legacies as black women."[17]

Unrestricted by the standards of academe, these pragmatic scholars' writings tended to connect the past to the present, address contemporary issues directly, target laypersons and youth in black communities, and in some cases sought to promote harmony between blacks and whites. This group included Gertrude E. H. Bustill Mossell, Leila Amos Pendleton, Laura Eliza Wilkes, Susie King Taylor, Elizabeth Lindsay Davis, Delilah Beasley, Elizabeth Ross Haynes, Drusilla Dunjee Houston, and black women teachers, activists, and researchers of the Association for the Study of Negro Life and History from its founding through the mid-1950s.[18]

There also existed a significant group of black female scholars who, though not professionally trained in history, were formally trained in other disciplines and used their scholarly expertise to produce historical scholarship. The two representatives of this group whom I discuss, longtime curator for the Moorland-Spingarn Research Center Dorothy Porter Wesley and the multitalented Shirley Graham Du Bois, applied their various scholarly skills to producing scientific and pragmatic historical scholarship and to promoting black history as a tool of racial uplift. During the era of Jim Crow segregation, Dorothy Porter Wesley published several historical articles and important bibliographical studies on African American history, collected and cataloged valuable primary sources, and helped countless researchers. Simply put, her work was as important as that of quintessential bibliophile Arthur Schomburg. At one level, Shirley Graham Du Bois was the most prolific scholar discussed in this chapter. From 1944 until 1955, she authored eight biographies on famous black leaders.

Professionally trained black women historians with PhDs before the emergence of the civil rights movement in the mid-1950s can be best categorized by the decade during which they earned their doctorates. In the 1920s, Anna Julia Cooper was the only black woman PhD in the field of history. In the decade after Cooper earned a doctorate, no black woman appears to have earned a history doctorate. This drought in the 1930s was followed by a decade in which the numbers of black female historians increased significantly. In 1940, Marion Thompson Wright earned a PhD from Columbia University. Other black women, recognized in the field and lesser known, followed in her footsteps during the remainder of the decade. The first distinguishable coterie of formally trained black women historians included Lulu M. Johnson, Susie Owen Lee, Elsie Lewis, Helen G. Edmonds, and Margaret Rowley. Merze

Tate, the first African American woman to receive a doctorate in government and international relations from Harvard (1941), was not formally trained in history, but her scholarly writings and activism qualify her as being a professional historian.[19] The seven black women who earned doctorates in history during the 1940s, including Merze Tate, can be subdivided into two main groups. Wright, Tate, Lewis, and Edmonds published significant historical scholarship and were active in the national black history movement of Woodson's time—and even, in some cases, joined the ranks of white historical associations. While they may have been first-rate historians and teachers, Johnson, Lee, and Rowley do not appear to have been active researchers and writers. In 1955, Lorraine Williams earned a PhD in history, becoming the last black woman to earn a PhD in the pre–civil rights movement.

When viewed together, black women writers and students of history from the late 1800s until the mid-1950s developed distinct approaches and helped redefine the historian's function and identity in the United States. These black women intellectuals stand out for many reasons. They produced insightful and at times groundbreaking scholarship; they proposed relevant and vital connections between the past, present, and future; they demonstrated abilities to balance scholarly writings with social and political activism; they struggled to transcend the gender barriers of their times; and they were committed to race vindication.

Black Female Novelist-Historians

Novelists Frances Ellen Watkins Harper (1825–1911) and Pauline E. Hopkins (1859–1930) meshed history with fiction in presenting and interpreting critical periods, events, and personalities in U.S. history. In 1892, at the age of sixty-seven, Harper—a feminist, public lecturer, poet, teacher, novelist, and, in Bettye Collier-Thomas's estimation, the "single most important black woman leader to figure in both the abolitionist and feminist reform movements"—published her most famous book, *Iola Leroy, or Shadows Uplifted*.[20] Perhaps the bestselling novel by an African American writer before the twentieth century, Harper's book was aimed primarily at black Sunday School teachers and female readers. As she had done decades earlier in her poetry on slavery, Harper critically revisited America's past in hopes of generating debate among her wide readership. As Hazel Carby has argued, she sought to "promote social change," "aid in the uplifting of the race," and "intervene in and influence political, social, and cultural debate" about black life during "the nadir."[21] While Harper's novel addressed many of the intricacies surrounding slavery, the wartime South, emancipation, and Reconstruction, it historicized the role and social responsibility of educated, privileged African Americans. Harper explored various issues in African American history until Reconstruction, but her message was applicable to the times in which she wrote. She made connections between the period of slavery and the present for pragmatic and political purposes. In analyzing *Minnie's Sacrifice* and *Iola Leroy,* Melba Joyce Boyd has suggested that "these novels provide a connection between the past horrors of slavery and the present terror of lynching. The radical history Harper preserves in both novels is a time continuum essential to a liberated vision in the future. In both instances, the works are written for the black reading audience." Harper acknowledged the complex inner workings of slave culture long before the slavery studies of the post–civil rights era highlighted enslaved blacks' agency. In *Iola Leroy,* Harper identified slaves "as participants in the struggle for liberation" and contrabands of war, probed the diversity within slave societies, and observed "the complex dynamics that characterize the master/slave relationship." Harper's fictional account of slavery was revisionist in nature and sensitive to notions of historical objectivity and detachment. "Harper's portrayals of the enslaved contradict popular opinion, manifesting vital, thriving voices of resistance. At the same time, Harper does not romanticize the slaves to benefit a counterargument." In dealing with Reconstruction, Harper also highlighted the significance of rebuilding the family for African Americans in the South.[22]

Frances Harper used history in order to help dictate a program for what W. E. B. Du Bois deemed the "Talented Tenth." In the novel, protagonist Iola, who had been living as a white person until her adult years, immediately accepted her African heritage upon discovering that her mother was "a quadroon." During the Civil War and following emancipation, this "Southern lady, whose education and manners stamped her as a woman of fine culture and good breeding" devoted her life to the black masses of the South as a nurse, a teacher, a church worker, and an organizer of mother's meetings. For Iola, being a servant and leader of the race "is a far greater privilege than it is to open the gates of material prosperity and fill every home with sensuous enjoyment." In response to Dr. Gresham's plea that she no longer serve her oppressed people and marry him, Iola passionately asserted, "It was through their unrequited toil that I was educated, while they were compelled to live in ignorance. I am indebted to them for the power I have to serve them. I wish other Southern women felt as I do. . . . I must serve the race which needs me most."[23] Harper stressed that middle-class, educated blacks owed a collective debt to black history, to the historical struggles waged by their enslaved ancestors. As Carby has observed, Iola and the other intellectuals and race leaders in Harper's "entertaining and instructive" opus "gained their representativeness or typicality from an engagement with history. They carried the past in their individual histories and were presented as a historical force, an elite to articulate the possibilities of the future of the race."[24]

Like Harper, Pauline Hopkins also employed her writings in the struggle for racial uplift. "In giving this little romance expression in print," Hopkins introduced *Contending Forces* in 1900, "I am not actuated by desire for notoriety or for profit, but to do all that I can in an humble way to raise the stigma of degradation from my race."[25] During the late nineteenth century and the early part of the twentieth, Hopkins was one of black America's most productive journalists. "The single most productive black woman writer at the turn of the century," from 1900 until 1905 Hopkins produced for publication four novels (one in book form); seven short stories; one brief, self-published historical booklet, *A Primer of Facts Pertaining to the Early Greatness of the African Race and the Possibility of Restoration by Its Descendants—with Epilogue* (1905); two dozen biographical sketches in the *Colored American Magazine;* and many essays, columns, and editorials. She has accurately been called by one scholar a "performer, playwright, orator, novelist, journalist, short story writer, biographer, and editor."[26]

A self-proclaimed historian, Hopkins introduced her best-known novel as being a historical study grounded in rigorous research. Philosophically, Hopkins argued that history was instructive because of its direct connection with the present and future. She viewed the present as being part of a larger historical continuum, part of a vast body of interconnected ideologies and events. Though she "tried to tell an impartial story," Hopkins was forthright in the need for black-authored revisionist historical accounts. "No one will do this for us; we must ourselves develop the men and women who will faithfully portray the inmost thoughts and feelings of the Negro with all the fire and romance which lie dormant in our history, and, as yet, unrecognized by writers of the Anglo-Saxon race."[27]

Hopkins emphasized that the conditions facing blacks during "the nadir" were essentially the same as those of the antebellum era. She rejected the notion of black progress from emancipation and Reconstruction that was widely celebrated by the majority of black spokespersons. "Mob-law is nothing new," Hopkins declared. "Let us compare the happenings of one hundred—two hundred years ago, with those of today. The difference between then and now, if any there be, is so slight as to be scarcely worth mentioning. The atrocity of the acts committed one hundred years ago are duplicated today, when slavery is supposed no longer to exist."[28] Similarly, in her serial novel *Winona,* set in Kansas during the turbulent 1850s, Hopkins sought to "justify the need in 1902 for the kind of organized resistance to racist violence led by the anti-slavery leader John Brown in 1856." Hopkins interpreted the historian's role not simply in terms of recounting past events, but, more important, as a source of motivation and direction for the future. Like *Contending Forces, Winona* drew from historical sources.[29]

"Throughout her tenure at [*Colored American Magazine*] (1900–1904), Hopkins acknowledged her obligation not simply to cultivate but to create an audience for her revisionist race history," C. K. Doreski has asserted. "She assumed the authority of race historian and mediated between the issues of race and gender to incite a readership to pride and action." Hopkins's historical approach as an editor and journalist for the *Colored American Magazine* was essentially pragmatic. She strove to translate "representative lives into authentic history" and compose "history from exemplary lives in the hope of 'elevat[ing] the image of the entire race." Seeking to inspire her readers to uplift themselves and the more unfortunate of their race, Hopkins translated the two dozen biographical sketches of "famous" black historical figures into "participatory exemplary texts."[30] According to Ira Dworkin, Hopkins was very much like George Washington Williams in documenting her histories with newspaper accounts, letters, and other revealing primary sources.[31] At the same time, Hopkins educated the significant white readership of *Colored American Magazine*, who made up about one-third of her total readership.[32]

Hopkins was also a forerunner of the black women's history movement and the Afrocentric movement. From 1901 until 1902, she published a series of biographical sketches entitled *Famous Women of the Negro Race* that highlighted "the achievements of Negro women who were beacon lights along the shore in the days of our darkest history." In her *A Primer of Facts*, Hopkins, the outspoken pan-Africanist, highlighted African Americans' connection with ancient Africa: "What is the obligation of the descendant of Africans in America?—To help forward the time of restoration. HOW MAY THIS BE DONE?—By becoming thoroughly familiar with the meager details of Ethiopian history, by fostering race pride and an international friendship with the Blacks of Africa."[33]

Progressive Era Amateur Black Women Historians

Other Progressive Era black women "historians without portfolio" offered their interpretations of history in nonfiction works. In 1894, Gertrude E. H. Bustill Mossell (1855–1948), editor, journalist, and feminist, first published *The Work of the Afro-American Woman*, a historical and contemporary assessment of black women intellectuals' and activists' monumental accomplishments since the era of the American Revolution. Joanne Braxton has posited that this volume was, "for the black woman of the 1890s, the equivalent of Giddings' work of the 1980s—in sum, a powerful and progressive statement." *The Work of the Afro-American Woman* is subdivided into various sections, "original essays and poems . . . part intellectual history, part advice book, and part polemic." Like Hopkins, Mossell introduced her scholarship as being a vehicle of race pride and inspiration. "The value of any published work, especially if historical in character, must be largely inspirational," Mossell proclaimed. "This fact grows out of the truth that race instinct, race experience lies behind it, national feeling, or race pride always having for its development a basis of self-respect."[34]

In the first two chapters of *The Work of the Afro-American Woman*, Mossell discussed a variety of black women historical icons and also offered some provocative thoughts on the deeper meanings of history to African Americans. In chapter 1, "The Work of the Afro-American Woman," while Mossell highlighted the achievements of her contemporary "industrious" black women social reformers as well as the contributions of well-known black women historical figures such Phyllis Wheatley, Sojourner Truth, Harriet Tubman, and F. E. W. Harper, she also noted the contributions of obscure women.[35] In another "tribute to black womanhood," titled "A Sketch of Afro-American Literature," Mossell prioritized history in the black struggle, validated social and oral history, and subdivided black history into three major "epochs." She was especially critical of the postemancipation period that was "defrauded of its substance by every means that human ingenuity could devise."[36] Mossell recognized the importance of using history within the African American community as a vehicle of racial pride and self-esteem and as a guide for the future.

In 1902, less than a decade after Mossell published *The Work of the Afro-American Woman*, Susie King Taylor (1848–1912) published the only black woman's account of the Civil War. In *Reminiscences of My Life in Camp with the 33rd U.S. Colored Troops, Late 1st South Carolina Volunteers*, Taylor recounted her experiences as a laundress, teacher, and a nurse behind Union lines. Taylor, whose mother was a domestic slave, served in the Union Army in various capacities from about 1862 until 1865.[37] Nearly four decades following the end of the war, she self-published *Reminiscences* while living in Boston. Thomas Wentworth Higginson introduced her account with a few words of praise, noting that *Reminiscences*, "delineated from the woman's point of view," constituted an important contribution to U.S. military history.[38] Taylor opened *Reminiscences* with a personalized history, tracing back her mother's family history and her own early life before the war. The bulk of Taylor's book is devoted to discussing the day-to-day experiences of the

33rd U.S. Colored Troops, renamed the First S.C. Volunteers. While glorifying Lincoln's Emancipation Proclamation as Booker T. Washington did in *Up From Slavery* (1901), she also challenged the mythic antiblack accounts of the Civil War, emancipation, and Reconstruction. Taylor wrote: "These white men and women could not tolerate our black Union soldiers, for many of them had formerly been their slaves; and although these brave men risked life and limb to assist them in distress, men and even women would sneer and molest them whenever they met them." She also celebrated the role of black women during the Civil War and, though brief, her thoughts were ahead of their time. "There are many people who do not know what some of the colored women did during the war," Taylor proclaimed, "There were hundreds of them who assisted the Union soldiers by hiding them and helping them escape. Many were punished for talking food to the prison stockades for the prisoners . . . These things should be kept in history before the people."[39]

Taylor's tone was openly patriotic. In her account, she separated history from polemics, saving her most scathing critiques of white America for a later chapter, "Thoughts on Present Conditions." Like Pauline Hopkins, she critiqued the mistreatment endured by blacks during "the nadir," pointing to the similarity between contemporary and past racial oppression. In a Woodsonian fashion, Taylor asked younger generations to remember and study history: "I look around now and see the comforts that our younger generation enjoy, and think of the blood that was shed to make these comforts possible for them, and see how little some of them appreciate the old soldiers. My heart burns within me, at this want of appreciation."[40]

Though perhaps not as widely known as Taylor, Laura Eliza Wilkes (1871–1922), a public school teacher from Washington, D.C., joined the ranks of early black women "historians without portfolio" by publishing two obscure historical studies: a brief pamphlet printed by Howard University in 1899, and *The Story of Frederick Douglass, with Quotations and Extracts*.[41] Two decades later in 1919, Wilkes wrote *Missing Pages in American History, Revealing the Services of Negroes in the Early Wars of the United States of America*, published in Washington, D.C. In a letter she wrote to Carter G. Woodson on July 22, 1921, Wilkes, "a paying member of the ASNLH," articulated her anger with Woodson for not reviewing her work in the *Journal of Negro History*. "I submitted my work to you as soon as it came from the press and yet for some reason it has not received the courtesy, I had every right to expect for it," Wilkes told Woodson.[42] She believed that she had a place among serious African American historians who met Woodson's high standards for rigorous, historical scholarship. In her letter to the Association founder, Wilkes also intimated that Woodson did not review her book because she was a woman. Wilkes's subtle accusation of sexism is understandable, but it is improbable, considering Woodson's progressive treatment of women during the early black history movement. Julie Des Jardins's assessment of this situation makes sense: Woodson's "response to her book had more to do with the lack of academic credentials backing it."[43]

Wilkes appears to have been the first black woman to chronicle the history of blacks in the military from the colonial era through the War of 1812. She dedicated six years to researching her study, taking great pride in the unwavering patriotism exhibited by black soldiers in America throughout history. "The facts found herein are taken from colonial records, state papers, assembly journals, histories of slavery, and old time histories of the colonies and of the republic," Wilkes assured, "The reader can easily verify this statement by using the bibliography at the end of the work."[44] *Missing Pages* contains only eighty-four pages of text on black soldiers from 1614 until 1815, yet the work is dense and covers a great deal of historical ground, drawing attention to black soldiers during the conflicts of colonial America, the American Revolution, the French and Indian War, and the War of 1812. Wilkes's book was written in an overtly objective manner; drawing from more than fifty sources and listing many "facts," Wilkes adequately recovered blacks' contributions from the margins. Her sentiments reflected the thought of many black thinkers of her time. In 1919, during what James Weldon Johnson deemed the "Red Summer," blacks increased their critiques of America's failure to acknowledge blacks' willingness to help preserve American democracy. Black writers like Wilkes strove to prove to white Americans that the denial of fundamental citizenship rights to blacks was unjust because of their contributions to the United States at home and abroad during World War I and all wars before it. "The Negroes of America," Wilkes professed, "have done their bit in every war and taken no small part in every military movement made for the salvation of their country from the time of its earliest settlement."[45]

In 1912, between the publications of Wilkes's two books, Leila Amos Pendleton, a seasoned educator and reformer from Washington, D.C., published *A Narrative of the Negro,* a brief work that she described as being "a sort of 'family history'" for the "colored children of America."[46] In 1915, Du Bois hailed his book *The Negro* as the first major study of African descendants throughout the diaspora.[47] Though not as scientific and analytical as Du Bois's work, Pendleton's study was ambitious and wide reaching. It addressed Africans' lives from ancient times through the era of colonialism—blacks in Haiti, Brazil, Jamaica, and Bermuda, and black American life from the colonial era through "the nadir." Her young audience did not prevent Pendleton from embracing a militant tone. She chastised King Leopold of the Belgian Congo and the violent nature of the colonial conquest, called slavery "evil," and condemned the "long series of brutal outrages, murders, maimings, beatings, burnings" and "barbarous lynchings" of African Americans.[48] The bulk of Pendleton's study addressed African American history from the American Revolution through "the nadir," and in the tradition of African American juvenile literature it relied heavily on many brief biographical sketches of a range of black leaders. Renowned Harlem renaissance novelist and *Crisis* literary editor (1919–1926) Jessie Fauset heralded Pendleton's book: "Now, at last, it would seem, we have an historian who has arisen in answer to our need."[49] Five years after *A Narrative of the Negro* appeared, Pendleton published a historically scientific article in *The Journal of Negro History*, "Our New Possessions—The Danish West Indies."[50]

In 1919, a year after writing "Slavery in California" for the *Journal of Negro History*, journalist and social activist (and historian for the NACW during the 1920s) Delilah Leontium Beasley (1871[?]–1934) published *The Negro Trail Blazers of California*. Beasley's monograph, the first major examination of blacks in California, contains vast amounts of valuable information still useful to those interested in the history of blacks in California and the West. When judged within its proper historical context, her study is exhaustive. She was committed to challenging the notion that blacks had not contributed to California's history. She worked diligently on *The Negro Trail Blazers of California* for close to a decade. Charlotte A. Bass, editor of the *California Eagle,* praised Beasley's commitment: "In gathering the data for this most unique volume, she has sacrificed money, and health."[51] Beasley was a thorough, innovative, and persistent researcher. She took courses in "Colorado and Spanish Colorado history" at the University of California in Berkeley while writing her study. She conducted meticulous research at the California Archives and the Bancroft Library at the University of California, Berkeley; incorporated oral history into her study by interviewing California's black pioneers "in every section of the state wherever a railroad or horse and buggy could go"; examined a wide array of California's newspapers; combed carefully through personal family papers, letters, and memorabilia; and contacted counties in the state, asking them for any materials dealing with African Americans.[52] Woodson acknowledged the value of Beasley's findings and "the numerous valuable facts in the book." However, he was very critical of her style, approach, and methodology, calling *The Negro Trail Blazers of California* "so much of a hodge-podge that one is inclined to weep like the minister who felt that his congregation consisted of too many to be lost but not enough to be saved."[53] At the same time, Beasley and Woodson were similar in their commitment to social activism. She wrote a regular column, "Activities among Negroes," for the *Oakland* Tribune during the 1920s and 1930s and was instrumental in getting an anti-lynching bill passed in California.

Several years after Beasley's study appeared, Elizabeth Ross Haynes (1879[?]–1953), a pioneering sociologist, author of juvenile literature, social activist, and "historian without portfolio," published *Unsung Heroes*, a 279-page collection of biographical sketches of seventeen black historical figures, three of whom are women and three of whom hailed from outside the United States. *Unsung Heroes*, published by Du Bois's short-lived Du Bois and Dill Publishers, was an attempt "to provide black children with historical biographies and was one of the books written especially for black children in the Twenties." In the brief foreword to her book, Haynes insisted that her story is about "the victories in spite of the hardships and struggles of Negroes whom the world has failed to sing about." Haynes sought to inspire black youth to "succeed in spite of all odds." As Francille Rusan Wilson has proposed, Haynes did not deviate from the basic "facts" of her subjects' lives and works, but she "invented dialogues and offered her young readers access into the inner thoughts of children on the brink of greatness."[54] Several years after *Unsung Heroes* appeared, Haynes's master's thesis, "Negroes in Domestic Service in the United States," was published in the *Journal of Negro History*.[55]

In the 1920s and 1930s, Elizabeth Lindsay Davis (b.1855), founder and longtime president of the Chicago Phyllis Wheatley Woman's Club, chair of the history committee for the NACW, and key figure in the creation of the Illinois Federation of Colored Women's Clubs, published two illuminating historical narratives detailing the lives and works of black clubwomen: *The Story of the Illinois Federation of Colored Women's Clubs* (1922) and *Lifting As They Climb* (1933). Davis's 1922 study chronicles the origins and evolution of the Illinois Federation of Colored Women's Clubs and provides an overview of the organization's contemporary achievements and leadership. Like Susie King Taylor, Davis believed that black history could help socialize black youth who "oftimes do not appreciate the fullness of organized effort." Davis offered her study as an historical blueprint for social activism for the younger generation. "My greatest desire in presenting this volume," Davis insisted, "is that those younger women among our ranks will find in it, information that will give them a greater appreciation of the work and usefulness of the 'Pioneers' and that through this greater appreciation, they will be inspired to 'Carry On.'"[56]

Davis's larger study, *Lifting as They Climb*, constitutes the first major effort at chronicling the contributions of the National Association of Colored Women. As the "official history" of the NACW, *Lifting as They Climb* recounts the thirty-five year history, activities, and leadership of the black women's club movement from 1895 until 1933. As Wanda Hendricks has noted, Davis's meticulous monograph still serves as an essential repository of primary sources and starting point for research on black clubwomen. The work, more than four hundred pages long and with more than twenty pages of photographs of black clubwomen from all over the country, served as inspiration for her black female readership and provides detailed records of annual NACW conferences, summaries of black women's club activism by region, and hundreds of brief biographical sketches of black clubwomen, many of whose contributions have not yet been explored by modern historians.[57]

During the Harlem renaissance, several years after Davis's first study appeared, self-taught historian and journalist Drusilla Dunjee Houston (1876–1941) became the first black woman to examine ancient African history. Drawing from the various books in her father's personal library, Houston published *Wonderful Ethiopians of the Ancient Cushite Empire* in 1926. While it is hard to pinpoint what sparked Houston to dedicate her life to chronicling ancient African history, W. Paul Coates has suggested that the race pride embraced by her family and her reading of Du Bois's *The Negro* played key roles in this regard. Houston's book represents a precursor to the black American Afrocentric tradition that has flourished since the Black Power era. Labeling black Americans "the modern Cushites," she wanted her black readership to claim Africa's ancient achievements, especially those of Ethiopia, as a source of cultural pride.[58]

Houston realized that the denial and falsification of black and African history bolstered the oppression of African peoples throughout the diaspora, that "the hatred of the races springs out of misunderstanding." With a sense of self-proclaimed authority and authenticity, Houston claimed that her facts were "convincing and absolute." She envisioned her scholarship as being an important platform for social reform. Like Marcus Garvey, Houston exhorted her audience: "Lift up your heads, discouraged and downtrodden Ethiopians. Listen to this marvelous story told of your ancestors, who wrought mightily for mankind and built the foundations of civilization true and square in the days of old." Equally significant, Houston transcended the limitations of a philosophy of blind race pride, demanding that her readers draw inspiration to achieve "a greater consecration to the high idealism that made the masteries of olden days."[59]

"Bibliomaniac" Dorothy Burnett Porter Wesley and Prolific Biographer Shirley Graham Du Bois

Unlike their Progressive Era predecessors, Dorothy Burnett Porter Wesley (1905–1995) and Shirley Graham Du Bois (1896–1977) received extensive training in academic areas other than history and used their expertise to generate significant historical scholarship. Like countless black women scholars, Porter Wesley intended to become a secondary school teacher. She shifted her focus to library science after working in the library of a Washington, D.C., school for teachers, Miner Normal School. After graduating from Howard in 1928, she pursued degrees in library science at Columbia University. Two years before earning a graduate degree in library science in 1932, Porter Wesley was appointed the chief curator for the Moorland-Spingarn Research Center, a position she held from 1930 until 1973. In more than four decades, she created a vital institution for researchers interested in the history of African descendants, especially African Americans. Porter Wesley received very little funding and support at Howard during her early years there. Since the university's library was not a priority, she became a very resourceful and persistent chronicler and collector of African descendants' history and culture. She recalled that in order to acquire materials, she had to "beg, beg, beg, and clean up people's basements, and find books anywhere."[60] Porter Wesley was close to many well-known black intellectuals and often received, as gifts, monographs and materials from them. Along with the countless other books and sources that she purchased, she added these to the Moorland-Spingarn collection. She was, as she called herself, "a bibliomaniac." Porter Wesley was also active in the early black history movement initiated by Woodson. She credited him with piquing her interests in her people's past. "I didn't know Carter Woodson until 1930, when I came to Washington," Porter Wesley remembered. "I went to see him in order to learn something about my history, which I knew he knew, which I did not know."[61]

In the tradition of Woodson, Porter Wesley used black history as a medium to help others—professional scholars, university students, and laypersons alike. Most important, as a public historian she secured rare, priceless items so that they could be useful to others, in turn paving the way to new discoveries and publications. Porter Wesley made certain that blacks at Howard University and the surrounding Washington, D.C., area were exposed to black history. With little funding, she persuaded many leading African American intellectuals, such as Sterling Brown, Langston Hughes, Arna Bontemps, Charles Wesley, and Gwendolyn Brooks to participate in Howard's Negro History Week activities; she brought Kwame Nkrumah to Howard as well. She must have been very persuasive since these scholars, on average, received $25 for their services. Equally important, Porter Wesley was able to mobilize students and the community to participate in her programs. "I always made certain that we had a roomful, because I never liked a person to come and talk to an empty room," she recalled, "I could get students. I'd go out and corral them in."[62]

Porter Wesley's most celebrated contribution to the black historical profession was her role as a curator, librarian, and resource. Researchers respectfully called her "a walking encyclopedia." In 1973, her colleague Benjamin Quarles praised her: "without exaggeration, there hasn't been a major black history book in the last 30 years in which the author hasn't acknowledged Mrs. Porter's help."[63] Porter Wesley's role as a guide to locating obscure primary sources in black history cannot be understated. Henry Louis Gates Jr. deemed Porter Wesley "one of the most famous black librarians and bibliophiles of the twentieth century, second only, perhaps, to Arthur Schomburg." Gates's recent discovery of Hannah Craft's *The Bondswoman's Narrative* (circa 1850s) owed a great debt to Porter Wesley, as this valuable manuscript was part of her personal collection.[64] Porter Wesley was also a published historian; before the modern civil rights movement, she compiled many comprehensive bibliographies on black history, her earliest being *A Selected History of Books by and about Negroes* (1936) and *Negro American Poets: A Bibliographic Checklist of Their Writings* (1945). In addition, during the 1930s, 1940s, and 1950s, Wesley published articles on antebellum black activists in the *Journal of Negro Education* and the *Journal of Negro History*. Well documented and based on close readings of primary documents, her scholarship was very much like that of Woodson's disciples, one of whom, Charles H. Wesley, she married in 1979.[65]

Though both women respected primary sources, Shirley Graham Du Bois's approach to black history was different from Porter Wesley's. Graham Du Bois, the first black woman to write and produce an all black opera, earned a master's degree in music history in 1935. She also worked on a doctorate in English and education at New York University. According to her leading biographer, Graham Du Bois was a "woman of many dimensions and talents" who "lived many lives."[66] Very much like her predecessor Pauline Hopkins, this creative artist and intellectual wore many different hats. She "was variously a composer, playwright, actress, drummer, biographer, editor, novelist, and political activist."[67] Though her contributions as a part-time, nonprofessional historian have been overshadowed by her social and political activism, between 1944 and 1976 Graham Du Bois published thirteen biographies of famous historical figures in African American history, half of which were published between 1944 and 1955. Her early biographies covered the lives of black male leaders like George Washington Carver, Paul Robeson, Jean Baptiste Pointe de Sable, Frederick Douglass, Benjamin Banneker, and Booker T. Washington, and all were published by New York's Jullian Messner, Inc. Creative, accessible to a broad readership, and often based on careful examinations of the available primary and secondary source documentation, Graham Du Bois's biographies produced during the era of Jim Crow segregation demonstrate her abilities as a historian.[68]

There Once Was a Slave, Graham Du Bois's biography on Douglass, for instance, received "the sixty-five hundred dollar Julian Messner Award for the best book combating intolerance in America." The competition was stiff; more than six hundred manuscripts were submitted to the contest. The book was released in 1947 (the same year that John Hope Franklin's *From Slavery to Freedom* was published), when black history was far from being mainstreamed but was making some significant progress. Graham Du Bois devoted most of the book to narrating Douglass's life after he gained his freedom in 1838. Like Elizabeth Ross Haynes in *Unsung Heroes,* Graham Du Bois created dialogues for her historical figures. She also occasionally quoted directly from *My Bondage and My Freedom, Life and Times of Frederick Douglass, The Liberator,* and Du Bois's *John Brown.* Her bibliography contains more than a dozen scholarly sources, including the *Journal of Negro History* (1935–1946). In the epilogue, she validated her scholarship, stating, "This is a true story."[69] In the tradition of Elizabeth Ross Haynes, Pauline Hopkins, Jane Dabney Shackelford, and other black women who wrote juvenile and popular literature, Graham Du Bois's scholarship sought to educate young adults and laypersons about black history. At the same time, the prolific Graham Du Bois was more sophisticated and advanced in her writing than her predecessors. An important nondoctoral historian of black America, "her aim was to preserve Black history and culture."[70]

Pioneering Generations of Professional Black Women Historians

Professionally trained black women historians coexisted with their laywomen counterparts, but they emerged later. On March 23, 1925, roughly thirty years after W. E. B. Du Bois became the first African American historian to receive a PhD, feminist pioneer, educator, and social activist Anna Julia Cooper became the fourth black woman to receive a PhD and the first to receive a PhD within the field of history and romance languages. Cooper, at age sixty-six, faced numerous challenges, including poor working conditions, a university bureaucracy, and a critical advisor.[71] Nonetheless, she earned her doctorate from the prestigious University of Paris, Sorbonne. Her dissertation, written in French, was entitled "L'Attitude de la France dans la question de l'Esclavage entre 1789 et 1848" ("The Attitude of France on the Question of Slavery between 1789 and 1848"). Cooper conducted meticulous research at the Library of Congress, various French archives, and the Bibliothèque

Militaire, while immersing herself in the relevant secondary source materials. She was questioned during the defense of her dissertation by leading French historians, including M. Sagnac, M. Cestre, and M. C. Bouglé.[72]

Cooper's achievements were remarkable on many levels. Author of the first major black feminist manifesto, *A Voice from the South* (1892), Cooper did not conform to the "cult of true womanhood," the prevalent ideology that a woman's place was in the domestic sphere. She directly challenged the leading male spokespersons of the Progressive Era for their sexism, declaring "only the BLACK WOMAN can say 'when and where I enter . . . then and there the whole Negro race enters with me."[73] Cooper maintained this stance throughout her life, was an outspoken advocate for the higher education of women, and embraced the National Association of Colored Women's "Lifting As We Climb" motto. She earned her bachelor's and master's degrees in mathematics, and as a doctoral student she studied literature, history, languages (French, Latin, and Greek), and phonetics. She was indeed multidisciplinary in her intellectual approach, combining her knowledge and expertise in history with other fields of intellectual inquiry to forge an original worldview. Moreover, she earned her doctorate while serving as guardian to five grandnieces and nephews.[74]

Cooper's dissertation went largely unnoticed in French and U.S academic circles, yet she translated it into English and used it when she taught adult education at Frelinghuysen University in the 1930s. Frances Richardson Keller has suggested that perhaps Cooper "hoped that her study would be an example of scholarly achievement, a case-in-point for doubting male examiners, a model for other women scholars."[75] Cooper's dissertation was a direct challenge to France's slaveholding past and that of the Western world at a time when blacks still suffered greatly from this past. Laying objectivity and scholarly orthodoxies to the side, she introduced her study with unwavering indictments of slavery on moral terms. "In the European colonies of America," Cooper emphasized, "black slavery was an institution founded solely on the abuse of power. In all aspects created by a barbarous and shortsighted politics, and maintained by violence, we shall see that it could be abolished by a stroke, a simple legislative measure."[76]

Ahead of her time and foreshadowing Walter Rodney, she also mentioned the devastating impact of the slave trade on Africa, estimating that for every one slave imported, four lost their lives.[77] Cooper's fundamental argument was that slavery had a profound impact on debates among the French during the French Revolution and that the French revolutionaries in part failed because of their reluctance to recognize how slavery went contrary to their ideas. The tone of Cooper's study is polemical at times, but she understood and employed the standard historical methods of her times.

Following Cooper, a distinguishable cadre of professionally trained black women historians emerged. While no black woman appears to have earned a PhD in history in the decade of the Great Depression, the 1940s was a watershed era for professional black women historians. In this decade alone at least six black women earned doctorates in history. This group was significant when viewed within the broader context of black women with PhDs. According to Stephanie Y. Evans, by the early 1940s nearly fifty black women had earned doctorates.[78] Though at times politically and ideologically diverse, these scholars shared some important traits. Born in the early twentieth century, they received their training from some of the most prestigious institutions in the country, often becoming the first black woman to earn a doctorate at their respective institutions. They often used the *Journal of Negro History* and the *Journal of Negro Education* as outlets for their scholarship. Like their contemporaries John Hope Franklin and Benjamin Quarles, these women tended to write very objective history, a strategy dictated by their times. It is not surprising that none focused on black women's history. These women often served as mentors for younger black female scholars and interpreted their roles as teachers very seriously, in turn developing new gendered strategies of education. As black female scholars, they developed mechanisms to cope with the sexism and racism prevalent in American society.

In 1940, Marion Thompson Wright became the first black woman to earn a doctorate in history in the United States. Her dissertation, *The Education of Negroes in New Jersey*, was published in 1941 by the Columbia University Teacher's College Series. After earning her degree, she returned to Howard University to teach, setting high standards for her students while influencing younger black women to at least consider the historical profession as a career. In the mid-1940s, she also created a student counseling service at Howard. She was active in the university counseling services throughout the 1950s and was known for her willingness to mentor and guide students. "Students often came to her Washington apartment with their work to ask for her criticism and help. She insisted on correctness of detail at the same time that she nurtured and supported them. She was unstinting in the number of hours she would give to her students."[79] While at Howard, Wright published articles on blacks in New Jersey in the *Journal of Negro History*, the *Journal of Negro Education* (for which she served as the book review editor), and the *Journal of Educational Sociology*.

Wright's *The Education of Negroes in New Jersey* was the first to study the "social and educational history of Negroes in New Jersey." She examined African Americans in New Jersey in five major periods from the late seventeenth century through about 1881. Wright's work is straightforward, objective, and free from passionate overtones—until the concluding chapters. In her closing chapter, "Implications for Education," Wright drew the connections between the history of black education in New Jersey with the contemporary times. "The history of education in New Jersey has . . . revealed that unequal opportunities have been the usual accompaniment of segregated schools," Wright asserted. "Recent investigations show how that at the present time it is still a matter of inferior facilities, limited opportunities . . ., and few openings in the field for teacher training and placement."[80] At the same time, Wright commended New Jersey for never passing laws that required segregation in public schools. Wright held the educator ultimately responsible for helping solve the contemporary problems facing blacks and education in New Jersey. She called upon educators to study history and help alleviate racial prejudice, a phenomenon that she believed harmed both blacks and whites. She challenged the state for stigmatizing black students.[81] Wright's critiques were perhaps more effective because she couched them in a discourse that seemingly praised positive efforts for reform. Wright concluded her study with a plea to white America's "educators of New Jersey and America" to "assume roles of leadership in telic or purposive planning instead of allowing themselves merely to reflect the sentiments, ideas, and practices of the social groups of which they are members."[82] Woodson and members of the ASNLH were especially impressed with Wright's scholarship. In 1943, "the first prize of One Hundred Dollars for the best article submitted to the *Journal of Negro History*" was awarded to Wright for "New Jersey Laws and the Negro."[83] In his review of *The Education of Negroes in New Jersey* in the *Journal of Education,* authority on the African American educational experience Horace Mann Bond praised Wright's scholarship, objectivity, writing style, and historicity. He applauded Wright for engaging in the "History of Education" at a time when most education scholars had "turned away" from this scholarly avenue "as from a sort of Dead Sea fruit." Bond concluded his review emphasizing: "Persons educating Negro teachers would be wise to spare time from methods, tests, guidance, or even the curriculum, to have their students read and digest this volume."[84]

Wright's scholarship revealed her commitment to social activism. Her research helped expose the negative effects of discrimination on U.S. culture. In 1947, the governor of New Jersey announced that he would address some of the issues raised by Wright's research. Several years later, in part influenced by Wright's research, New Jersey passed a new constitution, "the first in the country to forbid segregation in both public schools and state militia."[85] During the 1950s Wright was a researcher for the NAACP, amassing evidence for the *Brown vs. Board of Education, Topeka, Kansas* case.[86] She was a social activist on other fronts as well, holding membership in numerous civil rights and professional organizations.[87]

During her career as a professor at Howard University from 1941 until her untimely death in 1962, Wright faced significant gender discrimination. When she arrived at Howard, she was "one of only two female assistant professors." Margaret Smith Crocco has argued that sexism was common at Howard during Wright's undergraduate years. Several scholars have pointed out that Wright believed that the university did not adequately recognize her work because she was a woman. Her assessment appears to have been accurate. "The affirmation of her accomplishments was muted by the sexism of Howard University and the racism of the larger society." Wright was convinced that "black women's contributions to the cause of 'racial uplift' were widely underestimated within the black community." She was not outspoken about this deeply rooted intraracial problem, yet she did discuss black women's dilemmas in higher education in a 1944 article in the *Journal of Negro Education,* "Negro Advancement Organizations."[88]

In 1941, the same year that Wright's *The Education of Negroes in New Jersey* was published, Lulu M. Johnson earned a doctorate in history from Iowa State University. Her dissertation was titled "The Problem of Slavery in the Old Northwest, 1787–1858." This Rockefeller Foundation Fellow also published a manual entitled *The Negro in American Life* and taught at West Virginia State College.[89] In the same year that Johnson received her degree, Merze Tate became the first black woman to earn a PhD in government and international relations from Harvard University. Though not formally trained as a historian, Tate embraced an interdisciplinary approach. At Howard University, where she remained from 1942 until 1977, she taught courses in history and published several historical monographs, such as *The Disarmament Illusion* (1942) and *The United States Armaments* (1948). "A significant influence among undergraduate and graduate students, Tate saw the economic and social aspects of society as central to understanding history," Rosalyn Terborg-Penn recounted. "A mentor through the years, she taught outstanding African-American students who themselves have made contributions to public secondary education, higher education, and the history profession."[90] In 1943, Susie Owen Lee received a PhD in history from New York University; her dissertation was titled "The Union League of America: Political Activity in Tennessee, the Carolinas, and Virginia, 1865–1870."[91]

Three years later, in 1946 Elsie Lewis earned a doctorate in history from the University of Chicago. She completed her dissertation on the secession movement in Arkansas. In 1955, Lewis published a significant article, "The Political Mind of the Negro, 1865–1900," which analyzed black political thought from emancipation through "the nadir." Thus she became probably the second African American (and certainly the first African American woman) to contribute an article to the *Journal of Southern History*.[92] The article was also the first in the journal by an African American to focus on African American subject matter.

Based on a close and balanced reading of black convention proceedings, black newspapers, and a few black males' polemics, Lewis stressed that post–emancipation era African American male political activists embraced the patriotic rhetoric from the Declaration of Independence, fought tirelessly for "full citizenship rights and privileges," and drew upon "ethical teachings to bolster their arguments," while maintaining a commitment to their fundamental beliefs in natural rights, equal rights under the laws of government, and egalitarianism.[93] Lewis debunked the widely held myth of universal pre-FDR black support for the Republican Party and acknowledged the disagreements within this nonmonolithic group. She clearly drew inspiration from her subject matter, exclaiming in her opening paragraph, "As a group, they represented the highest type of professional and intellectual achievement of the Negro in America."[94] Yet, like her contemporaries Benjamin Quarles, John Hope Franklin, and many of Woodson's "Boys," she was committed to rigorous, objective historical scholarship. Lewis was one of the African Americans active early within the Southern Historical Association. She was also a member of the ASNLH, the American Historical Association, and the Organization of American Historians.[95]

Spanning from 1946 until 1977, Helen G. Edmonds's long career as a professional historian was shaped by the changes ushered in by the immediate post–World War II, Cold War, civil rights, and Black Power eras. Before Mary Frances Berry (PhD in history, University of Michigan, 1966) served as assistant secretary in the Department of Health, Education, and Welfare, as vice-chair of the Civil Rights Commission under President Carter, and as chair of the Civil Rights Commission under President Clinton, Edmonds was the most active black female historian in American politics. She was also arguably the most widely known black woman historian before the post–civil rights era. An outspoken supporter of the National Republican Party who in the 1960s told an audience of black churchgoers that "the Democratic Party is no friend of the Negro," she served in the Department of State, the Department of Defense, the National Advisory Council of the Peace Corps, and even as an alterative delegate to the General Assembly the United Nations.[96] She was especially active in the Eisenhower and Nixon administrations. In a 1961 newspaper article, "Dr. Helen Edmonds to Launch Education Week," Edmonds was praised for being a black woman "first": "Dr. Edmonds made history in 1956 when she became the first colored woman in the history of this country to second the nomination of a candidate for the presidency of the United States. At that time she seconded the nomination of President Dwight D. Eisenhower for his second term. . . . Dr. Edmonds has carved for herself a niche as an outstanding platform lecturer in this country as well as in Europe."[97] In more than a few issues of the *Pittsburgh Courier,* Edmonds was praised for her oratory skills, national reputation, and effective political career.[98]

Before receiving her PhD in history in 1946 from Ohio State University, she was active in promoting black history. For instance, a year after earning her master's degree in history in 1938, she developed a "Syllabus for the Study of Negro History in the High Schools of Virginia," which was used by St. Paul Normal and Industrial School and by the Virginia State Department of Education in 1940.[99] In 1951, she published her dissertation, *The Negro and Fusion Politics in North Carolina, 1894–1901,* a detailed examination of African Americans' role in North Carolina politics during the pivotal 1890s. She focused on "the fusion between Populists and Republicans from 1894 to 1898 that overthrew Democratic rule and inaugurated a significant, if short-lived, experiment in inter-racial democracy."[100] Her study, however, deals with both black political activism and the general political climate of North Carolina spanning roughly a century. *The Negro and Fusion Politics in North Carolina* was reviewed in many journals and was well received. Reviewers, many of whom were well-respected historians of the time, welcomed her analysis, objectivity, thoroughness, and meticulous examination of the available sources. One reviewer noted that "no fair-minded students of the stormy period of Fusion politics can afford to ignore this book." Rayford W. Logan praised Edmonds' "absorbing narrative" and called upon his colleague to "complete her analysis by a history of the Negro in North Carolina politics since 1901."[101] During the remainder of the 1950s, Edmonds did not publish significant historical scholarship and instead studied European history at the University of Heidelberg and traveled throughout Europe as a "leader specialist" in the Cultural Exchange Program under the U.S. Department of State.

Two decades after *The Negro and Fusion Politics in North Carolina,* she published a study on blacks in the government, *Black Faces in High Places* (1971). Edmonds was among the few black historians born during the Progressive Era who wrote a monograph focusing on black history on the eve of the civil rights movement. Edmonds was an important presence at North Carolina Central University (NCCU) in Durham, where she worked from 1941 until she retired in 1977. She held a host of positions at NCCU, serving as the chair of the Department of History from 1963 until 1964. In one of her biographical sketches from 1970, Edmonds wrote herself into history: "Dr.

Edmonds is the first and only Negro woman Dean of a graduate school of Arts and Sciences, a position she has held at North Carolina Central University since 1964."[102] Sometime during the 1960s, it appears that Edmonds was working on a project on the history of black women. In a 1967 interview with a reporter from the *Richmond News Leader*, Edmonds indicated: "My current book deals with the most neglected area in historical writing regarding the Negro. There has yet been no composite picture of the average woman."[103] As revealed by notes in her book proposal for *The American Negro Woman*, Edmonds planned to write a comprehensive history of black women from 1618 until 1956, in five major parts. She outlined her "suggested approach" as follows:

> Show her as the social product of Negro life of each period. Contrast her with the white female types which existed at the same time. (If this dual approach is agreed upon, then this must be maintained throughout the work. The technique of contrast becomes a device for delineation rather than a device for evaluation—and, as such, relieves us of the task of being too academically critical.) She will be painted against the backdrop of the growth of Negro society in American life, and then contrasted with the role of her counterpart, the white female, at these given periods we shall handle. This approach requires a penetrating analysis of the status of white females at each period.[104]

Edmonds never completed *The American Negro Woman*. If she had done so in the 1960s or 1970s, it would have potentially been the first major comprehensive history of black women by a professionally trained historian. Equally important, her proposed comparison between black and white women preceded Darlene Clark Hine's 1992 call for "crossover history" in the *Journal of Women's History*. Perhaps Edmonds's busy life in politics prevented her from completing this intriguing project.

In the late 1940s, Margaret Nelson Rowley closed out the decade for professionally trained black female historians, earning a PhD in history from Columbia University.[105] Rowley, who graduated summa cum laude from Hunter College in New York, encountered sexism as a doctoral candidate. According to her son, Dean Rowley, a Columbia professor told his mother that she was basically wasting her time pursuing a doctorate in history "because, chances were, she'd just get married and never make use of her degree or advanced education." Discrediting her foes, Rowley devoted her career to teaching history and mentoring young African American adults. She died on December 4, 2003, having spent the majority of her career as a historian based in Atlanta. For instance, she introduced African American Studies at Morris Brown College, chaired its history department, and served as one of its academic deans.[106]

During the civil rights movement, formally trained black women historians who came of age in the 1940s continued to be active in the profession,
especially Wright, Lewis, and Edmonds. Yet, like the 1930s, the 1950s appears
to have been a challenging decade for professionally trained black women
historians. Among the few black women to earn doctorates in history departments during the 1950s was Lorraine A. Williams (1923–1996). Focusing on American intellectual history, Williams received her doctorate from
American University in 1955 at the advent of the civil rights movement.[107]
Coinciding with the Black Power era and the black women's history and
studies movements, during the 1970s and 1980s many more black women
received doctorates in history. Many of these women later contributed to the
institutionalization of black women's history during the 1980s, 1990s, and up
through the present. Today, as demonstrated by Deborah Gray White's *Telling
Histories,* by an examination of current black historiography (especially in
the field of black women's history), and by black female participation in the
Association for the Study of African American Life and History, the ABWH,
the Organization of American Historians, and the Southern Historical Association, black women represent an important presence in the U.S. historical
profession.

The history of black women historians from the late nineteenth century
until the emergence of the classic civil rights movement is complex and vast.
It is a history that constitutes an illuminating record of intellectual struggle,
self-definition, and empowerment. Maneuvering around the different barriers before them, black women intellectuals declared themselves historians
with and without formal scholarly training. In publishing historical studies
for the black masses, white and black middle-class lay audiences, and for
their colleagues in academe, during the era of Jim Crow segregation African
American women created distinguishable and viable niches for themselves
among the chroniclers of America's past. They challenged the gender conventions of their times and entered the largely male-dominated public sphere
of academic discourse. The scholarship of these pioneering historians held
its ground and laid the foundations for many future historical endeavors.

In the decades following the modern civil rights movement, the numbers
of black women historians, especially those professionally trained, increased;
black women historians created vital organizational infrastructures such as
the Association of Black Women Historians; black women's history became a
popular and advanced subfield of U.S. history; and a handful of black women
historians rose to significant positions of power within academe and government. The scholarship, strategies, activism, and visions of pioneering black
women historians are essential components of black history and the black

historical enterprise. In order to properly understand the U.S. and African American historical professions, we must properly contextualize black female historians' scholarship, lives, and struggles. Their achievements give further credence to Nannie Helen Burroughs's motto for the National Training School for Women and Girls, founded in 1909 in Washington, D.C.: "We Specialize in the Wholly Impossible."[108]

5. "Shadow vs. Substance"

Deconstructing Booker T. Washington

I always make it a rule to make especial preparation for each
address. No two audiences are exactly alike. It is my aim to reach
and talk to the heart of each individual audience, taking it into my
confidence very much as I would a person. When I am speaking to
an audience, I care little for how what I am saying is going to sound
in the newspapers, or to another audience, or to an individual. At
the time, the audience before me absorbs all my sympathy, thought,
and energy.

—Booker T. Washington, *Up from Slavery*

"Easily the most striking thing in the history of the American Negro since
1876 is the ascendancy of Mr. Booker T. Washington," W. E. B. Du Bois remarked in *The Souls of Black Folk,* "But Booker T. Washington arose essentially as the leader not of one race but of two,—a compromiser between the
South, the North, and the Negro. . . . Mr. Washington represents in Negro
thought the old attitude of adjustment and submission," his "programme
practically accepts the alleged inferiority of the Negro races," and he "with-
draws many of the high demands of Negroes as men and American citizens."[1]
More than a decade later in an obituary for Washington in *The Crisis,* Du
Bois continued his critical assessment of his former adversary. "The death
of Mr. Washington marks an epoch in the history of America. He was the
greatest Negro leader since Frederick Douglass, and the most distinguished
man, white or black, who has come out of the South since the Civil War. . . .
On the other hand, in stern justice, we must lay on the soul of this man, a
heavy responsibility for the consummation of Negro disfranchisement, the
decline of the Negro college and public school and the firmer establishment
of color caste in this land."[2]

Since the early twentieth century, generations of scholars and historians
have hagiographically celebrated and further conceptualized more than a few
of Du Bois's enduring ideas, especially his theories of the "Talented Tenth,"

"double consciousness" or "two-ness," and "the problem of the color-line."[3] Equally noteworthy is that many scholars of the African American experience have embraced and expanded upon Du Bois's critical stance toward Booker T. Washington. With few exceptions, since the early 1970s historians have largely concurred with Louis R. Harlan's conclusion that the most important dimension of Washington's life was "the sources, nature, uses, and consequences of his power."[4] In various ways, historians have unpacked the meticulous details of Washington's public persona and identity, his shrewd racialized political tactics, and his role as the token black leader and spokesperson during the era described as "the nadir" of black life. On the other hand, less controversial issues such as Washington's hands-on programs for black farmers have received significantly less serious attention. In the late 1970s, one scholar observed in *Callaloo* that "Washington's current standing among scholars is fairly low."[5] Nearly thirty years later, the editors of a collection of essays on the Tuskegeean similarly commented: "Today, in many academic and social circles, it takes a lot of courage to even half-heartedly defend Washington's educational, economic, and social strategy, or attempt to place his strategies and tactics in a contextual framework."[6] With few exceptions, since the mid-1990s, more than a few leading African American public intellectuals, figureheads, and spokespersons as well as one of the most recent Washington biographers have tended to oversimplify Washington's leadership and legacy by largely focusing on the overt negative dimensions of his strategy of conciliation.[7]

While he has suggested a useful paradigm for understanding "the Tuskegee Institute approach to black development," Manning Marable has blamed Washington for black America's future economic, educational, and political predicaments. "Many social dilemmas confronting black American universities and educators today, a century later, are rooted in the conceptual and programmatic contradictions of Washington's educational and economic paradigms."[8] Similarly, in his controversial broadside against the black public intellectual, Adolph Reed Jr. grouped Washington with Cornel West, Henry Louis Gates Jr., bell hooks, Michael E. Dyson, and Robin Kelley. For Reed, Washington, like his twentieth-century black public intellectual disciples, was a "freelance race spokesman; his status depended on designation by white elites rather than by any black electorate or social movement."[9] In the 2005 Black History Month volume of *Black Issues in Higher Education*, economist, public intellectual, and the president of Bennett College, Julianne Malveaux, similarly dismissed Washington by placing him in direct opposition with the protest tradition: "Celebrating protest, beginning with the Niagara Movement, means celebrating those folks who refused to go along to get along, refused to smile and take the payola that Washington was offering. It means celebrating the Black Panther Party and its breakfast programs created to feed Black children so they could learn." Embracing the accommodation-protest dichotomy, Malveaux ignored the similarities between the Black Panther Party and Booker T. Washington. Many of the Panthers' practical programs, including the free breakfast for children program, mirrored those instituted by Washington in Macon County, Alabama.

Malveaux is more explicit in her critique of Washington in her polemic essay in Rebecca Carroll's anthology *Uncle Tom or New Negro?* (2006). "I think there are some things about Booker T. Washington that were purely evil," Malveaux wrote. "And then there's the fact that he, Mr. Social Segregation, allegedly had an affair with a white woman at the end of his life. Let's not leave that out. A syphilitic white woman, I believe." Beyond claiming that Washington had syphilis, Malveaux also misrepresents the well-documented so-called Ulrich Affair that occurred in mid-March 1911. Malveaux asserts: "In one of the biographies written about him, I'm not sure which, there was a mysterious occurrence toward the end of his life, and it was in all the white newspapers. He went to some brownstone in New York, in the East Sixties, and got into some altercation and got beat up. He claims he went to this house by mistake, but there was a white woman of ill repute there, and her significant went off—I'm not getting it entirely right, but it was scandalous. It was definitely scandalous." In 2006, medical doctors at the University of Maryland's conference on the causes of death of historical figures discovered that Washington did not have syphilis and instead died from high blood pressure. In 1915, a racist New York physician wrote that Washington died of "racial characteristics," a diagnosis that among white doctors in the South was synonymous with syphilis. As described in the *New York Times,* "Washington's records show that his blood pressure was 225 over 145, nearly double the 120 over 80 that is considered normal. The records also show that a blood test ruled out syphilis."[10]

In a recent monograph on Washington, *The Art of the Possible: Booker T. Washington and Black Leadership in the United States, 1881–1925,* Kevern Verney, who acknowledges Washington's complexity, describes Washington as being a self-centered, conservative, greedy, dictator-like, black conscious-less, despot who remained ideologically static between 1895 and 1915. Verney suggests what Washington could have done and assigns him various denigrating labels, such as the "rustic-minded Tuskegean," a man of "bucolic character," and a "turn of the century Forrest Gump."[11] On the other hand, the 2003 works by W. Fitzhugh Brundage and Jacqueline M. Moore present a more complete and complex portrait of Washington. The essays in

Brundage's *Booker T. Washington and Black Progress* are especially unique and unpredictable, recognizing the "multi meanings and polyvocality" of Washington's autobiography.[12]

Viewed in its totality, the historiography on Washington is more than a century old; is dynamic and fascinating; consists of many key transformations, developments, and debates; has been shaped by a wide variety of scholars; and serves as a revealing window into not only current perceptions of Washington, but also into the epistemology of African American history and the evolution of African American leadership history. "Epistemology is a philosophical inquiry into the nature of knowledge, what justifies a belief, and what we mean when we say that a claim is true."[13] An exploration of the historical scholarship on Washington provides an ideal exercise in epistemology and a deconstruction of the processes of how we know what we do about Washington. The historical studies on Washington have been compelling enough to attract the attention of more than a few scholars.[14] These scholars' analyses of Washingtonian scholarship, however, need to be updated and significantly elaborated upon.

This chapter critically explores significant scholarship on Washington published since the beginning of the twentieth century. Bearing the title of one of his countless "Sunday evening talks" to Tuskegee students, this chapter unravels how scholars have interpreted and characterized the "shadow" (the silhouette, perplexity, relative obscurity, and darkness) and "substance" (the core, essential nature and meaning, and significance) of Washington's life, leadership strategies, and philosophy. As epitomized in the epigraph from *Up from Slavery* that opens this chapter, Washington consciously portrayed himself in different ways to various audiences and publics, thereby influencing how scholars have characterized and judged him. Many Booker T. Washingtons can therefore be gleaned from the historical record. The student of history faces the challenge of deciphering Washington's place and meaning in the African American historical experience.

The historiography on Washington can be subdivided and analyzed in several ways. Chronologically, the first body of scholarship on Washington spans from the immediate aftermath of his death on November 15, 1915, until the middle of the twentieth century, and then from the mid-twentieth century to the present. The decade of the 1970s stands out as especially dynamic and revisionist. Thematically, scholars have analyzed Washington on many levels, focusing on his life story, leadership, autobiographical writings and rhetorical styles, educational theories and programs, relationships with his opposition, views on Africa, and his pragmatic outreach programs. I analyze both the chronological and thematic evolution of Washington historiography and explore predominant ways we have been encouraged to view Washington. Incorporating the wide range of scholars' interpretations and findings, I offer the beginnings of a framework with which historians can assess Washington and teach "millennials"—today's college and university students—about his role as a black leader.[15]

Washington Scholarship: An Annotated Chronology

From 1915 until 1950, there were eight biographies of Washington published. During the 1920s, 1930s, and early 1940s, he was one of the only black Americans featured in white-authored books about "great" American reformers, educators, and leaders. He was also the topic of a diverse range of articles pertaining to education and the history of African American leaders. *Booker T. Washington: The Master Mind of a Child of Slavery* (1915) by Frederick E. Drinker, "former city editor of the *Philadelphia Record* and an advertising agent," is the major first biography of Washington. Based on the standards of the historical profession during the Progressive Era in the United States, Drinker's study is well documented and quite comprehensive, drawing extensively from lesser-known, invaluable primary sources. He also included a rich collection of authentic photos. According to Drinker, Washington's educational outlook was "a radical idea" and a pioneering educational experiment, especially for its commitment to outreach activities.[16] The second and more recognized major biography of Washington, *The Life and Times of Booker T. Washington* by Benjamin Franklin Riley, was published in 1916. Carter G. Woodson praised Riley's effort, noting that the book was "of incalculable value in the study of the Negro during the last quarter of the century."[17] Though Riley's study received more attention than Drinker's, it did not supersede Drinker's in terms of analysis or information.

In January 1917, "The *Crisis* Advertiser" praised *Booker T. Washington: A Builder of a Civilization* by Emmett J. Scott and Lyman Beecher Stowe as being the "authorized biography of Booker T. Washington."[18] Woodson also welcomed their study, "deeming it an appropriate estimate of the man."[19] Scott and Stowe cited extensively from Washington's lesser-known writings, including many unpublished documents. It is not surprising that they defended Washington from his opposition and highlighted his outreach work for the black masses of Macon County. "Mr. Washington was the kind of leader who kept very close to the plain people," Scott and Stowe insisted, "He knew their every-day lives, their weaknesses, their temptations. . . . He knew exactly what they 'were up against' whether they lived in country or city."[20] As Washington's personal secretary and close confidant, Scott remained dedicated to Washington throughout his lifetime.[21]

From 1917 until 1939, five biographies on Washington were published.[22] In 1932, Washington's son, E. Davidson, offered scholars another window into his father's worldview by publishing a collection of his speeches.[23] None of these studies, however, surpassed those written by Drinker, Riley, and Scott and Stowe. Of the early biographies on Washington, Scott and Stowe's appears to be the most widely read, whereas Drinker's work has been the most overlooked. From the 1920s until the 1940s, white authors like Lyman Abbott, M. A. De Wolfe, M. S. Fenner, and Eleanor C. Fishburn included Washington as the representative token black leader in their writings.[24] In 1935, Merle Curti became one of the first white scholars to openly criticize Washington as an historical figure. While he praised Washington's educational program, directly comparing it to that of Dewey, he critiqued Washington because he "failed to see the problem of democracy in industry; he failed to seek an alliance with the labor movement, or with any group that sought to remake the existing order along more equitable and more stable lines."[25] Curti also argued that Washington lacked any appreciation for black America's African background, black southern folk culture, or the so-called "generally pleasant, easy-going ways of the black man."[26]

From 1922 until Gunnar Myrdal's *An American Dilemma: The Negro Problem and Modern Democracy* (1944), white scholars tended to applaud Washington, while black scholars and historians both openly critiqued and defended him. Du Bois critiqued Washington's program both during and following "the age of Booker T. Washington." Du Bois's position in "Of Mr. Booker T. Washington and Others" remained fairly constant in his later autobiographies.[27] Likewise, during the 1880s and 1890s, journalist and anti-lynching crusader Ida B. Wells-Barnett openly chastised Washington's failure to forthrightly denounce lynching. In her autobiography, Wells historicized her opposition to Washington. "We saw, as perhaps never before, that Mr. Washington's views on industrial education had become an obsession with the white people of this country. We thought it was up to us to show them the sophistry of the reasoning that any one system of education could fit the needs of an entire race."[28] The complexity of the relationship between T. Thomas Fortune and Washington was reflected in Fortune's published editorials on the Tuskegee principal.[29] Though he called Washington "submissive" in *Radicals and Conservatives*, Kelly Miller defended Washington from his critics of the New Negro literary renaissance in *Booker T. Washington: Five Years Later*, declaring that Washington's leadership tactics "must be at the basis of any future scheme of race reclamation and relationship."[30] Similarly, Monroe N. Work, sociologist, author of the biennial *Negro Year Book,* founder of the Department of Records and Research at Tuskegee Institute, and Washington ghostwriter, praised his employer in a 1925 *Journal of Social Forces* essay.[31]

Younger black scholars born and raised during Washington's rise to fame analyzed Washington in ways that overlapped with and diverged from those of their predecessors. For instance, in 1928 Charles S. Johnson vindicated Washington, calling for a reinterpretation of his strategy. "He advocated conciliatory rather than aggressive tactics in race relations. The principle has been confused both by his critics and his imitators of less vision and courage." Johnson continued, "It is not for us to determine whether he was less manly, or wanted less than those who insisted on their full rights."[32] Johnson claimed that Washington's program *was* the New Negro of the South, that Washington's ideas permeated the cultural consciousness of the 1920s. "The most effective interest of the present is art, and even of this it may be said that it is but an elaboration of Washington's principles of stressing work rather than the rewards of work."[33]

From the mid-1920s until the late 1930s, Horace Mann Bond offered thoughtful insights into Washington's program. In an article in the *South Atlantic Quarterly,* Bond criticized Washington for supposedly leaving behind no legacy and allowing his seeds to fall "upon fallow and unproductive ground."[34] Later, in *The Education of the Negro in the American Social Order* (1934), Bond defined the objectives of Washington's program as being character building and as informing vocational and teacher training. Bond viewed Washington's role as being multidimensional. "The formula which Booker T. Washington carried to his people was as simple as their own lives and understanding," he continued, "the theory of Booker T. Washington eschewed issues which were debatable. It was couched in such an eloquent, persuasive, and far-reaching vein that his sentiments could mean all things to all men."[35]

In *Negro Education in Alabama,* Bond called upon historians to not place too much emphasis on Washington's influence, whether positive or negative, on the status of African Americans because "we have inadequate statistical measure" of his "effect on human history."[36] Bond posited that Washington wore many hats, paying especially close attention to how he presented himself to whites. "The motives of Washington in appealing for money for the support of industrial education may not always have been the same as those of the men who gave him the money."[37] Despite Washington's tenuous relationships with advocates of black inferiority, Bond agreed with Scott and Stowe and concluded that he "was, indisputably, a man of the folk."[38] At the same time, in discussing Washington's legacy, Bond rejected Washington's optimistic claims of how Tuskegee improved blacks' conditions in Macon County.[39] In this sense, Bond foreshadowed the revisionist scholarship of Donald Spivey and James D. Anderson. "The influence of Tuskegee upon the school, and, through schools, upon the life of Negroes of Macon County, is hardly justified by the facts pertinent to their present status," Bond asserted. "The effect may have been a negative one."[40]

In his major study, *An American Dilemma: The Negro Problem and Modern Democracy* (1944), Gunnar Myrdal dichotomized black leadership and dubbed Washington an "accommodating black leader," the "great conciliatory leader of his people." Yet, unlike many of his African American research assistants, he appears to have been, in part, a Washington apologist. Myrdal noted that Washington "not only formally accepted segregation and implicitly the entire racial etiquette, but presented excuses for much more than that. . . . But in principle he never gave up the Negro protest against social discrimination." Myrdal ventured further, declaring that "it is wrong to characterize Washington as an all-out accommodating leader" because he "never relinquished the right to full equality in all respects as the ultimate goal." Unlike more than a few of his contemporaries and future scholars, Myrdal did not blame Washington for African Americans' setbacks during and following "the nadir."[41]

The papers of Booker T. Washington, "one of the largest collections of manuscript memorabilia," were "presented to the Library of Congress by the unanimous vote of the trustees of Tuskegee Institute" on June 27, 1943.[42] E. Franklin Frazier, who on September 1, 1942, "began his service as Resident Fellow of the Library of Congress in American Negro Studies,"[43] was instrumental in this monumental acquisition. As head of the Department of Sociology at Howard University, Frazier's work was more than a part-time occupation. In little less than a year's time, he traveled to Tuskegee Institute, New York City, Massachusetts, Connecticut, and Virginia.[44] Frazier visited Tuskegee in July to "inspect the packing and shipment" of Washington's papers, which reached the Library of Congress by 1943, with a smaller collection being added in 1945.[45] A year following the termination of his fellowship, Frazier wrote an article about Washington's papers in the *Library of Congress Quarterly Journal of Current Acquisitions*. He suggested that Washington's agenda "had envisioned the Negro as becoming a part of the industrial proletariat through industrial education,"[46] and he classified the material "under seven heads: correspondence with members of Washington's family; correspondence and materials relating to Tuskegee Institute; Washington's addresses and articles; correspondence with various philanthropic funds and foundations and private donors; correspondence with leaders in American life; correspondence with Negro leaders; correspondence and materials of the National Negro Business League."[47] Frazier also noted that many of the "valuable" papers were taken from the collection before being sent to the Library of Congress.

The Library of Congress Manuscript Division completed processing Washington's Papers on August 16, 1957. Exactly when Washington's papers were actually made accessible to the public is hard to decipher. Nevertheless, it is clear that this new repository of information soon influenced how Washington would be portrayed in academe. In the mid-1940s, historians began seriously using the Washington Papers. Seven biographies on Washington were published from 1948 until 1983, and beginning in the late 1940s several historians began publishing articles exposing his "secret life." From the late 1960s until the 1990s, a school of scholars explored Washington's intriguing relationship with Africa. During the same period, historians of the African American educational experience also published key studies on Tuskegee Institute and Washington's educational ideology.

The first major post–World War II biography of Washington was Basil Mathews's *Booker T. Washington: Educator and Inter-Racial Interpreter* (1949). Mathews, who claimed that there was no authoritative biography on Washington, drew largely from interviews with faculty, staff, close friends, and family. He highlighted Washington's multidimensional character and explored how Washington ran Tuskegee, instigated community involvement, and established a relationship with President Theodore Roosevelt.[48] Mathews is the first scholar to acknowledge that Washington was not a provincial man of the South, probing into Washington's activities in Liberia and Europe. Mathews's study is the most comprehensive Washington portrait before the biographies of the 1970s.

Samuel R. Spencer Jr.'s *Booker T. Washington and the Negro's Place in American Life,* published in 1955, was the second major biography of Washington after the Library of Congress's acquisition of Washington's papers. His work is one of the nineteen biographies in Oscar Handlin's "The Library of American Biography" series, and Washington is the only African American of the group. Spencer's study is brief yet wide ranging. Perhaps in response to some of the pioneering works that unveiled Washington's role in American politics and his use of the press, Spencer argued that "Washington's activities as a national leader, important as they were, never diverted him from his primary task. His heart was always at Tuskegee."[49] Spencer also acknowledged the value of the Washington collection at the Library of Congress. "This collection, crammed into some two thousand file boxes in a semiorganized fashion, awaits systematic examination and cataloguing before it can be used effectively. Even so, the Papers are rewarding."[50] While Spencer's book was widely reviewed, Shirley Graham's brief biography of Washington, published in the same year, was ignored.[51] After Spencer's and Graham's biographies quietly acknowledged the fortieth anniversary of Washington's death, it would be seventeen years until several serious biographies were published, with 1972 as a watershed year. Arna Bontemps, Barry Mackintosh, Bernard A. Weisberger, and (most important) Louis R. Harlan all published biographies on Washington that year. In addition, many scholars produced informative and enlightening articles using the collection at the Library of Congress.

During the 1950s, 1960s, and 1970s, a host of historians explored varied dimensions of Washington's life in scholarly articles and essays, some of whom began explicitly to dismantle the prevailing, oversimplified interpretation of Washington as a quintessential race man, pioneering educational reformer and innovator, and spokesperson for the Southern black masses. In his classic *The Negro in American Life and Thought: The Nadir, 1877–1901* (1954), Logan highlighted the significance of Washington's acceptance, as the newly crowned black leader, of an "inferior status for Negroes" and the "doctrine of compromise," an approach that was clearly established before Washington's 1895 Atlanta Compromise speech. Logan contributed to the historiography on Washington by being the first scholar to provide "a comprehensive analysis" of white Southern and Northern newspapers "just before and after the speech." Logan's investigation revealed near-universal praise for Washington's embracing of blacks' "subordinate status."[52]

During the 1950s, August Meier wrote four articles on Washington. "Booker T. Washington and the Negro Press" (1953) made use of the Washington papers to examine "his far-reaching influence among Negro editors and publishers" and how he financially supported and partially owned newspapers and magazines in New York, Boston, and Washington, D.C. Meier emphasized that Washington was an accommodationist.[53] "His disarming flattery of southern whites, his emphasis upon economic development and moral uplift rather than on oppression and injustices, his soft-pedaling of civil and political rights and higher education, and his placing the chief responsibility for the Negroes' difficulties and the burden of their advancement upon Negroes themselves, make his thought characteristically accommodating in tone."[54] In 1954 Meier published two articles that also relied heavily upon the Washington papers. In "Booker T. Washington and the Town of Mound Bayou," he briefly assessed the so-called failure of one of Tuskegee's offspring in Mississippi.[55] His second article of 1954 elaborates on Washington's unsuccessful attempts to squash Du Bois's Niagara Movement and the

NAACP.[56] In "Toward a Reinterpretation of Booker T. Washington" (1957), Meier called for a "re-evaluation of Washington's philosophy and activities" by exploring how he "covertly" attacked "segregation and black disfranchisement." Meier concluded that "the picture that emerges from Washington's own correspondence is directly at variance with the ingratiating mask he presented to the world."[57]

From the mid-1950s until 1972, many other interesting articles appeared on Washington, the majority of which were featured in the *Journal of Negro History.* In 1955, Mercer Cook explored French responses to *Up From Slavery* and called upon others to "examine all of the 1200 boxes of Washington's manuscripts."[58] In 1958, Emma Lou Thornbrough, who would later publish several other articles pertaining to Washington as well as edit an important Booker T. Washington reader, analyzed "the extensive correspondence" between Washington and T. Thomas Fortune, highlighting how Washington sought to secretly control the New York *Age.*"[59] In 1960, drawing largely from *The Crisis,* the Villard papers, and the Washington papers, Elliott Rudwick sought to debunk what he considered the popular myth that Washington contributed to the founding of the NAACP.[60] Emma Lou Thornbrough reentered Washington historiography with a paper first delivered at the 52nd Annual Meeting of the Association for the Study of Negro Life and History. She broke new ground by citing how many white supremacists were terrified by the interracial component of Washington's doctrine.[61] In 1969, John P. Flynn surveyed roughly fifteen years of scholarly articles on Washington, arguing in Washington's defense that "while one cannot assess accurately the motivations of Booker T. Washington, one can begin to see the possibility of his conciliation and accommodation as being necessary and effective for other than uncle tom objectives."[62] The last major article appearing in the *Journal of Negro History* before the 1972 avalanche was written by Willard B. Gatewood, who thoroughly investigated the ramifications of the assault on Washington by Henry Albert Ulrich in New York on March 19, 1911, the so-called Ulrich Affair. Echoing Thornbrough, Gatewood demonstrated that contrary to popular belief, Washington was not universally embraced by white America.[63]

Washington's Influence in Africa Considered

In the late 1960s scholars began increasingly exploring Washington's relationship with Africa. "Those who have thought of Booker T. Washington as a provincial southern American Negro, intellectually as well as geographically isolated from the rest of the world, will be surprised to find that he was substantially involved in African Affairs," Harlan asserted in 1966.[64] Among other issues, Harlan addressed Tuskegee's cotton-growing experiment in Togo, Washington's unique relationship with the South African government, his opposition to King Leopold's Congo Free State, his role in the Liberian Commission, his influence on African intellectuals, and the role of Tuskegee's International Conference of 1912. Overall, Harlan maintained that Washington projected the conventional civilizationist chauvinism of his times. Five years after Harlan's essay, J. Congress Mbata outlined fundamental connections between Washington with South African educator John Tengo Jabavu.[65] In "Booker T. Washington and African Nationalism," Manning Marable discussed how a variety of African leaders were influenced by Washington's philosophy of self-help and self-determination. Marable challenged Harlan's approach: "It would be a mistake to consider Washington's influence on the modern African mind by simply reviewing his direct associations with colonial administrators or his friendship with capitalist enterprisers." Marable added, "An astonishing amount of the correspondence of Washington, his secretary Emmett Scott, and his advisor, sociologist Professor Robert Park, with black nationalists implies Tuskegee's guarded support for black militant endeavors." Marable examined how Washington and Tuskegee's "independent advancement" influenced Pixley ka Isaka Seme, John L. Dube, the ANC leadership, Sol J. Plaatje, Duse Muhammed, Caseley Hayford, K. Soga, Edward Blyden, and John Chilembwe. According to Marable, "Washington's philosophy in both continents helped to create a nationalistic, proud and dynamic elite of black people."[66] In *The African Nexus,* Sylvia M. Jacobs disagreed with Marable and concurred with Harlan, arguing that, overall, Washington "helped to bolster the argument justifying colonialism."[67] In the late 1980s, Donald Spivey denounced Washington's educational program as contributing to Liberia's oppression, based on an analysis of Liberia's Booker Washington Institute from 1929 until 1984, which he argued upheld Washington's values.[68]

The popularity of Washington's influence in Africa resurfaced in the 1990s. In 1992, Michael West deemed Washington a pan-Africanist. He called for a new definition of pan-Africanism that included the Tuskegeean. "As far as the historiography of pan-Africanism is concerned, a major reason for the lack of attention accorded to the Tuskegee model is that it simply does not conform to the standard conception of pan-African movements."[69] Several years later, Mildred C. Fierce included Washington in *The Pan-African Idea in the United States, 1900–1910,* noting: "Irrespective of their ideological character," Washington's programs in Togo—West Africa in particular—revealed that he was very much conscious of Africa in his worldview.[70] In 1996, Edward O. Erhagbe concurred with Marable, West, and Fierce, declaring that Washington "played a major role in the Liberian diplomatic efforts to obtain US assistance in defense of the country's territorial integrity." Erhagbe went a step further suggesting that Washington acted "as one of the most important black Diasporan contributors to Africa during his age."[71]

Post–Civil Rights Movement
Interpretations of Washington

The 1970s was an important decade in Washington historiography. More than a few important articles were published in this decade; in 1972 alone, four book-length biographies on Washington were published. In 1972, Arna Wendell Bontemps published a novel-like biography that focused on Washington's "early days"; Barry Mackintosh, a former park historian at the Booker T. Washington Monument, published a concise assessment of Washington's life; Bernard A. Weisberger published *Booker T. Washington;* and Louis R. Harlan published his first biography on Washington.[72] In 1973, Joseph F. Citro wrote an exhaustive dissertation on Washington that examined the day-to-day dealings of the Tuskegee Institute from 1900 until 1915—something, he argued, that previous scholarship had ignored.[73] Citro also challenged Harlan's notion that Washington was the "master of the plantation." Not only did teachers, most notably George Washington Carver, challenge Washington's authority, but students—whether through vandalism, strikes, theft, dropping out, sexual misconduct, or grade changing—undermined his absolute power as well. Though at times a Washington apologist, Citro's conclusions are critical. "Thus as one goes through the Booker T. Washington Papers, one comes to feel that there existed at his school a pervasive defeatist prophecy. Students failed to learn and teachers failed to teach because everyone knew their efforts were likely to lead to failure."[74]

In 1975, Donald Spivey expanded upon Citro's findings and further challenged how Washington propagandized Tuskegee's program and success. In "Shine, Booker, Shine: The Black Overseer of Tuskegee," a revealing chapter from *Schooling for the New Slavery: Black Industrial Education, 1868–1915,* Spivey offered an important critique of Washington's educational philosophy, maintaining that Washington's program, "uplift through submission" and faith that "rights came with economic power," ultimately failed because Washington "alienated Tuskegee students and never gained the full support of the white South."[75] Spivey discussed the various "stringent rules and regulations" at Tuskegee as well as the student unrest that resulted. Challenging the once widely held belief that Tuskegee was an industrial, vocational, and trade school, Spivey argued that students' "training was primarily in 'how to behave' rather than how to become skilled tradesmen." "Higher Education at Tuskegee," Spivey declared, "was a sad joke."[76] Spivey's timely demystification of Washington's educational practices at Tuskegee were elaborated upon by James D. Anderson, who argued in *The Education of Blacks in the South, 1860–1935,* that "Washington and Tuskegee were Armstrong and Hampton in blackface," that Washington and Tuskegee focused on the drudgery of hard physical work, Jim Crow racial etiquette, obedience, and "the training of teachers on manual labor rather than on academic studies."[77] Spivey's conclusion about Washington as Tuskegee's principal was the harshest criticism since Du Bois: "His role was like that of the black overseer during slavery who, given the position of authority over his fellow slaves, worked diligently to keep intact the very system under which they both were enslaved."[78]

In the 1970s, following the appearance of Harlan's first volume of his official Washington biography, roughly one dozen scholars produced scholarship on the Tuskegeean, many of whom, despite Spivey's relevant observations, uncritically heralded Washington as an industrial educational guru and savior. Several examples suffice. In 1974, William DeLaney published *Learn By Doing: A Projected Educational Philosophy in the Thought of Booker T. Washington,* a work that celebrated Washington by comparing him with various European and white American educators. Donald Generals would echo DeLaney's approach at the dawning of the new millennium, comparing Washington to John Dewey and placing him within the context of progressive education.[79] In the mid-1970s, other scholars offered overviews of Washington's educational philosophy and contributions. Allen W. Jones's article is especially insightful. He detailed how Tuskegee Institute served as "a center for educating and uplifting more than 1,000,000 black farmers in the South" with agricultural education, the Tuskegee Negro Conferences, George Washington Carver's outreach work, the Farmer's Institutes and Fairs, the "Jesup Agricultural Wagon," and other extension activities.[80]

Another refreshing article in the 1970s was written by Laurence J. Friedman and also appeared in the *Journal of Negro History.* Friedman emphasized that Washington was a multidimensional figure who "was assiduously trying to present different images and arguments to different people."[81] At the same time, in the tradition of Du Bois and Oliver Cromwell Cox, Friedman called upon historians to ponder the various negative effects of Washington's shrewd behavior and propaganda. Although it would be very difficult, Friedman's plea for "a quantitative study of the economic effects of certain of Washington's words and deeds upon specific black populations" is still worthy of consideration. Friedman also asked historians to consider how Washington's unique disposition, specifically the insurmountable pressure under which he operated, must have affected his psyche and physical well-being.[82] This observation is especially relevant in light of the fact that Washington died from high blood pressure, an ailment that afflicted Martin Luther King Jr. and probably other black leaders.

From 1966 until 1989, Louis R. Harlan published a dozen articles and essays and two major biographies on Washington, as well as *The Booker T. Washington Papers* (14 volumes). Harlan has earned the designation "Washington's biographer." In 1949–50, he was one of the first scholars to explore the Washington papers. "When I saw them they were stacked in confusion in unlabeled boxes deep in the recess of the Library's Manuscripts Division," Harlan recounted, "In those easy-going days before tight security regulations, the authorities let me go into the stacks and poke around among the boxes for what I wanted. It was like discovering a new world, the private world of the black community hidden behind the veil and mask that protected blacks from the gaze of whites."[83] Yet many years would pass before Harlan began seriously researching Washington. Harlan mentioned Washington in passing in his first study, *Separate and Unequal* (1955).[84] Seven years later in a brief commentary published by the American Historical Association, Harlan called for a reevaluation of Washington.[85] In 1966, Harlan wrote his first major article on Washington in the *American Historical Review* and a year later began the Booker T. Washington Papers Project, the first major "project of its kind that dealt with the letters of a black person." With unprecedented access to the papers, he wrote eleven articles on Washington from 1969 until 1983. In 1972, Harlan produced the first of a two-volume biography, *Booker T. Washington: The Making of a Black Leader, 1856–1901.*

In this work, Harlan detailed Washington's life from his birth until the beginnings of his rise as a leading black spokesperson. He viewed Washington as a white-appointed black statesman. "Booker Washington's incorrigible humility made him the kind of symbolic black figure that whites accepted. His self-help advice to blacks shifted from whites the responsibility for racial problems they were thoroughly tired of. His economic emphasis took the question of Negro progress out of politics. His materialism was thoroughly American and attuned to the industrial age. His proposals of racial compromise promised peace not only between the races but between the sections."[86] Harlan portrayed Washington as "a man of action" who sought self-empowerment at all costs. According to Harlan, Washington's "thirst for power" began in his early twenties and his "aim was not intellectual clarity, but power. His genius was that of stratagem. His restless mind was constantly devising new moves and countermoves."[87] In the same year as his first biography on Washington, Harlan began publishing *The Booker T. Washington Papers.* Harlan and his large editorial staff carefully selected from the million items available, choosing no more than five percent of the total.[88] Two years after Harlan published the first volume of the papers, Daniel T. Williams, the archivist at Tuskegee Institute, finished cataloging and organizing 133 boxes of Washington's papers in *Booker Taliaferro Washington: A Register of His Papers in the Tuskegee Institute Archives.*[89]

In 1983, Harlan published the second volume of his biography on Washington. He pointed out that "Washington had multiple personalities to fit his various roles."[90] Harlan focused on Washington as a "power hungry" politician. "Readers who expect to find in this book a treatise on Washington's role in the history of education may be disappointed to find that his educational administration at Tuskegee Institute and his speeches and writings on education receive relatively brief attention. In view of the greater detail on this side of his life in the published *Booker T. Washington Papers,* and because I feel that he played an important but not remarkably innovative role in educational history, I have stressed what seems to me more important: the sources, nature, uses, and consequences of his power."[91] In doing so, Harlan explicated Washington's relationships with various groups of whites as well as his persistent attacks on and battles with his African American opposition. Harlan's approach dates back to Du Bois and echoes dimensions of the observations posed by August Meier, Elliott Rudwick, Emma Lou Thornbrough, Robert G. Sherer, Linda M. Perkins, June O. Patton, and V. P. Franklin—scholars who have addressed Washington's efforts to squash his black detractors and his ability to determine which black educational institutions would benefit from white philanthropy in the South during "the nadir."[92] With few exceptions, Harlan's scholarship has been celebrated. James D. Anderson and V. P. Franklin were among the few to critique Harlan's interpretations. While Anderson pointed out several "major shortcomings" and Franklin argued that Harlan failed to provide evidence of Washington's status as a genuine leader of the black masses, Harlan's interpretations have set the standard for analysis.[93]

In 2003, one of Harlan's disciples asserted that "there have been attempts to challenge his interpretation of Washington; none has succeeded."[94] Harlan could not agree more with his protégé. He held firm to his assessments of Washington several decades after his second biography on Washington was published. "Until another biographer brings convincing evidence of another view of Washington, I will stand by my own interpretation based on 20-odd years of scholarly labor," Harlan commented in 2006, "as a race leader . . . Washington seems to have been pretty much of a failure."[95]

Since Harlan's second biography and *Booker T. Washington in Perspective* (1988), several books have attempted to challenge Harlan's paradigm directly and indirectly.[96] In *Booker T. Washington and the Adult Education Movement* (1993), Virginia Lantz Denton charged Harlan with being overly judgmental and writing history with "an uneven voice" and "revisionist hindsight." According to Denton, Harlan's work "demands some caution from the serious reader." "Washington," in Denton's estimation, "was dominated by purpose, not power."[97] Denton celebrated Washington as being a man of the black masses, a revolutionary, a "prophet of the possible," as well as a pragmatic realist, and argued that adult education was the "special mission that made Tuskegee unique." While this modern Bookerite uncritically reiterates *Up from Slavery*, portrays Washington as almost being flawless, largely ignores his black detractors, and makes many observations that are not new, Denton is among the first scholars, in a book-length examination, to examine Tuskegee's extension activities. Echoing Allen M. Jones's 1975 piece "The Role of Tuskegee Institute in the Education of Black Farmers," she maintained that Washington's ultimate goal and driving cause célèbre was to create "social change through extension." Denton discussed in detail the Tuskegee Negro Conferences, the Movable School on Wheels, the Farmer's Institutes and Cooperative Demonstrations, Tuskegee's Bible School and Mother's Meetings, and Washington's commitment to health reform in the black community.[98] Though her outlook is unbalanced at times, the sixth chapter of Denton's study supplements Harlan's studies well.

Five years after Denton's book appeared, Karen J. Ferguson published an intriguing article in *Agricultural History* that explored Washington's Negro Cooperative Farm Demonstration Service (founded in 1903) in a more nuanced and critical manner than Denton. Ferguson argued that "Washington's self-serving motivations were complicated by his genuine commitment to black progress," and she critically reveals how such efforts were viewed by local whites, the black agents, and the black masses. Not only does she address the agents' elitism and cultural chauvinism, but she also provides evidence for resentment among black farmers whom the agents sought to reform. While she credits the efforts of "these self-help crusaders" and posits that "Tuskegee's agricultural extension programs had a subversive element," she concludes that the Negro Cooperative Farm Demonstration movement did not really change the material status of black farmers.[99]

A decade after Denton's book, the collection *Booker T. Washington and Black Progress: Up from Slavery 100 Years Later*, edited by Fitzhugh Brundage, appeared. The vast majority of the ten essays in the study are revisionist in nature, challenging the Washington as accommodationist school of thought and reaching "relatively positive conclusions about Washington and his program." Taken collectively, the contributors acknowledge the complexity of *Up from Slavery*. Especially intriguing is Peter A. Coclanis's assessment of

Washington's preoccupation with cleanliness; Patricia A. Schechter, David Leverenz, and Louise Newman's analyses of gender in *Up from Slavery;* and Hunt Davis's overview of *Up from Slavery* as appropriated by South Africans. Not only do the contributors to *Booker T. Washington and Black Progress* enhance Washington scholarship, but Brundage accurately concluded that "the riddle of Booker T. Washington endures" and "important questions remain about Washington's life and programs."[100]

In 2006, two studies on Washington were published, Michael Rudolph West's *The Education of Booker T. Washington: American Democracy and the Idea of Race Relations* and a collection of essays, *The Racial Politics of Booker T. Washington.* West's book is not a comprehensive biography on Washington; instead, focusing on the dynamics of Washington's life from 1856 until 1881, *Up from Slavery,* and the implications of his famous 1895 Atlanta Compromise speech, West explores Washington's ideas of "progress" and "race relations" as potential solutions to black America's dilemmas during "the nadir." He defines Washington's approach in broader terms as "Washingtonianism," "a set of attitudes, postures, and most of all an idea that rapidly amounts to a hegemonic solution to the Negro Problem, a set of requirements for responsible Negro leadership, and a platform upon which Washington stands as the leader with the only feasible solution to the problem."[101] West's critique of using an accommodationist paradigm for understanding Washington is refreshing, and he historicizes the "Negro problem" in Washington's rhetoric. His psycho-historical analysis of Washington is at times thought provoking. He also identifies many of scholars' tendencies in analyzing Washington. At the same time, several arguments that West raises, mainly in his introduction, remain underdeveloped, especially his assertion that Washington's thought and leadership strategies "lie back of the civil rights era's dramatic unfolding and ambiguous result."[102] Though intriguing, West's comparison between Martin Luther King Jr. and Washington also warrants further development and articulation.

Less recognized than West's book is *The Racial Politics of Booker T. Washington* (2006), a multidisciplinary anthology seeking to "prompt new interpretations" of Washington's life, thought, and leadership strategies. Drawing upon analytical frameworks from sociology, history, art history, anthropology, African American studies, literary studies, and political science, these scholars explore a wide range of issues, including Washington's diversified audiences and clientele; the similar and different views of his predecessors and contemporaries, especially Douglass and Du Bois; Washington's use of *Up from Slavery,* photography, and his Atlanta Compromise speech as tools of propaganda and self-representation; his influence on African American sociology; his relationships with coworkers like Monroe N. Work and Robert E. Park; and his travels to and views of Europe. The editors of the volume dub Washington a "broker-accomodationist."[103]

Openly challenging Harlan's paradigm, the most recent book-length publications on Washington defend and celebrate his accomplishments, legacy, and leadership while calling for new interpretations of his complex worldview and strategies. In 2008, three noteworthy revisionist studies were published on Washington. *Booker T. Washington: A Re-Examination* includes more than twenty short essays by scholars, political commentators and activists, and ministers who originally delivered these pieces as lectures at a 2006 symposium at Northwestern University celebrating the 150th anniversary of Washington's birth. All of the contributors, including three historians, sought to revive Washington's legacy, challenge the prevailing negative designation of Washington as an accommodationist, and apply Washington's philosophies and strategies to the present. "The principal reason I convened the symposium," conference organizer Lee H. Walker said, "is the firm conviction that the ideas of Booker T. Washington are even more relevant today than they were 150 years ago. . . . If blacks are to achieve the fullness of the American Dream, we need to move beyond political agitation and re-embrace the agenda of Booker T. Washington: quality education, self-reliance, character, and entrepreneurship." While this collection of essays does not add particularly new information to the research conducted by generations of Washington scholars and historians, it demonstrates that there is perhaps a shift occurring within the academy and among black political activists concerning the complex role and legacy of Washington. At the same time, the positive slant of these essays do not acknowledge the complete picture of how the Tuskegee Machine really operated.[104]

In *Booker T. Washington and the Art of Self-Representation*, Michael Bieze offers a genuinely new and refreshing analysis of Washington. "Until recently," he argues, "the scholarly portrait of Washington has almost completely ignored the important role he played in the development of African American visual art in general, and photography in particular." Using Harlan's "secret life" theory as a point of departure, Bieze identifies how Washington successfully used photography from the early 1890s until his death in 1915 to publicize and market the Tuskegee Machine, to construct and disseminate his "multiple identities" and "the layers of his self-representations in the media," to create a black aesthetic, and to challenge the racist and stereotypical images of African Americans in popular culture. Bieze goes a step further by deeming Washington "the first black media celebrity," "among the nation's first masters of mass marketing," and "an important patron of black artists and a supporter of black arts" and the New Negro movement.[105]

Familiar with the basic trends in Washingtonian historiography, Bieze demonstrates the value of employing a wide range of photographs of Washington and Tuskegee Institute to probe deeper into Washington's "secret life." "In historiographic terms," Bieze suggests, "the contextual interpretation of Washington photographs provides an important method of seeing the way photographic evidence does not verify objective truth but rather displays the many truths Washington hoped to have people accept. Therefore, photographs offer a way of studying agency, or a life of resistance not recorded in traditional, text-based archival materials, because of the way they so easily seem to convince viewers of facts without challenge."[106] Overall, Bieze's study draws from insightful art history and photography theories; contains important, new information regarding Washington's wide-reaching use of photographic technology during the Progressive Era and his relationships with white and black photographers; situates Washington within the U.S. arts and crafts movement; and, perhaps most important, showcases more than fifty unique photos and images of Booker T. Washington and the Tuskegee Institute. Perhaps more than any other scholar, Bieze directly challenges Harlan's limiting characterization of Washington as being an accommodating "man of action." Bieze demonstrates that Washington the intellectual and marketing guru "understood photographs as marketing tools, keepsakes, propaganda, and fine art. Most of all, he knew their power."[107]

Drawing from the wealth of historical scholarship on Washington, numerous Southern newspapers, Washington's papers, and the National Negro Business League Papers, David H. Jackson's *Booker T. Washington and the Struggle against White Supremacy: The Southern Educational Tours, 1908–1912*, explores the "educational tours" or "educational pilgrimages" that Washington and his co-workers took through Mississippi, Tennessee, North Carolina, Texas, and Florida between 1908 and 1912. A Washington apologist, Jackson highlights Washington's strategies of "double-talking" and "black survivalism" and argues that Washington went on these tours to inspire and psychologically empower blacks, expand the influence of the Tuskegee Machine, publicize and celebrate black progress and manhood, and, most important, to challenge and undermine white racism and supremacy. Through these National Negro Business League–sponsored speeches, Washington "reached around 1 million black and white people" and "saw the lives of countless people more intimately."[108] During these tours, he often spoke to audiences of thousands of people. In 1909, on one occasion in Mississippi he spoke to an audience of between seven thousand and ten thousand people. Though Jackson could have analyzed the content of Washington's various speeches in greater detail, his work helps broaden our interpretations of Washington's multifaceted program.

The most recent biography on Washington is Robert J. Norell's *Up from History: The Life of Booker T. Washington* (2009), an easy-to-read narrative account of the Tuskegeean's life. According to Norell, since the 1960s Washington has been vilified and misrepresented; "his story, therefore, deserves to be told anew."[109] Challenging Harlan's narrow yet widely accepted approach, Norell attempts to reveal a more complex Washington who embodied black achievement and who was ultimately committed to black uplift during "the nadir." Norell highlights that Washington was hated by many hostile white segregationists and nationalists who even had plans to assassinate him. While *Up from History* does not draw upon any previously overlooked primary source materials and basically reiterates the traditional story of Washington's rise to power and fame, Norell does explore many important dimensions of his life, such as his power-brokering politics, practical outreach reform projects, exhaustive fundraising efforts, relationship with his immediate family, oratory skills at Tuskegee, and interactions with U.S. presidents and influential white Americans. Revising Meier's and others' assertions that Washington only challenged segregation in behind-the-scenes efforts, Norell offers many examples of Washington's speaking out against racial injustices as early as the 1880s.

Norell is clearly among those historians who, contrary to the popular Harlan-influenced school of thought, characterizes Washington as an important forerunner in the black struggle for civil rights. Rejecting the notion of Washington the "Uncle Tom" or conservative, Norell asserts: "The almost universal characterization of Washington as an accommodationist to segregation is also inaccurate. Having conditions forced on him, with the threat of destruction clearly the cost of resistance, does not constitute a fair definition of accommodation. It is coercion. The accommodationist-protest binary has obscured the fundamental similarity of the substance of Washington's actions to the protest agenda put forward by the NAACP."[110] While I disagree with one reviewer's claim that *Up from History* totally recasts Washington within the larger context of the vast historiography on Washington, Norell's biography is a straightforward, comprehensive, and fairly balanced biography that is ideal for undergraduate students of black history.

Currents of Understanding

Based on nearly a century of historiography, there are three major interrelated lines of argument scholars and students have used in their analyses of Booker T. Washington. These specific tendencies evolved at different stages within Washington historiography and still reverberate today. Most important, Washington's philosophy has been defined as accommodationism, and his approach at Tuskegee has often been uncritically dubbed as industrial, vocational, and/or trade training. Also, W. E .B. Du Bois has often been used as the yardstick for measuring Washington. In addition, many laypersons and scholars often formulate opinions of Washington's ideology and leadership strategy based solely on his famous 1895 Atlanta Exposition address and *Up from Slavery* (1901).

Washington as Accommodationist

Washington has been labeled an accommodationist since the 1940s. A survey of historians' publications on "Negro thought" reveals that Washington's philosophy has been defined most consistently as accommodation, whereas his opposition, mainly Du Bois, has been celebrated as a forerunner for the black protest tradition. Since the cold war era, scholars have routinely characterized and analyzed twentieth-century black leadership in terms of this dichotomy, "categorizing black thought into sets of strategic or tactical dualisms (militance/moderation, protest/accommodation, integration/nationalism)."[111] In placing black leaders and spokespersons in only one of these camps, one overlooks the key similarities among black leaders of Washington's time, as Wilson Jeremiah Moses and Kevin Gaines have stressed.[112]

Moreover, scholars such as Houston A. Baker Jr. and V. P. Franklin have discussed the similarities in positions taken by Du Bois and Washington.[113] In the second half of the twentieth century, August Meier molded and promoted the accommodation/protest paradigm. Meier based many of his conclusions on ideas first formed by political scientist and "radical" Ralph Bunche, and Gunnar Myrdal. Their works, he recounted in 1991, "proved to be of incalculable value in developing the kind of conceptualization that underlay much of my future work." Along with many other bright, young, black scholars, Bunche was one of Gunnar Myrdal's African American "collaborators" for *An American Dilemma*.[114] Bunche did more than any other scholar for Myrdal's analysis of black leadership, completing "four memoranda dealing with black politics, leadership, ideologies, and betterment organizations. One, called 'The Political Status of the Negro,' ran 1,660 pages. (No wonder rumors persisted in the black community that Bunche wrote the *Dilemma*)."[115] In an unpublished essay entitled "Memorandum on Conceptions and Ideologies of the Negro Problem," Bunche explicitly dichotomized black leadership and argued that "roughly speaking all Negro ideologies on the Negro question fall into one or the other of two rather broad categories: accommodation, and release or escape."[116] For Bunche, accommodationists like Washington accepted the notion of black inferiority, while embracing education, self-help, interracial cooperation, "middle-class values," and a philosophy of "catching up with the white man."[117] Bunche located a "radical" ideology at the opposite pole.[118] At the same time, in another unpublished study, "A Brief and Tentative Analysis of Negro Leadership," Bunche subdivided black leaders into numerous groups, categories, and "types."[119]

Only a small part of Bunche's comprehensive analysis of black leadership laid the foundation for Myrdal's chapters on "Leadership and Concerted Action." "We base our typology of Negro leadership upon the two extreme policies of behavior on behalf of the Negro as a subordinated caste: accommodation and protest." Myrdal continued, "The first attitude is mainly static; the second is mainly dynamic."[120] Myrdal suggested that the accommodating black leader, whom he dubbed—using Bunche's language directly—the "'pussy-footing Uncle Tom,'" followed in the American tradition of exploiting mass passivity and served as "liaison agent" between blacks and whites. "Accommodating leaders" in Myrdal's estimation were more prevalent in the South than in the North. According to Myrdal, "pure protest leaders" rejected the accommodationist outlook, and "Booker T. Washington and W. E. B. Du Bois became national symbols for these two main streams of Negro thought. Two groups of followers assembled behind them."[121]

Expanding upon Bunche's and Myrdal's ideas, in one of his first articles Meier recognized the "great range of ideologies" in black thought, yet he dichotomized black leadership between the extremes of "total assimilation" and "complete withdrawal from the United States," concluding that blacks embraced "integration in American society."[122] Later, in his classic *Negro Thought in America, 1880–1915,* Meier divided black leaders into accommodationist and protest camps, and labeled Washington an accommodationist. "All in all, in viewing Washington's philosophy, one is most impressed by his accommodating approach."[123] Washington certainly accommodated to white power structures throughout the nation, especially in the Jim Crow South, in order to maintain his tenuous position of power, political influence, and access to financial support. However, the accommodation label, without adequate elaboration of the circumstances in which he operated and his multifaceted program and position, oversimplifies Washington. As Washington critic Rayford W. Logan observed more than fifty years ago: "The invitation to speak at the opening of the Cotton States and International Exposition in Atlanta on September 18, 1895, placed a responsibility upon Washington that few speakers have been called upon to accept."[124]

Washington as Foil for Du Bois

Since Myrdal's study, scholars have often portrayed Washington as being the opposite of W. E. B. Du Bois. In this scenario, Washington represents the accommodationist or conservative, whereas Du Bois is the agitator or the radical. Many of Du Bois's chief biographers, including Francis L. Broderick, Elliott Rudwick, Manning Marable, and David Levering Lewis, have tended to scrutinize Washington based upon a Du Boisian framework, in turn deifying Du Bois while at various levels demonizing Washington.[125] Post–civil rights era popular culture also seems to have followed in this trend. Referring to a black spokesperson as a modern day Booker T. Washington is no compliment. Lumping Washington together with powerful contemporary black conservatives like Colin Powell, Clarence Thomas, and Condoleezza Rice oversimplifies Washington and black conservatism. "The long history of black conservatism neither began nor ended with Booker T. Washington," one scholar of black conservative thought has observed. "Washington is often treated as an anomaly, a conservative exception to the dominant course of African-American history. This misrepresents Washington" and fails to account for those numerous black leaders who had "conservative dimensions to their thought."[126] In his recent book *Saviors or Sellouts: The Promise and Peril of Black Conservatism, from Booker T. Washington to Condoleezza Rice,* Christopher Alan Bracey acknowledges that Washington is the most recognizable black conservative, but he places him within the context of a much deeper trajectory of black conservatism and "American exceptionalism" dating back to the philosophies of Jupiter Hammon, Richard Allen, and James Forten. Bracey points out how "modern antigovernment [black] conservatives" like Glenn C. Loury have selectively harkened back to Washington's approach, adding: "It would be a mistake to conclude, however, that Washington's eschewal of an open civil rights agenda and promotion of industrial education marked him as a 'sellout.'"[127]

In February 1992, *The Crisis* magazine featured a Black History Month special issue, "Booker vs. W. E. B., The Great Debate: Has Time Provided the Answer?" In the longest article of the issue, "Who Won the Great Debate—Booker T. Washington or W. E. B. Du Bois," political scientist Charles Henry defined Washington's program based on his 1895 Atlanta oration and politicized the Washington–Du Bois conflict. "As we look forward to the 21st century, the question before us remains the one raised by Du Bois a hundred years ago. Are we fully satisfied with the values guiding our country's political and economic policy? For Clarence Thomas and others the answer appears to be yes. Like Booker T. Washington, they have attached their souls to those of the dominant power brokers. For those who challenge our nation's direction, they must turn to Du Bois. They must fashion a response rooted in the best alternative values to be found in black culture."[128] Julianne Malveaux's recent portrayal of Washington similarly dismisses him. Jacqueline M. Moore's

Booker T. Washington, W. E. B. Du Bois, and the Struggle for Black Uplift is among the few works to explore the Washington–Du Bois debate with a non–Du Bois bias.[129]

In his first biography on Washington, Harlan challenged, in passing, those who view Washington "as the intellectual opposite of W. E. B. Du Bois." At the same time, he ignored Washington's capacity as a thinker, claiming that he "was not an intellectual, but a man of action."[130] Though understandable, deeming Washington "a man of action" limits our analysis to his life as a race politicker and ignores his role as a political theorist and perhaps even a philosopher. Very few scholars deal with Washington's morally instructive "Sunday evening talks" or writings such as *Sowing and Reaping* (1900), his two-volume *The Story of the Negro*, and *Putting the Most Into Life* (1906), to name a few. In these writings, Washington offers philosophical inquiries—albeit in elementary ways—into issues such as religion, theory and practice, African cultural retentions in America, health, spirituality, history, and community building. It is widely known that Washington frequently employed ghostwriters, even in the case of *Up From Slavery*. Nonetheless, Washington delivered countless speeches and talks to a wide variety of audiences throughout the country.

Washington as Defined by His Two Most Famous Works

Despite the wealth of primary sources that have been accessible on Washington since the publication of *The Booker T. Washington Papers* and the reissuing of Washington's lesser-known works since the Black Power era, many non-Washington specialists, scholars, and historians, especially U.S. history textbook authors and editors of certain African American history anthologies, as well as secondary educators, still tend to define Washington based on two sources, his famous 1895 Atlanta speech and *Up from Slavery* (1901). To the general readership of black history, Washington's 1895 speech has become synonymous with his outlook. As one historian has recently claimed, "The ideas put forth by the Tuskegee educator in 1895 . . . remained, in many respects, unaltered during the last twenty years of his life."[131] Not only does this oversimplify Washington, but it further contributes to the uncritical acceptance of Washington's propagandistic portrayal of Tuskegee's goals, programs, and accomplishments. For instance, *Up from Slavery*—as well as other books like *Working with the Hands* (1904), *Tuskegee and Its People* (1905), and *My Larger Education* (1911)—presents aspects of Tuskegee students' experiences in a mythical manner that is not consistent with the historical record as exposed by Donald Spivey, James D. Anderson, and others.

Unfortunately, for many, *Up from Slavery* has come to epitomize Washington's worldview. Before and in some cases into the second half of the twentieth century, many of Washington's biographers simply reiterated this inspirational story. It has been well established that Washington used *Up from Slavery* as a way to present himself in a nonthreatening manner to his potential white donors and supporters. As Houston Baker Jr. has argued, Washington deliberately manipulated stereotypical images of blacks, language, and forms.[132] Since the 1970s, dozens of literary theorists and historians have read deeply and creatively into Washington's autobiographies. Critical examinations of Washington's autobiographical writings represent an established genre within the study of African American autobiography.[133] Roger J. Bresnahan, Charlotte Fitzgerald, and Donald Gibson have scrutinized how Washington presented himself in different ways to different audiences in his various autobiographical accounts, especially *Up from Slavery* and *The Story of My Life and Work*. The "Atlanta Compromise" and *Up from Slavery* are invaluable resources into reconstructing Washington's worldview, yet the wealth of his other writings must be acknowledged.

Few scholars have offered comprehensive frameworks for holistically analyzing Washington's worldview and program.[134] Because he so obviously decided to play (in Ralph Bunche's words) "the role of Negro leader and spokesman by white election" and worked hard and consistently to silence his black opposition, scholars since the modern civil rights movement have interrogated and unearthed the abuses of Washington's power. Fewer scholars have considered, among other dimensions, his various extension activities, his relationship to the southern black masses, the validity of his so-called grassroots leadership style, the realities of students' experiences at Tuskegee, and the overall complexity and multidimensional nature of his leadership. As this chapter demonstrates, the century of scholarship on Washington is expansive and multileveled. Still, there are more than a few issues and pressing questions that we can grapple with to better decipher Washington's place in African American history, especially when explaining his leadership to younger generations.

A leader of the masses?

In his classic 1947 *From Slavery to Freedom,* John Hope Franklin highlighted Washington's "weaknesses" but ultimately concluded that "the vast majority of Negroes acclaimed him as their leader," that "Washington's influence was so great that there is considerable justification in calling the period" from 1895 until 1915 "The Age of Booker T. Washington."[135] On the other hand, in 1951, Oliver C. Cox asserted that Washington's leadership was "spurious" and that he "was not a leader of the masses in the Garvian sense." Three decades later, V. P. Franklin echoed Cox and offered a more direct challenge to the presumption that Washington was a genuine black leader. For Franklin, Washington's leadership strategies "were contrary not only to the objective social, political, and economic interests of the southern black masses, but also to the predominant cultural values and objectives of the majority of African Americans living in the United States." Franklin pointed out that many of the black Southern masses did not listen to Washington's advice, as tens of thousands migrated to Northern and Southern cities after 1900. Franklin argued that "Washington did not represent the values and interests of the black masses and therefore should not be considered as their 'leader.'"[136]

Most scholars appear to have sided with John Hope Franklin and have assumed that Washington was a major black leader of the black masses. Cox and V. P. Franklin stand out for their insights. Future scholarship on Washington should test their observations. Was Washington a leader of the African American masses of the South? Was Washington really in tune with the daily lives of the rural Southern black masses as he often claimed? Did he have a closer relationship with the black masses in the South than did the Northern "intellectuals" whom he openly criticized in *My Larger Education* and elsewhere? Are there any valid counternarratives to Spivey's and Anderson's provocative arguments about the failure of Tuskegee to truly educate its students? Though quantitatively measuring their influence is perhaps impossible, what was the impact of the wide array of pragmatic outreach programs and extension activities that Virginia Lantz Denton has credited Washington with pioneering?

Perhaps more than any other leader in African American history, Washington has been viewed in many different ways by different peoples. He wore what Paul Lawrence Dunbar eloquently depicted as "the mask" more than any other major black leader. Washington presented himself and his program in different ways to different audiences. At times simultaneously, Washington spoke to many audiences in the United States, including white philanthropists and industrialists in the North and South, Tuskegee students, Southern black farmers, and black middle-class leadership in the North and South. Washington also had significant audiences abroad. When speaking to audiences that included a wide cross-section of the population, as was the case with the so-called "Atlanta Compromise," Washington used encoded language and tended to be very careful so as to not offend his white listeners. In *Up from Slavery,* Washington excused slavery, declared Reconstruction a success, claimed that the Ku Klux Klan no longer represented a threat, praised nearly all whites with whom he interacted, and reinforced the myth of the "Old South." At the same time, he offered his black readers messages of self-help, perseverance, faith, self-determination, struggle, and education, key "Afro-American values and cultural traditions."[137] In his numerous "whistle-stop" speeches and educational tours in Southern communities, Washington motivated and inspired blacks to persevere. The black masses made conscious decisions to attend his speeches in droves. He was a master at code-switching and, as Michael Bieze has passionately argued, black America's first celebrity.

Washington as moral philosopher

Since the 1950s, scholars have creatively tapped into Washington's papers, exploring a wide variety of topics and themes. Yet, many scholars continue to define Washington based on his 1895 oration and *Up from Slavery*. Textbooks and anthologies in American and African American history, with few exceptions, continue to be preoccupied with these two selections of Washington's work. Though aided by ghostwriters, Washington nonetheless authored a dozen books from 1899 until *The Man Farthest Down* (1912). He also delivered countless speeches to different audiences, employing different rhetorical strategies for each one. Washington, the "fireside chatter," delivered hundreds of "Sunday evening talks" to Tuskegee students; these expose us to Washington's straightforward moral and spiritual philosophies and deserve to be further analyzed.[138] As one scholar has observed, "Washington never purported to be a philosopher. On the other hand, we would be unfair to dismiss Washington and his corpus of public writings, speeches, and letters as the collected thoughts of a black institution builder who lacked broad intellectual perspective and a morally serious vision of people and society."[139] Challenging the Harlan school, African American intellectual historian Wilson Jeremiah Moses has argued that Washington was indeed an intellectual. "Washington was not a simple man" and was not "lacking as a thinker." On the other hand, Moses has suggested, he "was aware of the contradictions and the implicit ironies in the oxymoronic position of separate-but-equal assimilationism, but he wasted little time explaining, to those who were sometimes deliberately obtuse, the obvious fact that militancy could accomplish nothing in the Alabama of 1900. Washington's reluctance to draft extended philosophical statements did not stem from a shallow philistinism, but from a belief that overt intellectualism could be dangerous."[140]

"Learning to sew, with the ultimate end of becoming a full-fledged dressmaker, has been the height of ambition with the major part of our girls," Booker T. Washington's third wife Margaret Murray Washington, Tuskegee

Institute's Director of Instruction for Girls, put forth in an essay "What Girls Are Taught and How" (1905). "Girl life at Tuskegee is strenuous. . . . Although each Tuskegee girl is expected to become proficient in one trade at least, all are required to attend the cooking classes."[141] The education that young black women received at Tuskegee Institute during "the nadir" conformed to the widely accepted gender norms of early-twentieth-century U.S. society and resembled the type of training that black women received at other vocational and industrial schools throughout the Jim Crow South. A committed social and community activist, Margaret Murray Washington was "at the center" of the black women's consciousness movement of the late nineteenth and early twentieth centuries and was a pivotal figure in the National Association of Colored Women from its founding in 1896 until her death in 1925. While she embraced her husband's philosophies on many issues, as Jacqueline Anne Rouse has pointed out, she was not simply an extension of her husband.[142] Knowing what we do about Booker T. Washington's authoritative leadership style, he must have been comfortable with how Mrs. Washington shaped the experiences of female students at Tuskegee. Washington certainly shared his wife's conviction that black women would help build the black community by laying the foundations in the domestic sphere.

While Washington spoke highly of his mother in all of his autobiographies, he did not speak extensively about the role of women in his uplift movement. After becoming black America's leading spokesperson, he passed this responsibility on to his wife Margaret. In the future, scholars could definitely delve more into Washington's relationships with his family and his three wives, Fannie Smith, Olivia America Davidson, and Margaret Murray, and into his notions of gender and black womanhood. Each one of Washington's wives played instrumental roles in helping him run Tuskegee and though he was routinely away from home for significant amounts of time every year after his 1895 Atlanta oration, family was very important to Washington. Washington was also unlike other black male leaders of his time in that during the six decades of his life, he had three wives. While Monroe A. Majors, Louis R. Harlan, Wilma King, Jacqueline Anne Rouse, and Carolyn A. Dorsey have unearthed the contributions of Washington's wives, fewer have addressed Washington's notions of gender. Adele Logan Alexander has probed into Washington's ideas of black womanhood in her intriguing essay on allegations of sexual harassment at Tuskegee in 1906 and 1907. Alexander's analysis of the "Penney-Ridley case" suggests that Washington embraced the Victorian sexual ideology.[143]

* * *

Thirty years ago, Lawrence J. Friedman suggested that Washington's wearing of "the mask" may have "inadvertently inflicted physical as well as psychological damage upon himself."[144] This observation is still worth probing. In discussing Washington's father-son relationship with S. C. Armstrong, Harlan engaged in a bit of psychohistory. Historians still need to probe deeper into Washington's psyche, in light of the enormous pressures under which he operated. Washington's apologists insist that his strategy of accommodation was justified considering the social-historical context in which he operated. Likewise, historians like John Bracey, August Meier, and Elliott Rudwick have conceptualized black nationalism in order to include nearly all black leaders to some degree.[145] Challenging orthodox environmentalist historians' notion that Washington's times left him with no other possible options, social critic Adolph Reed Jr. has argued that in justifying accommodation scholars have underestimated the possible range of viable political options for fin de siècle black leaders.

Could Washington have achieved the positive accomplishments that he did without assuming an accommodating, conciliatory tone when needed? How do his accomplishments compare with those of other African American spokespersons from the South during the Progressive Era? How do we explain the ideological relationship between Washington and more militant and radical black organizations and leaders like Marcus Garvey, the Nation of Islam, and even the Black Panther Party? In Washington's case, did the ends justify the means? Was there a balance between Washington's contributions to African American advancement and his relentless attacks on his black opponents, particularly those in the Niagara Movement? Did Tuskegee Institute help positively reform the masses of blacks in Macon County, Alabama during Washington's times? How effective were Washington's outreach programs? How did wearing "the mask" affect Washington's psyche? What is Washington's legacy, and how have major black spokespersons, public figures, and white-appointed black leaders, like Barack Obama for instance, unconsciously and consciously borrowed from Washington's demeanor? Such questions could help us frame future investigations into Washington's contributions, legacy, and worldview. Washington's "ascendancy" and unique role in American and African American history will continue to engender debate. As the reader reads this book, another article and book on Washington is probably in the making or has already been published. The most powerful black leader of the early twentieth century will continue to have elementary and secondary schools named after him throughout the country and he will continue to be the representative black American, "the safe Negro," that many schoolteachers introduce when talking about black history with their students. In his talk to

Tuskegee students, "Shadow vs. Substance," Washington repeatedly instructed his students to avoid "grasping at the shadow instead of the substance."[146] As we continue on into the most advanced phase of African American historiography, we are no longer "grasping at the shadow" of Washington, but rather grappling with his "substance." As it is the case with all historical phenomena, Washington must be viewed holistically from many, often seemingly contradictory, vantage points. Just as Washington was complex and multidimensional, so too is the historiography surrounding him.

6. Genocide and African American History

[T]he oppressed Negro citizens of the United States, segregated,
discriminated against and the long target of violence, suffer from
genocide as the result of the consistent, conscious, unified policies
of every branch of government.
— William L. Patterson, *We Charge Genocide: The Historic Petition
to the United Nations for Relief from a Crime of the United States
Government against the Negro People*

Since William Lorenzo Patterson (1891–1980) and the Civil Rights Congress first accused the United States of committing genocide against African
Americans in their historic and controversial petition in 1951, delivered to
the U.S. Secretariat in New York by Paul Robeson and by Patterson to the
United Nations in Paris at the Palais Chaillot where the Fifth Session of the
General Assembly congregated, many radical black activists, nationalists,
and self-proclaimed revolutionaries, especially during the Black Power era,
have leveled similar charges against the United States government. Since the
1970s, a small group of scholars has exposed and analyzed various expressions
and manifestations of genocide within contexts of the African American
historical experience. Several decades after Patterson and his Civil Rights
Congress co-workers published *We Charge Genocide: The Historic Petition
to the United Nations for Relief from a Crime of the United States Government
against the Negro People* (1951), Patterson avowed that African Americans
continued to be victims of genocide and genocidal conditions in the United
States. Although during the Black Power era he publicly criticized the self-
defense strategy of the Black Panther Party and called upon them to engage in
coalition building with communists, Patterson also applauded the organization and defended them from what he viewed as being genocidal treatment.
"Racism," Patterson asserted, "had been pushed to genocidal proportions
in Oakland," the birthplace of the Black Panther Party. "An image of Black
militants as rampaging terrorists is being created, and every branch of the
government is involved in the process," Patterson insisted. "Never, since the

Reconstruction period, has this country witnessed such racist savagery as is now condoned and abetted by government." Encouraged by Patterson, Ossie Davis, Angie Dickerson, and Charlene Mitchell organized the "Emergency Conference for the Right of the Black Panther Party to Exist" in Chicago late in 1969. According to Mitchell, one of the conference's resolutions was "to collect signatures on a second petition to the United Nations, once again raising the issue of genocide. Pat, as ever, was helpful with ideas and suggestions. We called for the presentation of the petition to the U.N. in October 1970."[1] Twenty years after *We Charge Genocide* appeared, Patterson maintained: "Now, nearly two decades later, the charges made then can be materially enlarged. Characteristic of life in the United States today are the murderous brutality visited upon Black citizens in and out of the ghettos in which they are forced to live; the use of state troopers to suppress their demonstrations, and the use of Black nationals as armed gendarmes to force America's brand of democracy upon foreign peoples."[2]

Beginning primarily during the Black Power era, scholars from various fields of study have experimented with employing the highly politicized and controversial term *genocide* to describe the treatment of various historical groups of African Americans and their ancestors who were victimized by the Atlantic slave trade, colonial conquest, and other dehumanizing and violent forms of racial oppression. In the early 1980s and later in the early 1990s, Marimba Ani coined the term "Maafa," a Kiswahili word meaning "disaster," to "describe over five hundred years of warfare and genocide experienced by African people under enslavement and colonialism and their continued impact on African people throughout the world."[3] Black studies scholars, especially outspoken Afrocentric thinkers, have enlisted Ani's concept in theorizing the violent oppression experienced and witnessed by various groups of African descendants. Since the ratification of the U.S. Constitution, most notably during "the nadir," many incidences of the mass murdering and drastic mistreatment of African Americans have occurred that could be described as genocide based not only on the 1948 definition of genocide detailed (albeit in ambiguous and problematic terms) by the Convention on the Prevention and Punishment of the Crime of Genocide (hereinafter the Genocide Convention), but also based on the numerous definitions of genocide suggested by a group of leading genocide studies scholars who did not consider African Americans legitimate victims of genocide.

While professionally trained scholars began seriously dealing with issues of genocide and African American history in the second half of the twentieth century, especially in the post–civil rights era, black activists have addressed whites' genocidal behavior toward blacks centuries before Raphael Lemkin invented the term genocide in the 1940s. As Calvin H. Sinnette passionately underscored in 1972, "to suggest that blacks have only recently discovered the genocide issue is but another example of the ignorance of racist arrogance." The modern expression of this thought, he maintained, "is an old consciousness reawakened and applied to the internal dynamics of a people in search of liberation."[4]

During the antebellum era, in his famous 1829 *Appeal to the Colored Citizens of the World,* David Walker exclaimed: "The whites have always been an unjust, jealous, unmerciful, avaricious and blood-thirsty set of beings, always seeking after power and authority. . . . The whites, . . . where they have the advantage, or think that there are any prospects of getting it, they murder all before them, in order to subject men to wretchedness and degradation under them. . . . The whites have had us under them for more than three centuries, murdering, and treating us like brutes."[5]

Two decades later in an editorial in the *North Star,* Frederick Douglass remarked, "Already are our enemies gravely speculating upon our final extinction, and even venturing upon the probable time it will take to blot us out from the face of this nation."[6]

In her 1895 pamphlet, *A Red Record,* antilynching crusader Ida B. Wells chastised white America for its "barbarism" and genocidal treatment of African Americans: "Not all nor nearly all of the murders done by white men, during the past thirty years in the South, have come to light, but the statistics as gathered and preserved by white men, and which have not been questioned, show that during these years more than ten thousand Negroes have been killed in cold blood, without the formality of judicial trial and legal execution. And yet, as evidence of the absolute impunity with which the white man dares to kill a Negro, the same record shows that during all these years, and for all these murders only three white men have been tried, convicted, and executed. As no white man has been lynched for the murder of colored people, these three executions are only the instances of the death penalty being visited upon white men for murdering Negroes."[7] Preceding black communists, Patterson, and Malcolm X, in the early 1890s Wells traveled abroad (to England, Scotland, and Wales) and internationalized the genocide faced by African Americans.

During "the nadir," a significant group of white scholars, including Walter Wilcox, Frederick Hoffman, Joseph Tillinghast, Francis A. Walker, Alfred A. Stone, R. M. Cunningham, and leading figures in the American Economic Association, promoted what William Darity Jr. has defined as "the disappearance hypothesis," the belief "that the black presence would diminish over time in American society."[8] In an effort to challenge this widespread brand of academic racism, social Darwinism, Spencerian reasoning, colonialism, and cultural imperialism, W. E. B. Du Bois published an important essay, "The Future of the Negro Race in America" (possibly a play on Booker T. Washington's optimistic 1899 book, *The Future of the American Negro*), in a 1904 volume of *The East and the West: A Quarterly Review for the Study of Missions*. Not surprisingly, Du Bois's tone was much more analytical and critical than Washington's. Du Bois opened with these words: "There are, as it seems to me, four ways in which the American negro may develop: first, his present condition of serfdom may be perpetuated; secondly, his race may die out and become extinct in this land; thirdly, he may migrate to some foreign land; and fourthly, he may become an American citizen."[9] Darity points out that "Du Bois did not dismiss the second possibility as nonsensical. . . . [He] had raised the issue genocide of American blacks in 1904!"[10]

Du Bois explained how "the extinction of the negro in America" could possibly occur:

> It may easily happen too that circumstances and surroundings which favour one race may be fatal to another. And it is here that those who look for the extinction of the negro in America may legitimately take their stand. If, for instance, under conditions of civilised life as favourable as ordinary justice can make them a race of people have not the sheer physical stamina to survive, then, however pitiable the spectacle, there is little that surrounding civilisation can do. . . . If all authority is stripped from a people, their customs interfered with, their religion laughed at, their children corrupted, and ruin, gambling, and prostitution forced upon them—such a proceeding will undoubtedly kill them off, and kill them quickly. But that is not survival of the fittest—it is plain murder. Turning, then, to the second possible future of the negro in America— namely, that he may die out—it must be candidly acknowledged that this is quite possible.[11]

Du Bois proceeded to suggest that if blacks continued to be oppressed in all facets of their lives, then "it is quite possible . . . that the American negro will dwindle away and die from starvation and excess" adding "a few million more murders to the account of civilisation." At the same time, holding faith in black historical ability to persevere over oppression since "the horrors of the African slave trade," Du Bois surmised that if they "keep up their courage and hope" blacks' chances of "dying out are exceedingly small." Still, he underscored that "if extinction comes, it will be a long and tedious process covering many decades, accompanied by widespread crime and disease, and caused by unusual race bitterness and proscription."[12]

In New York City on July 8, 1917, Marcus Garvey indicted the U.S. government for not protecting African Americans who were massacred in the East St. Louis riot. In his famous speech, "The Conspiracy of the East St. Louis Riots," Garvey highlighted the American government's hypocrisy for speaking out against the Armenian genocide while ignoring the fundamental human rights of twelve million "of her own citizens." Garvey pronounced to repeated cheers: "For three hundred years the Negroes of America have given their life blood to make the Republic the first among the nations of the world, and all along this time there has never been even one year of justice but on the contrary a continuous round of oppression. At one time it was slavery, at another time lynching and burning, and up to date it is wholesale butchering. This is a crime against the laws of humanity; it is a crime against the laws of the nation, it is a crime against Nature, and a crime against the God of all mankind."[13] Following in the tradition of Walker, Douglass, Wells, Du Bois, Garvey, and many other black activists and race representatives active before the cold war era, since the dawning of the 1950s, from Patterson and the Civil Rights Congress to Conrad W. Worrill and the National Black United Front, a diverse group of black activists continued to indict the white American power structure for its blatant dismissal of African Americans' humanity and perpetuation of antiblack genocidal conditions.

In this chapter, I bring together a diverse body of scholars' theories from genocide studies and African American studies and history, as well as the pleas of many black activists hailing from different generations, in order to explore how genocide can be used as a revealing lens for understanding and interpreting African American history, for both conceptualizing the realities of the African American historical experience and for teaching about it. I discuss dehumanizing and violent historical injustices perpetuated against blacks that have historically conjured up notions of genocide within African American communities and popular culture, such as the slave trade and the middle passage, slavery, segregation, lynching, the Tuskegee Syphilis Experiment, the AIDS epidemic, and sterilization experiments. This chapter also unravels the ideas, social activism, and influential struggles of those African Americans who have boldly challenged the United States government and culture in general of committing genocide against African Americans primarily after the term formally entered America's and the world's vocabulary with Raphael Lemkin's writings of the 1940s. These thinkers include William L. Patterson, members of the Civil Rights Congress, Malcolm X, Nation of Islam spokespersons, a coterie of Black Power–era activists, Conrad W. Worrill and members of the National Black United Front, and a group of Afrocentric scholar-activists. Because of his important role in the evolution of conceptualizations of genocide and his central role in the international and global African American struggle for human rights, I highlight Patterson's life and worldview, paying particular attention to the monumental *We Charge Genocide.*

Genocide: Origins of the Word and Concept and Its Relevance to African American History

In his widely read and well-received *Axis Rule in Occupied Europe* (1944), Polish-Jewish émigré Raphael Lemkin coined the now hotly contested term genocide.

> New conceptions require new terms. By 'genocide' we mean the destruction of a nation or of an ethnic group. This new word, coined by the author to denote an old practice in its modern development, is made from the ancient Greek word *genos* (race, tribe) and the Latin *cide* (killing), thus corresponding in its formation to such words as tyrannicide, homocide, infanticide, etc. Generally speaking, genocide does not necessarily mean the immediate destruction of a nation, except when accomplished by mass killings of all members of a nation. It is intended rather to signify a coordinated plan of different actions aimed at the destruction of essential foundations of life of national groups, with the aim of annihilating the groups themselves. . . . Genocide has two phases: one, destruction of the national pattern of the oppressed group; the other, the imposition of the national pattern of the oppressor.[14]

In the 1950s in one of his many unpublished essays, Lemkin added to his definition of genocide, observing among other things that "genocide is a gradual process and may begin with political disenfranchisement, economic displacement, cultural undermining and control, the destruction of leadership, the break-up of families and the prevention of propagation. Each of these methods is a more or less effective means of destroying a group. Actual physical destruction is the last and most effective means of genocide."[15]

Lemkin developed the term genocide "to shock listeners as one which would have much greater impact than the earlier terms 'crimes of barbarity and vandalism.'"[16] While Lemkin was arguably "the driving force" behind the Genocide Convention, as one scholar has suggested "it is not clear, however, that his vision of genocide is embodied in the Convention."[17] At the same time, Lemkin was certainly among the most committed and influential campaigners and lobbyists for making genocide an international concern and crime. Extending Lemkin's conceptualization, the General Assembly of the United Nations, with its resolution 96 on December 11, 1948, in the immediate aftermath of World War II, deemed genocide "a crime under international law," recognizing that at "all periods of history genocide has inflicted great losses on humanity." In article II, the Genocide Convention construed genocide as "any of the following acts committed with the intent to destroy, in whole or in part, a national, ethnical, racial or religious group, such as: (a) Killing members of the group; (b) Causing serious bodily or mental harm to members of the group; (c) Deliberately inflicting on the group conditions of life calculated to bring about its physical destruction in whole or in part; (d) Imposing measures intended to prevent births within the group; (e) Forcibly transferring children of the group to another group."[18] It is worth noting that the U.S. Senate, with the backing of President Reagan, finally authorized ratification of the United Nations Genocide Convention on February 19, 1986.

Since the late 1940s, many scholars have revised and expanded upon Lemkin's and the Genocide Convention's definitions of genocide. From the late 1940s until the early 1980s when, according to Samuel Totten and Steven Leonard Jacobs, "the study of genocide came into its own as an academic field," Jessie Bernard, William Patterson and his Civil Rights Congress coworkers, Pieter Drost, Hannah Arendt, Jean-Paul Sartre, and Hugo Adam Bedau, among others, grappled with alternative definitions of genocide.[19] Epitomized by an upsurge of scholarly journal articles, monographs, and anthologies, the publication of the *Encyclopedia of Genocide* (1999), the organizing of many national and international conferences and research institutes on genocide, and the inauguration of the *Journal of Genocide Studies* in 1999, by the mid- to late 1990s, genocide studies constituted an established and dynamic field of scholarly inquiry. Since the late 1990s and the beginning of the new millennium, numerous thought-provoking anthologies have been published on genocide. "The number of books on genocide has tripled within less than a decade" and by 2001 one scholar identified more than twenty major definitions of genocide. Indeed, as Dan Stone posits, genocide studies is "one of the fast-growing disciplines in the humanities and social sciences."[20] Countless scholars have debated what genocide entails in various historical and modern manifestations. Reflecting on his research on the Armenian Genocide, Rouben Paul Adalian remarked: "When all is said and done, the emergence of a field called genocide studies represents a sea change in the academy and in the intellectual community—both of which long ignored the topic or frowned on the subject as a facet of the preoccupation of historically-persecuted minorities whose representatives were thought to be engaged in self-interested exercises of historical interpretation."[21]

Many scholars have explored incidents of genocide in Africa involving different African ethnic groups that have occurred in countries like Algeria, Sudan,

Ethiopia, Nigeria, Uganda, Burundi, and Rwanda, where an estimated 951,018 people, overwhelmingly Tutsis, were killed during the spring and summer months of 1994. Yet, during their field's early years, genocide scholars tended to embrace Eurocentric worldviews, often focusing on the Holocaust and other exemplar genocides of the twentieth century. As more than a few genocide scholars have observed, early scholarship on genocide was indeed Holocaust-centered, using the Holocaust as the epitome and primary case study of modern genocide. At the same time, today there seems to be a consensus among genocide scholars that the slaughter of more than 60,000 Herero and Nama men, women, and children in German South West Africa at the hands of the German government, General Lothar van Trotha, and German troops between 1904 and 1908 "was one of the first genocides of the twentieth century" and in many respects, as Sven Lindqvist argued in *"Exterminate All the Brutes": One Man's Odyssey into the Heart of Darkness and the Origins of European Genocide,* laid the ideological foundation for the Holocaust.[22] On August 14, 2004, the German Minister for Development and Economic Cooperation, Heidemarie Wieczorek-Zeul, "officially" apologized and accepted "historical and moral responsibility" for her ancestors who committed "atrocities . . . [that] would today be termed genocide." According to Jurgen Zimmerer, this is not only the first major apology of its kind, but it "can be considered a landmark event in dealing with genocides in the colonial context."[23]

Nonetheless, genocide scholars have been strikingly silent about discussing genocide as it relates to African descendants in the United States.[24] Of the numerous anthologies on genocide, only a few have included essays that have addressed African Americans. *Genocide* (2001), edited by William Dudley, includes an essay by Robert Johnson and Paul S. Leighton titled "African Americans: Victims of Indirect Genocide," and in *Gendercide and Genocide* (2004), edited by Adam Jones, there is an article by Augusta C. Del Zotto titled "Gendercide in a Historical-Structural Context: The Case of the Black Male Gendercide in the United States." Further, in 2008, Ann Curthoys and John Docker became among the few mainstream genocide scholars to seriously acknowledge the importance of Patterson's and the Civil Rights Congress's *We Charge Genocide.* Yet several leading and influential genocide studies scholars have in passing downplayed and dismissed using genocide within the context of African American history. Contemporary genocide studies scholars appear to have followed in the footsteps of Raphael Lemkin who, for a variety of reasons, was openly opposed to African Americans' appropriation of genocide to describe the masses of their people's historical experience.

When Lemkin first arrived in North Carolina to teach at Duke University in 1941, his "first impressions was that the discrimination practiced against the black population in the South bore certain resemblance to the unfair treatment meted out to Jews in prewar Poland." As a "lone campaigner" in a struggle to make genocide an international crime against various European ethnic groups, however, he was angered because "an early civil rights movement accusing the United States government of genocide against its own population incited a caucus of Southern senators to block the ratification of the convention in the Senate." In late 1951, Lemkin spoke out against William L. Patterson's attempt to charge the United States of committing genocide against African Americans. According to the *New York Times,* on December 17, 1951, Lemkin "assailed . . . a 240-page petition to the world organization accusing the United States Government of committing genocide against Negroes. . . . Dr. Lemkin said the accusations were a maneuver to divert attention from the crimes of genocide committed against Estonians, Latvians, Lithuanians, Poles and other Soviet-subjugated peoples."[25] Several years later again in the *New York Times,* positing planned extermination as a prerequisite for genocide, Lemkin contended that blacks were not victims of genocide. "By no stretch of the imagination," Lemkin surmised, "can one discover in the United States an intent or plan to exterminate the Negro population, which is increasing in condition of evident prosperity and progress." Several scholars have suggested that Lemkin's refusal to accept blacks' claims to genocide was influenced by his Eurocentric disposition, racist attitudes, sympathies toward colonialism, and anticommunist posture.[26]

"For those who would instruct others on the meaning of the Holocaust and genocide in general, there is a need to avoid degrading this whole tragic theme by spreading its meaning to include cultural deprivation or the punishment of select individuals, even if they symbolically represent the whole population," Irving L. Horowitz has commented. "The lynching of American blacks in the Reconstruction period was terrible. But at its worst epidemic proportions just prior to the First World War it could be measured in hundreds each year. The bulk of the black population were suppressed and discriminated against, but were not summarily liquidated. In this very fact there is an essential distinction to be made between a democratic United States and a totalitarian Nazi Germany."[27]

Helen Fein similarly dismissed the views of African Americans who believed that their people have perhaps been the victims of genocide. In pointing out how genocide has been misconstrued, Fein asserted: "The wave of misuse and rhetorical abuse parallels the alphabet: abortion, bisexuality, cocaine addiction, and dieting have also been labeled as examples of genocide—as well as suburbanization. At times such labeling verges on the paranoid and incendiary, as when Westerners or Jews are accused of genocide by giving Africans or African-Americans AIDS."[28]

Horowitz's and Fein's statements are oversimplistic and problematic for various reasons. Contrary to Horowitz's assessment, as Patterson, the Civil Rights Congress, and others argued, lynching—the often ritualized and systematic killing of African Americans who posed threats to America's racial and social order, especially, but not exclusively, in the South mainly during the era of Jim Crow Segregation—can be described as a form of genocide based on the Genocide Convention's and various scholars' definitions of the term. Many onlookers even postulated that during the 1940s and 1950s U.S. politicians were opposed to the Genocide Convention because they feared that their country would be accountable for lynching. Horowitz also misrepresented the number of African Americans who were actually lynched. Between the 1880s and 1944, the records from Tuskegee Institute indicate that at least 3,417 lynchings of blacks were documented and detailed by newspapers and investigators throughout the nation. In the 1890s, Ida B. Wells estimated that 10,000 black men were lynched between 1865 and the 1890s, and Dorothy Sterling "who combed through many thousands of documents and oral histories in preparation of a noted compendium of the Reconstruction era, cited 20,000 as the number killed by the Klan just in the four years 1868–71." Philip Dray, who has called lynching a "holocaust," has made an insightful observation that refers to the numbers of those innocent blacks lynched in the United States. "Efforts to establish precise numbers are extremely useful but become, at a certain point, meaningless; whether people were being killed for an alleged criminal act, a transgression of social norms, or for holding minority political views, whether their number was 500, 5,000, or 25,000, by the time the antilynching movement got under way just before the turn of the century it was evident that the threshold for mob murder in America had long since been crossed."[29] Equally important, Horowitz ignored that state officials and the U.S. government encouraged the murdering of blacks by failing to institute antilynching legislation. As one scholar recently commented: "What [white] United States citizen has ever been imprisoned or executed for lynching a Black person? Failure of authorities to pursue the perpetrators of lynching, hundreds if not thousands of whom are still alive, is tacit approval of the motive and act of lynching . . . Why has law enforcement failed to track down and hold members of the lynch mobs responsible for their crimes?"[30]

Fein's dismissal of African Americans' claims of genocide is equally as problematic. She intimates that there are significant cases in which "Westerners or Jews" have "been accused of giving AIDS" to African Americans. Indeed, many blacks have referred to AIDS as being a form of genocide against their people at the hands of the government, but except for maybe Louis Farrakhan and a few others (whom Fein does not mention by name), most commentators do not accuse Jews of this action in the outspoken fashion Fein suggests. There is a large body of provocative thought, moreover, that discusses AIDS as a man-made disease that should not be dismissed in such a cavalier manner. Blacks' views of genocide and AIDS warrant further discussion. Fein's concern over excessive "genocide-labeling" and genocide semantic gymnastics is valid and understandable. Certainly, every act of violence, murder, and mistreatment against a group should not be labeled genocide. However, to dismiss blacks' critical views of genocide and AIDS, or genocide in general, without any discussion of this phenomenon not only devalues the African American experience, but, more important, is rooted in the assumption that African Americans as well as other groups do not have the right or license to use genocide as a paradigm for looking at their experiences in the United States.

The various groups of blacks' views of AIDS as being a form of genocide deserve to be examined more closely. It is much more than the paranoia and mislabeling that Fein reduces it to. In the September 1990 issue of *Essence* magazine, Karen Grisby Bates wrote an intriguing article titled "AIDS: Is It Genocide?" While Bates ignored the many complex conceptualizations of genocide offered by rigorous genocide studies scholars, she delved into the so-called far-fetched belief among "a growing number of African Americans" that AIDS was a manufactured virus aimed at killing off Africans, African Americans, and others. Drawing upon the controversial ideas of Robert Strecker (MD and PhD) and Alan Cantwell (MD), she explicated the conspiracy theory that AIDS "was created as a tool for biological warfare." At least one black physician, Barbara J. Justice, has argued that "there is a possibility that the virus was produced to limit the number of African people and people of color in the world who are no longer needed." Bates's article is by no means one-sided; she provides the views of those, like Fein, who find such claims to be ludicrous. More important, however, Bates provides an elementary explanation as to why some blacks may have thought about AIDS within the context of genocide, noting "since slavery, there have always been those who thought that white America has targeted us for extinction, just as soon as we outlive our collective usefulness."[31]

Several years after Bates's essay appeared, Lorene Cary, then contributing editor to *Newsweek*, contextualized the "paranoid" mindset that Fein referred to in reference to blacks' notion of genocide. In "Why It's Not Just Paranoia,"

Cary briefly historicized blacks' genocidal beliefs and conspiracies within the context of slavery, emigration schemes, Reconstruction, Jim Crow segregation, lynching, and the infamous Tuskegee Study:

> No one could take the Plan seriously if it weren't true that from the beginning of the Union, from the writing of its Constitution, Americans in power legislated a lesser legal status for people of color—and that American science, theology and philosophy tried to prove that those same people did not merely deserve slavery but needed it to work their way, through God's plan and Dixie's cotton, out of degradation and sin. Now that's a Plan: neat, cosmic, inescapable. It wasn't genocide, because the object was to keep people alive and working; but the cost in human lives, not to mention spirits, was high indeed. First came at least a million and a half dead on shipboard . . . and several millions from the beginning of the marches from the interior of Africa to final landing in the Americas. Then there were the dangers at the destination. . . . We Americans continue to value the lives and humanity of some groups . . . more than others. This is not paranoia. It is our historical legacy and a present fact. . . . It is no longer true that an African-American's life can be bought outright; and U.S. laws no longer allow token penalties for the murder of a black person. But it is true that African-American life in the United States has long been, and is still, devalued. The fact is, to quote Gwendolyn Brooks's poem: 'We die soon.'"[32]

In *I Heard It Through the Grapevine: Rumors in African-American Culture* (1993), Patricia A. Turner became one of the first scholars to explore various black urban legends and rumors, including blacks' views of AIDS as being a form of genocide against blacks, and to contextualize blacks' views of genocidal conspiracies. According to Turner, many blacks' beliefs and rumors that AIDS is a form of genocide against African people are rooted in a history of real oppression. Since Turner's study, many scholars, including Cathy J. Cohen, Vanessa Northington Gamble, Dorie J. Gilbert, Ednita M. Wright, Jacob Levenson, and Gil L. Robertson, have contextualized and explained blacks' views of AIDS as possibly constituting a form of genocide against blacks.[33] According to Gamble, associate professor in the department of health policy and management at the Johns Hopkins Bloomberg School of Public Health and deputy director of the Center for Health Disparities Solutions, the "shadow" of the Tuskegee Study as well as the history of medical experimentation on African Americans dating back to the antebellum era, has immensely contributed to many blacks' distrust in clinical trials, organ donation, HIV/AIDS prevention and treatment programs, medical and public health institutions overall, as well as blacks' "fears about genocide." Echoing Turner, for Gamble "there is a collective memory among African Americans about their exploitation by the medical establishment" and the prevalent

"beliefs about the connection between AIDS and the purposeful destruction of African Americans should not be cavalierly dismissed as bizarre and
paranoid."[34]

A "bewildering array of definitions"

Since the late 1950s and increasingly by the 1990s, an ideologically diverse
group of social scientists have pinpointed the various problems and limitations with Lemkin's and the Genocide Convention's definitions of genocide.
Defining genocide has for the last several decades constituted a dynamic and
hotly contested subfield of genocide studies. One scholar has observed that
conferences on genocide often turn into "a merry-go-round of definitional
debates."[35] Major anthologies on genocide routinely begin with outlining the
variety of definitions of genocide. There is indeed a "bewildering array of
definitions" of genocide, and with these varied conceptualizations "and the
ambiguities surrounding both the Genocide Convention and historical interpretation, it is not surprising that nearly every posited case of genocide will
be discounted by someone else." The challenge, in John K. Roth's estimation,
is "to find definitions that are not, on the one hand, so broad as to trivialize
genocide and to render the uses of the term frivolous or, on the other hand,
so narrow that cases of mass death are unreasonably excluded from the
category of genocide. . . . The likelihood is that we will never possess a fully
adequate definition of genocide, at least if we expect universal agreement
about its meaning and about how to apply its meaning to the particularities
of political circumstances."[36]

While genocide studies scholars have been almost universally silent on
genocide in the context of the African American experience, more than a few
genocide studies scholars have put forward nonexclusive and wide-reaching
definitions of genocide that can be employed in useful ways to describe and
analyze various episodes of collective violence, mass murder, and genocidal
behavior against African Americans before and following World War II. David E. Lorey and William H. Beezley, for instance, have defined genocide as
"the purposeful murder of a group of people by another group that takes them
to be somehow distinct ethnically or culturally."[37] In addition to providing
a detailed "typology of genocides," Peter du Preez defines genocide broadly
as "the deliberate killing of people primarily because they are categorized as
being of a certain kind, with certain attributes." His notion of "hegemonic
genocide"—"the mass murder of various groups of people in order to force
the survivors to submit to their authority of the state"—is especially applicable
to African Americans during and before the era of Jim Crow segregation.[38]

Drawing from philosopher Thomas W. Simons's definition, Frank M. Afflitto and Margaret Vandiver have defined genocide as "the intentional killing of members of a group, negatively identified by the perpetrators, because of the victim's group membership. . . . Genocide is perpetrated on victim groups due to the fact that the perpetrators perceive threatening qualities intrinsic to the victim group. . . . Ethnicity or race, the 'geno factor,' is a mask for other threatening and identifying phenomena. . . . Victim groups are dehumanized to the point that they become mere 'functions' of their undesirable and threatening qualities."[39]

While he would probably not include African Americans within his theory of genocide, Leo Kuper has offered a notion of "domestic" genocide that applies to African American history. Domestic genocides, in Kuper's estimation, "are those which arise on the basis of internal divisions within a single society. They are a phenomenon of the plural society, with its marked divisions between racial, ethnic, and/or religious groups. Plural society theory deals with the relations between these groups, and the conditions promoting peaceful cohabitation, integration, or violent polarization leading to genocide."[40]

Israel W. Charny has offered among the broadest, and unsurprisingly controversial, definitions of genocide that would certainly be applicable to the African American experience. "I propose that whenever large numbers of unarmed human beings are put to death at the hands of their fellow human beings, we are talking about *genocide*." Charny's "generic" definition of genocide is equally applicable to African American history. "Genocide in the generic sense is the mass killing of substantial numbers of human beings, when not in the course of military action against the military force of an avowed enemy, under the conditions of the essential defenselessness and helplessness of the victims."[41]

While Lemkin's pioneering definition of genocide is not directly or ideally applicable to white Americans' indiscriminate and planned killing of African Americans since the revolutionary era primarily because whites in power never sought to totally destroy, annihilate, and exterminate black people, the United Nation's definition, as adamantly argued by Patterson and the Civil Rights Congress more than fifty years ago, can be interpreted to apply to black America's treatment by segments of U.S. society. In article II, the Genocide Convention noted that genocide meant various acts, including killing, causing serious bodily or mental harm, and inflicting on the group conditions of life "committed with the intent to destroy, in whole or in part, a national, ethnical, racial or religious group." The convention also sets forth that the perpetrators of genocide could include "constitutionally responsible rulers, public officials or private individuals." Throughout U.S. history, especially during the first two phases of the African American experience (1789–1965) "private individuals," often supported by "constitutionally responsible leaders," have killed tens of thousands of innocent African Americans, an "ethnical" and "racial" group, "with the intent" of destroying them, "in part." In murdering blacks engaged in slave conspiracies and revolts, by working blacks to death in the convict-lease prison system, and by lynching blacks, for instance, groups of "private individuals" sought to "destroy" a "part" of black America in order to maintain America's racial order and hierarchy. Furthermore, "constitutionally responsible rulers," "public officials," and "private individuals" have throughout U.S. history "deliberately" inflicted on African Americans "conditions of life calculated to bring about its physical destruction . . . in part." In other words, without abstraction, African Americans like William L. Patterson and others were not being far-fetched in proclaiming that certain white Americans committed genocide against African Americans.[42]

William L. Patterson: "The man who cried genocide"

In 1951, a sixty-year-old William L. Patterson delivered the Civil Rights Congress's historic petition to the United Nations' General Assembly in Paris, charging the U.S. with committing genocide against African Americans. In his words, "the petition was a detailed documentation of hundreds of cases of murder, bombing, torture of Black nationals in the United States. It dealt unsparingly with 'mass murder on the score of race that had been sanctified by law' and it stated 'never have so many individuals been so ruthlessly destroyed amid so many tributes to the sacredness of the individual.'"[43] This bold act represented the manifestation of his long evolution as a radical black activist. In the immediate post–World War II era, Patterson was for African Americans what Lemkin was for various victimized European groups. In order to understand and appreciate Patterson's petition, it is necessary to explore his dynamic maturation as a scholar-activist. Patterson's life mirrors that of black intellectuals, scholars, and activists who were born during the Progressive Era or "the nadir" of black life. He shared with many other black scholar-activists of his generation a poor, working-class background. Patterson belonged to a group of black scholar-activists born in the late nineteenth and early twentieth century who profoundly shaped the black struggle for civil and human rights during the era of Jim Crow segregation. Equally important, post–civil rights activists, notably members of the Black Panther Party, also drew upon the ideas and legacies of Patterson and his contemporaries.

While historians of black radicalism and black activism during the pivotal yet understudied cold war era have acknowledged Patterson's contributions, scholarship on "the man who cried genocide" is relatively scant. In 1971 at age eighty, Patterson wrote his engaging autobiography, *The Man Who Cried Genocide: An Autobiography,* which stands as part the African American autobiographical tradition. Kenneth Mostern's idea that "*nearly all* African-American political leaders (regardless of politics; self-designated or appointed by one or another community) have chosen to write personal stories as a means of theorizing their political positions" is certainly applicable to Patterson.[44] Like black autobiographers before him, Patterson offered his life story in great detail as an object lesson for his contemporaries and future generations. "May the record of my experiences in this battle add some useful first-hand evidence from one man who was deeply involved."[45]

Looking back at eight decades of his life, Patterson described it as being a "journey through the jungles of bigotry." He soon discovered that "the horrors of color prosecution and poverty could only be fully grappled with in a struggle against economic and social forces that had spawned them." As an activist, he wore many hats: he was simultaneously a committed "race man," a communist, and socialist. He also placed blacks' struggles for human and civil rights in the context of oppressed peoples throughout the world. By his twenties, he believed that socialism was the solution, that black and white workers needed to unite in a concerted struggle against capitalism and imperialism. Patterson's worldview was profoundly shaped by his early years and upbringing. Though his birth records were destroyed by an earthquake and fire in San Francisco, Patterson believed that his "correct birth date is August 27, 1891." His mother, Mary Galt, was born a slave in Virginia in 1850 near Norfolk. Her father, and his namesake, William Galt, was an "anti-racist" activist in California during the postemancipation era. Patterson described his mother as being "a fighter when she knew what the fight was about."[46]

Patterson's father, descended from a Carib Indian mother and a "full-blooded African" father, was born in St. Vincent in the British West Indies. A self-taught man, during Patterson's childhood he defied the Chinese Exclusion Act and smuggled Chinese into San Francisco and then became a Seventh Day Adventist missionary. Patterson did not have the fondest memories of his father. "If I never learned to love him, I didn't hate him either. The severity with which he beat us when he thought we had failed to observe some religious tenet was frightening." Patterson's father abandoned a young Patterson, his mother, and his brother and sister. Patterson recalled that his mother, a domestic like many black women of her generation, "was always on the desperate verge of survival." Patterson was inspired by his mother's strength and faith. "Only much later did I come to appreciate fully the great inner strength that helped my mother to carry on. She possessed an everlasting hope for something better. All poor mothers, regardless of their color or creed, have some of this unbounded strength, but the mothers of the Black poor are forced to draw upon it more constantly. . . . My mother could only respond to the hardships that poverty forced on her by increasing her sacrifices and her labors."[47]

Patterson traced his race/class consciousness back to his early years. As a youth in California, he attended predominantly white schools and was called a "nigger" by a classmate on at least one occasion. As Malcolm X testified in his autobiography, such insults affected the psyche of young blacks existing in a white-dominated environment. "A deep resentment arose in me," Patterson recollected. "This and subsequent incidents made me feel I was the object of color prejudice." At the same time, Patterson had some positive relationships with some poor whites. For instance, one time after his mother was evicted "some of the white boys" in his neighborhood helped him and his mother move into another residence, a rat-infested "shack." Foreshadowing Malcolm X's observations after he made his momentous pilgrimage to Mecca, Patterson asserted: "Here life came in conflict with my growing belief that all whites were prejudiced. I was perplexed."[48]

Like many black children of his generation, Patterson secured a variety of odd jobs to supplement his struggling family's meager household income. After graduating from high school in 1911 at age twenty, Patterson enrolled in the University of California—San Francisco to study law. While a student, he disagreed with Du Bois and openly opposed the United States' and black America's participation in World War I. He refused to participate in the university's mandatory military training and was dismissed. In 1915, he enrolled in Hastings College of Law at the University of California—San Francisco. He worked in a hotel in order to pay his school fees and was provided with basic lodging. As a "discontented Black law student," Patterson found comfort and affirmation by reading The Crisis, the Masses, and the Messenger. He was particularly impressed by A. Philip Randolph's and Chandler Owen's analyses of "the source of Black oppression" and its connection with "the international revolution against working-class oppression and colonialism." While a law student, he befriended Anita Whitney who recruited him to participate in the Tom Mooney Defense Committee. At this point in his life, Patterson embraced Garvey's "race first" notion and decided not to participate in the campaign to defend Mooney. During the height of World War I, Patterson befriended Colonel Charles Young and heard first-hand about Young's mistreatment at the hands of the U.S. government and he developed a more radical antiwar posture. Patterson was arrested in Oakland, California, for publicly speaking out against the war and then began to interact with other socialists during the World War I era, discerning "that class, caste and color were all involved in the triple exploitation of the Black man in the United States."[49]

After graduating from law school in 1919, Patterson failed California's bar and boarded a ship headed from London, thus developing his international perspective. He briefly worked for the *Daily Herald* in London and returned to Harlem in 1920. He would later pass the bar in New York. Though he noted that his "inability as a lawyer to offer a solution" bothered him, that "for the Black masses law and courts seemed a treadmill," and that he resented black lawyers who reaped profits from blacks' misery, in 1923 he formed (with Thomas Benjamin Dyett and George Hall) Dyett, Hall, and Patterson in New York City. The office on Seventh Avenue became a meeting place for radical lawyers. In Harlem in the mid-1920s, Patterson began to study the Soviet Union and Marxist-Leninist philosophy, applying it to black America. Upset with the "Talented Tenth," at the urging of Richard B. Moore he became involved in the defense of Ferdinando Nicola Sacco and Bartolomeo Vanzetti. An advocate of human rights, Patterson explained his decision to join this struggle: "I had either to join the battle for the lives of two innocent Italians or to ignore my kinship with these men." Along with other black communists, including Moore, Cyril Briggs, Otto Huiswood, Lovett Fort Whitman, and Grace Campbell, Patterson believed that the Sacco-Vanzetti case "was directly related to the legal lynching of Black people."[50] The execution of Sacco and Vanzetti in August 1927 in Massachusetts represented a major turning point for Patterson; in its aftermath he became more radicalized.

As a developing anti-imperialist thinker, he visited the Soviet Union and Germany. After returning, he proclaimed that socialism provided the solutions to African Americans' problems and he became a major Communist Party organizer in Harlem. With the International Labor Defense, he became active in the "Scottsboro Boys" case and moved to Chicago where, in 1938, he became the editor of the *Daily Record*, a newspaper that challenged racism and fought for the rights of the working class. After two years, the *Daily Record* folded, and he founded the Abraham Lincoln School that was committed to critiquing and dismantling imperialism and racism. Constantly under FBI surveillance, the school closed its doors after three years and Patterson devoted his energies to the Civil Rights Congress (CRC). Founded in Detroit in 1946, the CRC was created by the coming together of three organizations that had communist leanings, the International Labor Defense, the National Negro Congress, and the National Federation for Constitutional Liberties.

From 1946 until 1956, the CRC embraced the motto "self-definition for the Black Belt" and "fought for and established a number of civil liberty rulings that expanded the rights of all in the United States." According to the organization's leading historian, Gerald Horne, the "CRC was *not* the CP, yet it performed militant and often successful tasks" and won the support of many popular black entertainers, leaders, and personalities.[51] Patterson described the CRC as being "non-partisan" and "the Red Cross of the defenders of peace, constitutional rights, justice and human rights." With ten thousand members nationally dispersed in numerous chapters, the CRC publicized and internationalized the mistreatment of African Americans through "'mass action'—picketing, demonstrations, petitioning."[52] During its decade of existence, the CRC was important because its members challenged police brutality decades before the Black Panther Party; they were essential forerunners in the modern civil rights movement while challenging the tactics of mainstream civil rights organizations of their times; they brought together a diverse group of activists; they injected cases like the Willie McGee and Rosa Lee Ingram cases, the Trenton Six, and the Martinsville Seven into international arenas; and they made history by charging the United States with committing genocide against African Americans. While they suffered from internal conflicts, their demise in 1956 resulted from attacks by the state of New York, the FBI, the IRS, and the Subversive Activities Control Board.

While working to save the Martinsville Seven, seven black men who were accused of raping a white woman in Virginia in 1951, Patterson began to investigate the black prison population in Virginia. In the early 1950s, he observed that "there was not a single state in the Union in which the Black prison population was not in excess of the Black man's percentage of the general population." With University of Michigan sociologist Oakley Johnson and communist Elizabeth Lawson, Patterson wrote an unpublished study entitled "Genocide under Color of Law" that linked genocide to the killing of the Martinsville Seven. "The murder of the Martinsville Seven," Patterson noted, "fitted into the national social and political mosaic as neatly as patches fit into an intricate quilt pattern." As the national executive secretary of the CRC, Patterson began to recognize that the U.N. Charter of Human Rights was not applied to blacks. "I could not fail to recognize that just as the United States, under cover of law, carried out genocidal racist policies in police murders of Black men, framed death sentences, death that came from withholding proper medical care to Black people, just so had Hitler built and operated mass death machines under cover of Nazi law," Patterson continued, "It goes without saying that this analogy was not clearly seen by the masses in Western countries and by the masses of Americans."[53] Patterson was convinced that African Americans needed to situate themselves within the context of oppressed peoples throughout the world.

Patterson was not alone in his thinking. After Lemkin began his campaign and after the Genocide Convention was established, writers for the *Chicago Defender* and the *New York Amsterdam News* discussed the implications of genocide to African Americans. In a 1946 editorial, "Much-Needed New Word," the *Chicago Defender* observed: "Thus, this new interpretation of international law might give America the much needed weapon with which to combat the evil of lynching. It could easily be applied against any state in the union or against the country as a whole wherever and whenever a lynching occurs and the lynchers are not promptly apprehended and punished. For certainly, lynching comes within the context of Genocide." A year later, in the *Defender,* writer Willard Townsend noted that in the U.S. white racists with their "genocidal ravings" victimized African Americans. "The deliberate practice of social and economic genocide against Negroes in America," Townsend added, "gets its results in disease-ridden communities, high mortality rates and a collective group frustration that slowly destroys the spiritual and moral fibre of the victim." A year before *We Charge Genocide* appeared, an editorial in the *New York Amsterdam News* posited that "lynching of Negroes in the United States . . . would come under" the Genocide Pact agreed upon by (at that point) twenty-four nations. Hence, before *We Charge Genocide* was published, the black popular press was critically thinking about genocide's relationship to the black community.[54]

Patterson and members of the CRC, especially Richard O. Boyer, Howard Fast, Stetson Kennedy, John Hudson Jones, Leon Josephson, Oakley Johnson, Yvonne Gregory, and Elizabeth Lawson, wrote *We Charge Genocide* because they thought that it would be helpful "to all peoples fighting for freedom, and would be particularly helpful here at home among both Black and white citizens where the potentialities of the UN were not too well understood and appreciated. It would point out to Black men and women the broadening avenues through which this struggle might move forward." Patterson sought to have the petition "expose the reactionary role that the racists of the United States were preparing to play in world affairs, especially its danger to world peace. No government bound up with racism could want or seek world peace."[55] Patterson described the petition as being an "all-out ideological attack" at the "center of the world stage" against the United States' mistreatment of African Americans. Patterson and the CRC mailed letters introducing the petition to "prominent" black and white liberals throughout the country. According to Patterson, the replies were, "in the main, along the color line. A majority of the Negroes polled believed that the Genocide Convention should be invoked; a majority of white liberals and personalities were of the contrary view." Raphael Lemkin wrote to Patterson, stressing "vehemently that the provisions of the Genocide Convention bore no relation to the U.S. Government or its position vis-à-vis Black citizens."[56] In one week, the CRC sold five thousand copies of *We Charge Genocide* and in doing so incited debates within the black community, U.S. political circles, and international settings.

Patterson strategically decided to personally deliver the petition to the delegates at the United Nations' Assembly meeting in Paris. He sent sixty copies to Paris, London, and Budapest and carried twenty copies with him to Paris. He arrived in Paris on December 16, 1951, and his mission was covered not only in the communist press like *L'Humanite,* but also in Paris's mainstream presses. Those black leaders present at the U.N. General Assembly in Paris included Channing Tobias and Ralph Bunche, both of whom opposed Patterson's petition. Considered by many to be sympathetic to blacks' struggles for civil rights, Eleanor Roosevelt as acting-chief of the U.S. delegation to the U.N. and the head of the U.N. Human Rights Commission had mixed feelings toward the CRC's petition. In January 1952 she told a correspondent for the *New York Amsterdam News* that the petition was "well done as a petition" and "based upon sound and good documentation." She added, however, that "the charge of Genocide against the colored people in America is ridiculous in terms of the United Nations definition."[57]

Although in a brief telephone conversation the American Embassy in France cancelled Patterson's passport and demanded that he return to the U.S.—to which he responded a defiant "well, you go to hell"—and none of the delegates significantly supported the adoption of *We Charge Genocide,* Patterson viewed the petition as being successful. He reasoned that none of the delegates supported his cause because "the Negro question was inextricably bound up with the liberation struggles of all mankind, but the forces at work were complex." A victorious Patterson emphasized: "An ideological and moral victory had already been won; the moral bankruptcy of U.S. leaders even in the UN had been exposed." Patterson continued, "The Negro struggle had been lifted up to a new level; American reactionaries were afraid of the exposure of the cold, hard, murderous character of those who, since the time of Lincoln, had prescribed terror—not law and order, not constitutional government—as a policy toward one-tenth of the citizenry of the country."[58] Patterson's petition received some attention in the United States, especially in the black press. According to Patterson, forty-five thousand copies of *We Charge Genocide* were sold in the United States and many more were purchased in the Soviet Union, Czechoslovakia, and Hungary. After Patterson returned from Paris, he was detained at the airport in New York, questioned, and strip-searched. Why did U.S. officials respond to Patterson's and the CRC's petition in this manner?

To say that this document epitomizes twentieth-century black radicalism in an understatement. Although she considered Patterson's charge of genocide against the U.S. "ridiculous," Eleanor Roosevelt was on point in telling a correspondent for the *New York Amsterdam News* that *We Charge Genocide* was "well done" and "based upon sound and good documentation."[59] Several decades ago, Gerald Horne eloquently captured the significance of *We Charge Genocide*: "The CRC's genocide petition still stands in hindsight as a major landmark on the path to equality in the United States and sanity in U.S. foreign policy, and it set precedents still followed regarding the value of internationalizing the struggle against racism."[60] It is not far-fetched to still say that *We Charge Genocide* is the most thorough and well-argued critical assessment of the U.S. government's systematic oppression of African Americans and failure to live up to its ideal democratic values that has ever been written. The petition's authors provided its readers with countless irrefutable cases detailing how, through a complex and systematically orchestrated system, the U.S. government since Reconstruction did very little to protect blacks' most fundamental civil and human rights. Though Patterson's passion and anger flavors this petition, it was written in a scientific, scholarly manner. In using official records, reports, and statistics from the U.S. government, Patterson and the CRC engaged in what Audre Lorde problematized as using the "master's tools to dismantle the master's house." After reading *We Charge Genocide*, it is hard to believe that only several genocide scholars have acknowledged its significance within the context of the evolution of interpretations of genocide. The scholarship of Ann Curthoys and John Docker has perhaps signaled the beginnings of a shift within genocide scholarship. "This petition had until fairly recently been largely forgotten by genocide studies," Curthoys and Docker underscore. "*We Charge Genocide* needs to be featured in the conceptual history of genocide . . . *We Charge Genocide* is a remarkable document."[61]

In introducing *We Charge Genocide*, Patterson referenced articles II and III of the Genocide Convention—especially the clause referring to "acts committed with intent to destroy in whole or in part a national, ethnical or religious group"—and declared that "the oppressed Negro citizens of the United States . . . suffer from genocide as a result of consistent, conscious, unified policies of every branch of government." Patterson viewed himself and the CRC as being representatives and spokespersons for the disempowered, internally colonized black masses mainly in the South's Black Belt, "for every black American whose voice was silenced forever through premature death at the hands of racist-minded hooligans."[62] The CRC called upon the U.N. to hold the government of the United States accountable for its strategically "synchronized" mistreatment of African Americans.

"Here we present the documented crime of federal, state and municipal governments in the United States of America, the dominant nation in the United Nations, against 15,000,000 of its own nationals—the Negro people of the United States. These crimes are of the gravest concern to mankind. The General Assembly of the UN, by reason of the United Nations Charter and the Genocide Convention, itself is invested with power to receive this indictment and act on it."[63] According to the CRC, the U.S. government and the Supreme Court did not use its authority to protect innocent African Americans from systematic killing. By not enforcing the 14th and 15th Amendments, among other essential pieces of legislation, the U.S. government enabled genocide, the CRC argued. The CRC asserted, "Our case is strong because it is true." Armed with undeniable evidence, they asked the General Assembly of the U.N. "to condemn this genocide on the score that it is not only an international crime in violation of the United Nations Charter and the Genocide Convention but that it is a threat to the peace of the world."[64]

In introducing the petition, Patterson and the CRC stressed that the "institutionalized oppression" of African Americans was directly linked to the international struggle for "democracy on a universal scale." While prominent black leaders and intellectuals like Ralph Bunche did not support the CRC's petition, close to one hundred activists signed it, including Du Bois, Harry Haywood, Claudia Jones, Maude White Katz, Louise Thompson Patterson, Paul Robeson and his son, and Mary Church Terrell. *We Charge Genocide* is subdivided into five parts: "The Opening Statement," "The Law and the Indictment," "The Evidence," "Summary and Prayer," and an "Appendix." In "The Opening Statement," Patterson and the CRC provided an assessment of the "historical background of the genocide being committed against the Negro people of the United States" and highlighted that the systematic and openly practiced genocide experienced by thousands of African Americans "for more than three hundred years" is unprecedented. They proceeded to place acts of genocide inflicted upon African Americans within the U.N.'s Genocide Convention, focusing on legal and extralegal murder and economic and political genocide. They pinpointed the capitalist motivations: "The foundation of this genocide of which we complain is economic. It is genocide for profit. The intricate superstructure of 'law and order' and extra-legal terror enforces an oppression that guarantees profit."[65] They characterized the genocide against African Americans as constituting "domestic genocide," yet they also linked this victimization to genocide throughout the world, cautioning that the systematic oppression of African Americans will bolster the oppression of other victims of genocide worldwide. Preceding the internal colonialism theories prevalent during the Black Power era, they described the oppression endured by African Americans as being of the "colonial type." They pointed out that African Americans were murdered and discriminated against because of their "ethnic origin."[66] Though they acknowledged the long history of genocide against their people, Patterson and the CRC focused on providing detailed evidence from January 1, 1945, until June 1951, including lynching, murder, and death at the hands of the police. The CRC acknowledged that the history of genocide against African Americans was rooted in slavery, yet they emphasized that by the mid-twentieth century "murder on the basis of race by police and courts" constituted "an American phenomenon" and "is increasing."[67]

Like Ida B. Wells in her accounts of lynching, they also stressed that their evidence was incomplete. "But by far the majority of the Negro murders are never recorded. . . . The unrecorded deaths are the rule rather than the exception—thus our evidence, though voluminous, is scanty when compared to the actuality."[68] Patterson and the CRC outlined the murders of Willie McGee, James Leon Jr., Charles Trudell, the Martinsville Seven, the Trenton Six, and others as well as numerous cases "typical of police killings" and other murders. They exposed how "high government officials" including the Senate and the House of Representatives participated, in rhetoric and action, in denying blacks their fundamental civil and human rights and, in turn, justified genocide. Patterson and the CRC called out American political leaders for facilitating an environment in which groups like the Ku Klux Klan could terrorize and murder blacks without any consequences.

In "Law and the Indictment," the CRC carefully analyzed the articles of the Genocide Convention as they related to the U.S. government's mistreatment of African Americans. They indicated that contrary to popular belief, genocide is not simply "the complete and utter extermination by force and violence of a people or group" and instead highlighted the clause "acts committed with intent to destroy in whole or in part." The CRC avowed that the U.S. government violated not only the Genocide Convention but also the charter of the United Nations. "The refusal of the United States to carry out the promise of the Charter of the UN is not only an international offense but also a violation of a cardinal principle of the United States law."[69] The CRC stated that members of the U.S. Senate Committee on Foreign Relations, the American Bar Association, and others opposed the ratification of the Genocide Convention because then the U.S. would be guilty based on its treatment of African Americans and would not be able to "continue its present lawless terror."[70]

In part III, "The Evidence," the CRC chronologically cataloged known acts of genocide against African Americans from 1945 until the summer of 1951 that were recorded in leading black newspapers and by civil rights organizations. The CRC detailed the murders of more than 150 blacks at the hands of white civilians and police officers. Building upon scholarship dealing with the psychological impact of segregation and second-class citizenship on blacks, the CRC then listed numerous cases (forty pages of text) of beatings, rape, discrimination, intimidation, and torture that, as stated in article II (b.) of the Genocide Convention, caused "serious bodily and mental harm" to African Americans. The petitioners cited rigorous scientific scholarship that pointed out how these individual cases affected the entire community, socializing them within a genocidal environment. The CRC then indicted the U.S. government under article II (c.) for "deliberately inflicting on the group conditions of life calculated to bring about [blacks'] physical destruction in whole or in part." They argued that many blacks died each year because of ghettoization, unemployment, inferior medical treatment, and other byproducts of segregation. Drawing from Office of Vital Statistics reports for the blacks who died because of genocidal living conditions, they proclaimed: "The number of United States Negroes killed each year by legal and extra-legal lynching is relatively small in comparison with the number wiped out by the imposition of genocidal living conditions."[71] Patterson and the CRC deduced: "Approximately 32,000 United States Negroes are killed each year through the imposition of inferior living and health conditions. This adds up to the snuffing out of almost 200,000 lives by this means alone since the United States signed the United Nations Charter."[72]

The CRC identified the interconnectedness between blacks' deteriorating health conditions (especially diseases), poverty, inferior segregated housing facilities, the American penal system, education, and capitalism. "We find law, wage scales and other economic facts, the legal opinions of the courts, the incitements of officials, the policies and measures of government, legislative acts and failures to act, the deliberate use of the police and the courts, the discriminatory practices of Big Business, discrimination and segregation by federal, state and county governments, all combining over a long period of years to one invariable result—the systematic institutionalized genocidal oppression of the Negro people of the United States for profit."[73] According to the CRC, the profits were beyond several billion dollars. The CRC also dubbed the U.S. a world imperial power whose large profits abroad were directly related to their exploitation of a disenfranchised agricultural and industrial black laboring class who was held in "economic bondage." For the CRC, the denial of black people's right to vote was also crucial. "It is through this device of robbing millions of Americans of their vote that the economic-political conditions for the profitable oppression of the Negro people are maintained." Equally important was the "genocidal nature of segregation." According to the CRC, segregation lead to "'killing members of the group,' to 'serious bodily harm to members of the group,' to 'deliberately inflicting on the group conditions of life calculated to bring about its destruction in whole or in part.'"[74]

In part IV, "Summary and Prayer," Patterson and the CRC underscored that the genocide against blacks by the U.S. government "is an undeniable fact" and asked the General Assembly of the United Nations to find the United States guilty. In the lengthy "Appendix," Patterson and the CRC included cases of violence against blacks in Georgia from 1940 until 1950, cases involving black men disproportionately charged with raping white women in Louisiana, a study of the economic exploitation of blacks in the South, a record of Congress's failure to protect African Americans' rights, and a bibliography.

Internationalizing the African American Struggle against Genocide and Post-CRC Pleas

While *We Charge Genocide* was not adopted by the United Nations and was dismissed by the U.S. government, it contributed to the post-Lemkin evolution of conceptualizations of genocide and helped internationalize African Americans' struggle for human rights during the Cold War era. During the modern civil rights movement and especially the Black Power era, black activists, namely nationalists, radicals, and self-appointed revolutionaries, extended the arguments of Patterson and his CRC co-workers. Though he was not the only driving force behind this post–Cold War movement, Patterson did certainly influence future generations of blacks who cried genocide on behalf of the disempowered and victimized of their people. Hailing from a different generation, Patterson, very much like Ella Baker vis-à-vis SNCC, was sympathetic to the Black Panther Party's program and he spoke out in defense against the violent repression they faced. At the same time, the Black Panther Party was not always enthusiastic about Patterson's paternalistic stance toward them. For instance, in *The Black Panther* (1970) Huey P. Newton offered a direct rebuttal to Patterson's "The Black Panther Party: A Force against U.S. Imperialism," asserting that Patterson presented "a most narrow interpretation" of his organization's program and philosophical roots and underpinnings.[75] The differences between Patterson and Newton were as much philosophical as they were generational.

During the modern civil rights movement, several African American spokespersons accused the United States of committing genocide against their people. After severing his ties from Elijah Muhammad and the Nation of

Islam and then founding the Organization of Afro-American Unity (OAAU) in 1964, Malcolm X (echoing Patterson) moved toward internationalizing the African American struggle. Under the motto "Freedom by any means necessary," at the first public rally for the OAAU in Harlem on June 28, 1964, Malcolm described his organization's international perspective: "One of the first steps we are going to become involved in . . . will be to work with every leader and other organization in this country interested in a program designed to bring your and my problem before the United Nations. This is our first point of business," Malcolm declared. "We must take it out of the hands of the United States government. And the only way we can do this is by internationalizing it and taking advantage of the United Nations Declaration of Human Rights, the United Nations Charter on Human Rights, and . . . bring it into the UN before a world body wherein we can indict Uncle Sam for the continued criminal injustices that our people experience in this government."[76] On February 16, 1965, in one of his last speeches at Corn Hill Methodist Church in Rochester, New York, Malcolm stressed that traditional struggles for civil rights were no longer adequate because they fell "within the jurisdiction" of the U.S. government that denied blacks' their fundamental rights. "For as long as you call it 'civil rights,'" Malcolm explained, "your allies can be the people in the next community, many of whom are responsible for your grievance. But when you call it 'human rights' it becomes international. And then you can take your troubles to the World Court. You can take them before the world. And anybody anywhere on this earth can become your ally." For Malcolm, "our problem was no longer a Negro problem or an American problem but a human problem. A problem for humanity."[77]

Several weeks after founding the OAAU, Malcolm traveled to Cairo, where the Organization of African Unity was meeting. He was received as a delegate for African Americans and "some of the delegates at the meeting even 'promised to officially assist the OAAU in its plan and to give their support during the following session of the United Nations.'"[78] Malcolm sent a petition to the United Nations charging the United States with committing genocide against 22 million blacks. According to Alphonso Pinkney: "As ultimately outlined the petition charged the government of the U.S. with economic genocide, mental harm, murder, conspiracy, and complicity to commit genocide."[79] Like Patterson, Malcolm proclaimed that the United States violated its own constitution, the charter of the United Nations, the Declaration of Human Rights, and the Genocide Convention. In the late 1960s, more than a few black leaders and intellectuals, including Charles V. Hamilton, H. Rap Brown, Samuel DeWitt Proctor, Floyd B. McKissick, Julian Bond, Stokely Carmichael, and Adam Clayton Powell, evoked genocide in reference to African American historical and contemporary life. In the late 1960s Carmichael and other Black Power era radicals claimed that the drafting of black men during the Vietnam War was a form of genocide, and McKissick boldly charged the United States with seeking to exterminate blacks: "Would America systematically destroy 22 million Blacks? My answer is: Look at the record! More specifically, I believe they can. I believe they will."[80] From the early 1960s through the 1970s, the Nation of Islam's paper, *Muhammad Speaks,* routinely used genocide to describe the dangers facing African Americans and regularly cited from the Genocide Convention and charged the United States with orchestrating genocide against African Americans.

In a 1970 *Muhammad Speaks* article, "U.S. Fears to Sign Treaty against Genocide," Lonnie Kashif declared that blacks had "borne the brunt of U.S. genocidal lust" and surmised that the United States failed to sign the Genocide Convention because "the many forms of domestic lynchings and unbridled discrimination so prevalent in the U.S. will be shown to the world."[81] During the Black Power era, Patterson also used *Muhammad Speaks* as a platform for continuing his cause. In "We (Still) Charge Genocide," Patterson maintained that the charges made in *We Charge Genocide* were still valid. "Racism," he pronounced in 1970, "is now a phase of the drive towards a fascist state in the U.S.A." Patterson insisted that the "discriminatory conditions" fostered by the U.S. government resulted in a shorter life span for African Americans, and he compared the killings of black youth in Chicago, New Haven, and Jackson with the killings of civilians in Korea, Cambodia, and Vietnam. "The man who cried genocide" concluded his essay by reiterating that the treatment of blacks in the United States violated the UN's Declaration of Human Rights and the Genocide Convention: "1. Killing of members of the group is notoriously true. 2. The psychological impact of those murders and of jim-crow and segregation in their subtle and covert forms does extreme mental harm to the group. 3. America's racism is bringing about in part the physical destruction of the group and its span of life reveals that fact. 4. Measures to prevent birth within the group are practiced in several states."[82]

On June 18, 1970, as spokesperson for the Committee to Petition the United Nations, Ossie Davis announced to a crowded press conference at the Overseas Press Club in New York that his organization, composed of black and Native American activists, was seeking to secure one hundred thousand signatures charging the United States of committing genocide against "men, women and children of red, brown, yellow and particularly black Americans." The short-lived Committee to Petition the United Nations focused its charges on "savage police activities," "murderous attacks on black youth," "legal frameups," and "the forces of hunger, ignorance, and disease" that "work their natural course," resulting in genocide.[83] Several weeks later, the National Committee of Black Churchmen (NCBC) issued its "Declaration of Independence" in the *New York Times*. With the backing of nine hundred members and some of the most prominent black churchmen of the Black Power era, the NCBC protested against at least fifteen "different forms of 'white racism and repression and genocide' against the black man" and sent their declaration to thousands of churches with black members, "urging the clergy to use it and other materials" for its Sunday services.[84] Calling for an end to the enduring "genocidal practices" employed by the U.S. government, the NCBC adopted the revolutionary rhetoric of the Declaration of Independence and proclaimed: "The history of the treatment of Black People in the United States is a history having in direct Object the Establishment and Maintenance of Racist Tyranny over this People." African Americans, they added, had been repeatedly "lynched, burned, tortured, harried, harassed and imprisoned without Just Cause" and "gunned down in the streets, in our churches, in our homes, in our apartments and on our campuses, by Policemen and Troops who are protected by mock Trial, from Punishment for any Murders which they commit on the Inhabitants of our Communities."[85]

During the early 1970s, discussions of genocide proliferated in black popular culture. As William L. Van Deburg has argued, Black Power era artists and writers "who understood that there was great utility in knowing the enemy" often "warned of genocide" in their novels, plays, poetry, and films. Popular magazines and journals, such as *Jet, Ebony, Freedomways,* and *Essence,* also addressed the issue of genocide during the early 1970s. According to scholars who conducted quantitative research on fears of genocide among blacks toward the end of the Black Power era, "genocidal fears are widely held in the black population" and "factors of age, sex, region and educational level are related to the prevalence of these fears." Moreover, "these results indicate that black Americans have a great deal of fear and distrust of white Americans."[86]

At one level, Dick Gregory—comedian, civil and human rights activist, and leader in the Committee to Petition the United Nations—was probably among the first to popularize discussions of genocide in black middle-class circles during the Black Power era. The featured cover story for *Ebony* magazine in October 1971, arguably black America's most popular magazine at the time, was Gregory's article "My Answer to Genocide."

"My answer to genocide," Gregory opened his commentary, "is eight black kids—and another baby on the way." Gregory challenged Planned Parenthood's suggestion to American families to have two-and-a-half children and considered birth control and abortion "against Nature" and "obvious tactics of genocide." Though not in great detail, Gregory then accurately reviewed

Lemkin's and the United Nations' definitions of genocide, claiming that "less-open acts of genocide occur in America every day" in black communities, acts such as police raids on "black militants," segregation, and mental abuse "that is insidiously and deeply woven into the fabric of the American system." Echoing Patterson, Gregory argued that "segregated housing" made "the ghetto areas breeding grounds for rats, disease and death" and that this "pattern is 'deliberate.'" Gregory also compared blacks' confinement in ghettos to Native Americans' confinement on reservations: both produced high poverty and mortality rates. Gregory concluded his bitterly comedic think piece with a plea to the U.S. government to ratify the Genocide Convention, "exposing this nation to the full weight of international opinion on the matter."[87]

Toward the end of the Black Power era, Robert G. Weisbord published *Genocide? Birth Control and the Black American* (1975), an extension of a 1973 essay he published in *Demography,* "Birth Control and the Black American: A Matter of Genocide?" In his book, Weisbord explored how during the 1960s and early 1970s various groups of African Americans believed "that birth control programs constitute a thinly disguised white plot to commit genocide against people of African extraction in the United States and elsewhere." The importance of Weisbord's study, however, is that he also explored the rising concern with genocide in general among blacks during the Black Power era. Defining genocide based on the Genocide Convention's fundamental definition, Weisbord argued that "an effort to eradicate a portion of a people thus qualifies as genocide insofar as international law is concerned." Weisbord historicized blacks' views of birth control as amounting to genocide by revisiting the "racial drama" of America's past dating back to the violent and murderous nature of the Atlantic slave trade, enslavement, and slavery. "The whole of black American history comprises the back drop against which the genocide fear has evolved," Weisbord asserted.[88] In contextualizing blacks' skepticism toward birth control, Weisbord revealed the troubling history of sexual exploitation, medical experimentation, castration, and sterilization in black communities.

According to Weisbord, blacks began to seriously scrutinize and grapple with birth control after Margaret Sanger founded her clinics and the Birth Control Federation created a Division of Negro Service. The majority of the black leaders and spokespersons during the first half of the twentieth century, however, embraced efforts to encourage blacks, especially the poor, to control and reduce their birth rates. In 1945, pathologist Dr. Julian Lewis became among the first seriously to deem birth control a form of "race suicide," a term later replaced with genocide.[89] Building upon the ideas of Lewis, many African American spokespersons, cosigning with the ideas of many of their counterparts throughout the diaspora, believed that birth control went against the survival of African descendants. Weisbord dubbed this the "'strength in numbers' school of thought." According to this line of thought, if blacks had more representation in an America dominated by pervasive white racism, they would be better equipped to survive, persevere, access power, and combat genocide.

Expanding on Dick Gregory's comments, many African Americans, including H. Rap Brown, Julian Bond, William Darity, Julius Lester, members of the Black Panther Party, writers for the *Black News,* conservative black clergymen, and especially Elijah Muhammad and other spokespersons for the Nation of Islam, "subscribed to the theory that governmental birth control programs designed for indigents are an attempt at genocide" against African Americans.[90] While during the Black Power era a significant group of black feminists and female political figureheads like Shirley Chisholm and Barbara Jordan rejected the argument that birth control was a form of antiblack genocide, other black women, including Nation of Islam and Black Panther Party women and Frances M. Beal, were outspoken in labeling birth control genocide against blacks. "Punitive sterilization" programs like those instituted in Mississippi in the late 1950s and in Illinois and Ohio in the early 1970s, Weisbord noted, also increased blacks' views of birth control as genocide. In response to these policies, SNCC circulated a pamphlet entitled *Genocide in Mississippi.*[91] Even though these "punitive sterilization bills" do not mention race, black women and families were the most affected because blacks were "represented on the welfare rolls out of all proportion to their percentage of the overall population. To that extent an involuntary sterilization requirement would disproportionately affect Afro-Americans." Citing Fannie Lou Hamer's claims, Weisbord rooted blacks' fears of birth control in the guise of sterilization as a form of genocide against black women because there have been rumors that numerous black women were sterilized "through means of deceit and trickery." Weisbord provided a host of controversial case studies, largely overlooked by the mainstream media, that surfaced during the 1970s to argue his point. The Black Panther Party and the Nation of Islam were among the major black organizations to respond to these cases, deeming them "deliberate" acts of "genocidal sterilization."[92]

After analyzing a diverse group of blacks' views of birth control as a form of genocide against African descendants, Weisbord concluded that "contraception, abortion, and sterilization have never been systematically used to exterminate black America." At the same time, he surmised that "there is much in the historical record and in contemporary societal developments to sustain black fears about the existence of such a plan." While sympathetic,

Weisbord rejected radical blacks' claims and "paranoia" of birth control as genocide but understood their roots and adequately contextualized them. Based upon research conducted in the early 1970s, Weisbord concluded that theories of genocide were likely to persist, especially among young black males. "Genocide polemics," Weisbord emphasized, "will surely continue to be heard, for black 'paranoia' is anchored in historical reality." He was correct. Weisbord ended his provocative study, essentially an overview of several decades of black thought regarding the relationship between birth control and notions of genocide, by calling upon the United States to grant black people their fundamental human rights so that "the genocide rhetoric will be muted."[93]

During the 1970s, especially until the decline of the Black Power era in approximately 1975, a diverse group of black activists used genocide as a concept for describing various episodes in African American history as well as contemporary conditions faced by the masses of poor African Americans. Much fewer in numbers, during this pivotal period scholars like Weisbord and Ronald Walters published scholarly studies that transcended their counterparts' rhetoric and polemics. Post–Black Power era scholarly discourse on genocide in the context of the African American experience is scant. In the 1980s, several scholars explored genocide and black America in the *Journal of Black Studies*. Beginning in the 1990s, a group of Afrocentric scholars and Reparations scholar-activists developed genocide paradigms for black American history. And, in the new millennium, several anthologies on genocide have seriously considered using genocide within the context of the African American historical experience.

In 1983, acknowledging the "lack of unanimity within the scientific community regarding the importance of genocide as an issue among Afro-Americans," Walter C. Farrell Jr., Marvin P. Dawkins, and John Oliver examined "the presence of fears of race genocide in a context of selected social background factors in a random sample of Blacks in a rural Texas community."[94] Such a study was conducted a decade ago by two scholars who explored the fears of genocide among 1,890 blacks living in Philadelphia and Charlotte.[95] Farrell, Dawkins, and Oliver conducted similar quantitative research in Waller County, Texas, that had a 53 percent black population. These social scientists interviewed a total of 190 respondents (104 females and 86 males) and recorded their responses pertaining to the relationships between genocide in black communities and birth control and abortion, black population reduction, and attacks on black "militants." These scholars' findings suggested that in this rural, predominantly black Texas community there were noteworthy fears of race genocide, especially among the black male participants.

Among other recommendations, Farrell, Dawkins, and Oliver called for more research on how age influenced blacks' views of genocide and insisted that "organizations be cognizant of the effect of genocide fears on their service programs for the Black community."[96]

Several years later in 1986, Sidney M. Willhelm updated his earlier research in a lengthy article, "The Economic Demise of Blacks in America: A Prelude to Genocide?" arguing that the members of the black underclass were being increasingly and systematically excluded from "the labor market where they are immersed in the economics of exploitation and are entering into the . . . 'economics of uselessness'" and that during the early to mid-1980s the "economic circumstances permit a stronger racialist policy of conditional genocide."[97] Willhelm's argument was certainly controversial. "In other words," he emphasized, "Blacks are hostages to White America today just as surely as they were owned by a White America during slavery. They are not held in bondage as mere particles of ownership, but, nonetheless, their fate remains bound to the same kind of White people, namely, people holding vast resources in the form of property. Just as Whites acted out of property interests to keep Blacks in slavery, today Whites perform in accord with their property interests to eliminate the Black person from the labor processes of production."[98]

In explaining the economic peril that blacks, especially males, faced in the United States, Willhelm borrowed from Jean-Peal Sartre and equated the racial separation and post-*Brown v. Board of Education* segregation that characterized American culture during the 1980s as "conditional genocide." Willhelm contended that blacks have been systematically removed from the viable workforce and that these "genocidal conditions" have forced blacks, especially males, to participate in underground, illegal, and criminal activities. This is the explanation that Willhelm offers with regard to the disproportionate number of black men in the prison industrial complex. He concluded that "several recent developments," such as the "vanishing black family" phenomenon, unequal systems of justice, and blacks' overall "economic demise," resulted in "conditional genocide." Willhelm insisted that "the vanishing Black behind the visible wall of separation under conditional genocide is now beyond dispute."[99]

Maafa: The Disaster of Negation

In the 1990s, economist William Darity Jr. critiqued the National Research Council's report for ignoring "the issue of evidence about the construction and execution of genocidal social policies directed toward the black poor." Darity charged "members of the managerial elite" of creating public policies that embraced "a strategy of preemptive elimination of unborn black babies via population control targeted at the black poor"; for ignoring the heath dilemmas devastating black communities; and for subjecting "black males, in particular, to environments where they can be forgotten or they can die." Darity's conclusions in 1990 were not optimistic. "The most troubling prospect of all is not considered in the NRC report: that a continued black presence is by no means assured. In the transition from capitalism to managerialism, those relegated to the surplus population will find their physical and cultural existence threatened."[100]

Beginning primarily during the 1990s, Afrocentric thinkers expanded on Marimba Ani's theories and described the violent mistreatment and destruction of African peoples for five hundred years as "Maafa," a Kiswahili term meaning "disaster."[101] During the 1990s Ani's conceptualization of "Maafa" became popularized within Afrocentric circles, and she addressed the concept in her exhaustive *Yurugu: An African-Centered Critique of European Cultural Thought* (1994). In *Yurugu,* Ani posits that European and white American culture "has an enormous capacity for the perpetration of physical violence" against those, especially African peoples, they transform into cultural others and render nonhumans. Ani cited the Tuskegee Study and the AIDS epidemic as attempts "to destroy African people," charging the U.S. Public Health Service "with antihuman, genocidal behavior." In discussing AIDS, Ani contended that people of African descent were in the 1980s "being set up as objects of 'justified' genocidal behavior by people of European descent."[102] Asante is among the Afrocentric thinkers who has used genocide and "Maafa" to describe episodes in African American history, borrowing Ani's concept in calling for reparations for African descendants in the United States. Others, including John Henrik Clarke, C. T. Keto, Erriel D. Roberson, Nancy Boyd-Franklin, Delores P. Aldridge, Carlene Young, Kobi K. K. Kambon, and Wade Nobles, have referenced Ani's notion of "Maafa" in characterizing the oppression faced by Africans throughout the diaspora.[103]

In a 2002 essay, psychologist Wade W. Nobles expanded on the importance of the "Maafa" concept. "The Maafa," Nobles said, "is a continual, constant, complete, and total system of human negation and nullification. Fundamentally, the Maafa is the 'denial of the validity of African people's humanity,' accompanied by a collective and ever-present disregard and disrespect for the African and people of African ancestry's 'right to exist.' It gives license to the continual perpetuation of a total systematic and organized process of spiritual and physical destruction of African people both individually and collectively. Hence we cannot be lulled into believing that the experiences of oppression, discrimination, and dehumanization of African American people are past history."[104] A year later, veteran African American studies scholars Delores P. Aldridge and Carlene Young expanded further on Ani's conceptualization in relationship to genocide, highlighting that "Maafa" is "a culturally distinct, self-determined naming of the genocide experienced by Africans under western colonialism and slavery." They continued, "In this context Maafa serves much the same cultural psychological purpose for Africans as the idea of the Holocaust serves to name the culturally distinct Jewish experience of genocide under German Nazism."[105]

Indirect Genocide: The Destruction of the Black Underclass

In the late 1990s, Robert Johnson and Paul S. Leighton published an essay, "American Genocide: The Destruction of the Black Underclass," in a mainstream genocide anthology, extending Willhelm's argument that the black underclass faces genocide in the United States. "We argue that the various calamities and catastrophes to which poor, inner-city African Americans are exposed reflect the operation of genocidal forces in their lives." Johnson and Leighton noted that while genocide scholars have ignored genocide in the context of African American history and many social commentators have scoffed at black activists' charges of genocide against the U.S., "it is entirely possible that the paranoia alluded to is figurative and the feared genocide literal." Drawing on a rather inclusive definition of genocide suggested by Ervin Staub, they avowed that the plight of the black underclass "crosses the threshold of genocide."[106] For them, "the key concept at the core of the notion of genocide is the attempted destruction of a group—an end that can be pursued in various ways." Johnson and Leighton described the genocide that affected the African American underclass as being "indirect genocide," "the imposition of destructive life conditions" that "undermine" blacks' "existence" and contribute significantly to their oppression and decreased life spans. The indirect genocide that African Americans faced in the ghettos persisted, the authors maintained, because it was more subtle. The black masses, in their estimation, lived in a "genocidal environment" that leads to poverty, crime, and other death-inducing situations or "self-inflicted genocide." According to Johnson and Leighton, genocidal conditions and indirect genocide were easily ignored by the white power structure, the perpetrators, because of indirect genocide's subtle nature and its existence outside of the gaze of white America. More than most Afrocentric advocates of "Maafa," Johnson and Leighton grappled with leading genocide scholars' conceptualizations of genocide and concluded that African Americans faced "indirect genocide." "In the face of genocide . . . 'to persist' with destructive policies" that lead to the deaths of members of the black underclass "'is to intend the death of a people.'"[107]

Of the seemingly countless anthologies on genocide published in the new millennium, only a few have included essays on genocide and African Americans. While Ann Curthoys and John Docker have called for the inclusion of *We Charge Genocide* into the complex processes of conceptualizing genocide in *The Historiography of Genocide* (2008), only one essay on blacks has been published in a major mainstream genocide anthology. In *Gendercide and Genocide* (2004), edited by Adam Jones, Augusta C. Del Zotto wrote an essay titled "Gendercide in a Historical-Structural Context: The Case of Black Male Gendercide in the United States." According to Del Zotto, "Unlike many instances of gendercide, when practices involving the systematic elimination of males are situated within specific events involving warfare and political prosecution, the practice of gendercide against African American males follows a long historical continuum and is contingent upon an outspoken de facto war involving race and class."[108]

Gendercide: The (Self-)Destruction of the Black Male

Del Zotto begins her historically rooted discussion by explaining that the "social engineering" of enslaved black males increased their subordination and effectiveness as producers. During the era of slavery, black males were violently coerced to work, weeded out, and "indirectly" killed off when in their old age they were no longer productive. After slavery, Del Zotto proposes, "The public spectacle of targeting and eliminating the black male," especially through lynching, "was a common feature of U.S. society." Moreover, during the era of Jim Crow segregation, poor whites were enlisted by whites in power to help violently control black men. In America during the post–civil rights era, Del Zotto argues that black males have been relegated to the margins of society through direct and indirect genocides. Largely because of negative media portrayals, Del Zotto intimates that black males are criminalized and abused by law enforcement. Black males, for instance, are the victims of police brutality more than any other group. At the dawning of the new millennium, Amnesty International pointed out that there is a problem in the United States concerning the beating, torturing, and killing of "black (overwhelmingly male) motorists who have committed no crime, or who have committed minor violations such as speeding." Building upon the "black male seasoning" theory proposed by Jawanza Kunjufu, Del Zotto indicates that black males are socialized by U.S. society and culture to internalize these negative social constructions and view themselves as being "dangerous and worthless . . . which in turn evolves into acts of self-destruction" and "black-on-black male violence—the first phase of indirect genocide." Del Zotto proposes that while young black men do not commit suicide in great numbers, they do engage in dangerous and death-causing acts in hopes of destroying a self that was created and simultaneously demonized by white America. Del Zotto's essay is intriguing and reiterates several of the arguments posed by Patterson and the CRC, Willhelm, and Johnson and Leighton regarding the "genocidal conditions" experienced by the masses of impoverished African Americans.[109]

Del Zotto's argument belongs to a scholarly trajectory concerning the plight of the black man that dates back to the Black Power era and its immediate aftermath and certainly earlier as well as to a broader body of writings that focus on black men. As the *Washington Post* staff observed in *Being a Black Man: At the Corner of Progress and Peril* (2007), "Over the past 100 years, perhaps no slice of the U.S. population has been more studied, analyzed and dissected than black males. Dozens of governmental boards and commissions have investigated their plight, scholars have researched and written papers on them, and black men have been the subject of at least 400 books."[110] In 1985, the NAACP Legal Defense and Educational Fund labeled young black men "an endangered species." Though they did not directly invoke notions of black male gendercide, they clearly helped introduce the life threatening challenges that black men were facing to the various publics.

In the aftermath of the Black Power era, scholars foreshadowed Del Zotto's argument. In 1978, for instance, James B. Stewart and Joseph W. Scott argued that the imbalance in the sex ratio in the African American community was a byproduct of the "coordinated operation of various institutions in American society which systematically remove Black males from the civilian population." These scholars employed the term "institutional decimation" to describe "the process by which Black males are programmatically eliminated from the Black community." Stewart and Scott argued that there were intimate and complex interconnections between the decimation process of black men, the "politico-socio-economic situation" of black men, the criminalization and militarization of black men, the black male unemployment rates and black males' "economic frustration," poor health care, high mortality rates, "homicidal behavior," and the overall status of the entire black community, especially in economic terms. These scholars concluded their essay in a cautious tone: "If the institutional decimation of the Black male is not halted, we can expect to witness the progressive genocide of Black culture."[111] A decade later, contributors to Jewelle Taylor Gibbs's *Young, Black and Male in America: An Endangered Species* (1988) elaborated on some of the issues raised by Stewart and Scott.[112]

* * *

Since *We Charge Genocide* appeared in 1951, a small group of scholars has proposed analyzing African American history and contemporary life through the complicated lens of genocide. Collectively, these scholars have created an intriguing, important body of scholarship that deserves further consideration and elaboration. Though largely ignored by leading genocide studies scholars, their ideas contribute to ongoing debates concerning what genocide means and can possibly entail. As Dan Stone has underscored, such debates are useful because they can engender "considerable energy and vigor to historiography and broader cultural debates." Black human rights activists, often under the banner of the Reparations movement, have continued charges that Patterson, the CRC, and Malcolm X leveled against the U.S. government for perpetuating genocide against African Americans. Beginning in 1996, responding to what they deemed "revelations that the CIA was involved in the explosion of crack/cocaine in the African communities in America," the National Black United Front (NBUF) instituted a "Genocide Campaign." Founded in 1980, the NBUF has been most concerned with issues such as "quality education for Black children, police and Black community relations, electoral politics, women's affairs, economic development, housing and international affairs," reparations, and the anti-apartheid movement.[113] On May 21, 1997, they submitted petitions with 157,000 signatures from African Americans "who agreed that the United States was involved in acts of genocide against African people in this country" to the Officer in Charge of High Commissions of Human Rights, Centre for Human Rights in Geneva, Switzerland. Recently, in 2007, Conrad W. Worrill, the National Chairman of the National Black United Front, called upon *Chicago Defender* readers and others to rally behind the Reparations movement and the struggle to hold the U.S. accountable for its past and contemporary genocidal treatment of African Americans. "We must continue to make our case in the streets with the masses of people in America that the United States Government is involved in acts of genocide against African people in America and that we are owed reparations," Worrill proclaimed.[114]

For more than half a century, many scholars and activists have offered intriguing arguments for using genocide in reference to black America's past, present, and future. For those familiar with the tragic dimensions and "facts" of the African American historical experience, these thinkers' ideas are informative, relevant, valid, and, at a minimum, understandable. As William L. Patterson and the CRC lamented in 1951, "It was easy for your petitioners to offer abundant proof of the crime. It is everywhere in American life. And yet words and statistics are but poor things to convey the long agony of the Negro people. . . . Three hundred years is a long time to wait."[115] On the other hand, for those uninformed about the harsh realities of black life in North America during the seventeenth and eighteenth centuries and in the United States from 1789 until the present, these thinkers' concepts seem exaggerated, unsubstantiated, radical, and paranoid. It is refreshing that the focus of genocide studies has moved beyond a preoccupation with the widely known genocides. While I concur with Dan Stone that it would be helpful for scholars to develop a somewhat universal definition for genocide, such a consensus is very unlikely. In the poignant words of two scholars, "We can say that as a concept, genocide, born in the turmoil of a world war in one of humanity's most dreadful centuries, continuously interacting with always-disputed historical situations, will continue to be passionately argued and fought over, for it brings to the fore the most fundamental of questions: the character of humanity as a species, history as progress, the ethical bases of societies, and the honour of civilizations and nations."[116] Hopefully, as the ideas of the various scholars and activists surveyed in this chapter have revealed, a lot can be learned by interrogating, exploring, and viewing the African American historical experience through the lens of genocide and genocide studies.

Conclusion

The scholarship and worldviews of members of each of the more than five generations of professionally trained black historians since W. E. B. Du Bois earned a PhD in history from Harvard University in 1895 have been inevitably and distinctly molded and influenced by their upbringings and experiences as well as by the overall historical contexts in which they existed. Black historiography, our collective knowledge of the black experience in America, and the African American historical profession will certainly continue to develop, transform, and blossom with the unknown changes that will occur in the future. Carter G. Woodson's enduring fear that black history needed to be recorded so that African Americans would not become "a negligible factor in the thought of the world" is no longer a realistic concern that causes black scholar-activists anxiety. Still, as we proceed into the twenty-first century, the black historical enterprise stands at an important crossroads, and black historians should think carefully about their roles in the enduring struggle for black equality and cultural and psychological empowerment and liberation. We currently have the luxury of being able to reflect upon more than a century of scholars' and thinkers' thought-provoking interpretations of black history and innovative approaches to the black historical craft. As John Hope Franklin observed in the 1980s (the decade of black history's significant legitimization in "whitestream" higher academe), during the Black Power era the standards for publishing works, especially anthologies, on African American history with profit-seeking publishers were often very low. Today, in part as a result of history PhD programs throughout the nation attempting to graduate students in a more timely fashion than perhaps in previous decades, it is often problematical for nonexceptional history graduate students to discover and pinpoint original dissertation research topics that they can revise and rework as their first monographs. Assistant professors of African American history, moreover, face many challenges in publishing their scholarship. Not only is it becoming increasingly more arduous for them to secure book contracts with leading university presses in African American history and studies, such as the University of Illinois Press, University of North Carolina Press, Indiana University Press, New York University Press, Oxford University Press, Duke University Press, University of Chicago Press, Harvard University Press, and a few others, but there remains one major journal that concentrates on dimensions of African American history, the *Journal of African American History,* the oldest existing scholarly journal devoted to African American history.

Each succeeding generation of black historians encounters a greater responsibility in advancing historiography, demarcating the function of African American history, and rethinking and identifying the multiple meanings and future of the African American historical profession. Since the mainstreaming of African American history in higher education and the inauguration of Black History Month in the post–Black Power era, African American history as a field of critical scholarly inquiry has undergone enormous growth. Today, all major periods of black life from the era of the American Revolution through the modern civil rights movement have been scrutinized and amended, and historians are now expected to acknowledge and explore the vital intersections between a host of factors that highlight the diversity within the black community, including ethnicity and skin complexion, class, region, gender, sexual orientation, religious and political beliefs, and age. Today, there are numerous subfields in African American history that are based on the different major phases and time periods of the African American experience and that recognize those factors that have contributed to the black community's nonmonolithic nature. African American history has also become more theoretical in orientation. Black women's history has developed immensely in the decades since its early formative years in the immediate post–Black Power era. The "four major phases" of black American women's history that Francille Rusan Wilson identified in the Association of Black Women Historian's twentieth-anniversary anthology at the dawning of the twenty-first century have been expanded upon over the last decade.

The historiography on the Black Power era and the period's most characteristic organization, the Black Panther Party, is especially refreshing and innovative. While those active during this crucial period have written and reminisced about the so-called shift from mainstream civil rights tactics to more militant approaches toward black liberation, a dynamic group of hip-hop generation African American historians born during the Black Power era have spearheaded a revisionist historiography, dubbed "Black Power Studies" by Peniel Joseph, author of the most recent encompassing and popular study of the Black Power era, *Waiting 'Til the Midnight Hour: A Narrative History of Black Power in America* (2006). Not only has this new generation of "Black Power Studies" scholars helped deromanticize this period of black cultural rejuvenation, but the young participants of "the new Black Power Movement historiography"—as exemplified by Jeffrey O. G. Ogbar's *Black Power: Radical Politics and African American Identity* (2004); *The Black Power Movement: Rethinking the Civil Rights–Black Power Era* (2006); the *Journal of African American History* 2007 Special Issue, "New Black Power Studies: National, International, and Transnational Perspectives"; and *Souls: A Critical Journal of Black Politics, Culture and Society* 2007 volume on "The New Black Power History"—have also argued that the roots of Black Power precede Stokely Carmichael's and Willie Ricks's 1966 pleas for "Black Power;" that the civil rights and Black Power eras were intimately intertwined; that the social history, and "ordinary" people, of this movement are important; and that "Black Power Studies" requires multidisciplinary approaches. As demonstrated by the numerous articles, monographs, anthologies, plenary sessions, and conferences on dimensions of the Black Power era, this subfield of African American history is one of the most popular and fastest growing in the African American historical enterprise. At a well-attended plenary session at the 93rd Annual Association for the Study of African American Life and History Meeting in 2008, "Perspectives on the New Black Power Scholarship," three hip-hop generation historians explored the dynamic relationships between Black Power–era ideologies, gender, and contemporary African American politics.

At the same time, historians have not yet adequately unraveled the nuances of African American life during the post–Black Power era, 1975 until the dawning of the new millennium. While many political scientists, sociologists, black studies practitioners, and other social scientists and critics have critically examined the contours of black life from the mid-1970s until the present, black historians—perhaps avoiding the perils of presentism or the challenges of contemporary history—have tended to overlook black history in the post–Black Power era. Historians Manning Marable and Robin D. G. Kelley are among the few exceptions. Founder of the Center for Contemporary Black History at Columbia University, Marable has published many important studies on post–Black Power era black history, including *From the Grassroots: Essays toward Afro-American Liberation* (1980); *How Capitalism Underdeveloped Black America: Problems in Race, Political Economy and Society* (1983); *Race, Reform and Rebellion: The Second Reconstruction in Black America, 1945–1982* (1984); *Black American Politics: From Washington Marches to Jesse Jackson* (1985); *Beyond Black and White: Transforming African-American Politics* (1995); *Black Liberation in Conservative America* (1997); and *Living Black History* (2006). Kelley's early scholarship focused on black communists in the South during the Great Depression, yet beginning with *Race Rebels: Culture, Politics, and the Black Working Class* (1994) and *Yo' Mama's Disfunktional! Fighting the Culture Wars in Urban America* (1997), he began exploring post–Black Power era and contemporary dimensions of the African American experience. His *Into the Fire: African Americans Since 1970* (1996) and his chapter in *To Make Our World Anew* (2000) remain several of the most clear and concise studies of post–Black Power era African American history by a professionally trained historian. Other comprehensive and wide-sweeping studies and textbooks on the African American historical experience have also explored in general terms the contours of black life in the 1970s, 1980s, 1990s, and new millennium. Post–Black Power black history will certainly become a popular field of study in African American historiography in the next several decades or so.

More than five years ago, I argued that the black history popularization efforts of Woodson and his co-workers of the early black history movement were more effective and practical than those of the 1990s and early 2000s. I still hold this assessment to be accurate, especially when considering the recent unprecedented developments in multimedia technology and the internet. We have still not fulfilled Woodson's dreams of transforming "Negro History Week," now Black History Month, into what he envisioned as "Negro History Year." During the mid-1950s, still feeling the effects of Woodson's death, in the *Negro History Bulletin* Charles H. Wesley called upon young scholars to be "servants" to "a number of publics," to support the ASNLH, and to help popularize black history. Wesley's plea is still relevant. Hip-hop generation historians can play leading roles in shaping the future of the ASALH, the oldest existing African American historical organization in the world.

At this point, we have the necessary resources and knowledge to truly incorporate black history into U.S. and world history at all levels of education. Sam Wineburg's and Chauncey Monte-Sano's recent findings that black leaders Martin Luther King Jr., Rosa Parks, and Harriet Tubman are the most "famous" historical figures for a diverse group of high school students are intriguing, yet misleading. Based on a simple questionnaire that they distributed to two thousand eleventh and twelfth grade high school students in each state, they optimistically intimated with some precaution that high school teachers throughout the nation, with the help of updated and progressive textbooks, have succeeded in mainstreaming African American history. For those of us engaged in teaching African American history at large, predominantly white universities and elsewhere, Wineburg's and Monte-Sano's findings and conclusions deserve to be scrutinized. At colleges and universities throughout the nation, African American history is still treated as a separate entity from "whitestream" U.S. history, and African Americans appear to still be treated as marginal figures in mainstream U.S. history in all levels of education. At the vast majority of large colleges and universities, black studies courses are disproportionately filled with African American students.

Despite the attacks on black studies in the early part of the present decade in the *Chronicle of Higher Education* and elsewhere, black studies continues to grow in institutions of higher education. As of 2008, there were nearly a dozen universities with doctoral programs in African American Studies, including Temple University, Harvard University, Yale University, University of California-Berkeley, Michigan State University, Northwestern University, Indiana University-Bloomington, the University of Massachusetts Amherst, University of Wisconsin-Milwaukee, Brown University, and the University of Pennsylvania. At the same time, as several black studies scholars noted in a 2008 issue of *Diverse Issues in Higher Education,* no HBCU has a PhD program in African American studies. In 2000, Sundiata Keita Cha-Jua stressed in his essay "Black Studies in the New Millennium: Resurrecting Ghosts of the Past" that black studies scholars needed to return to the ideas of 1960s-era black intellectuals and recognize "the unity of research and social action." Indeed, we need to embrace the National Council of Black Studies' motto of "academic excellence and social responsibility," a fundamental characteristic of the black historical enterprise dating back to its formative years. As Earl E. Thorpe emphasized in his "justification" for black history in the late 1950s and then again in the early 1970s, black history is important because it, simply put, advances our knowledge of the past. Equally important, it remains as a testimony to a people's self-determination, humanity, and abilities to persevere.

Throughout the chapters in this book, I have contended that critically unraveling and deconstructing how scholars and intellectuals have conceptualized and taught about black history and theorized the deeper meanings and potential of the black historical profession are important starting points for understanding the African American experience with all its nuances and complexities. The study, teaching, and popularization of African American history was born in a struggle for liberation and advancement for people of African descent in the United States. In the new millennium, I am certain that I am not alone in having faith in the belief that the historians of the African American experience will continue to correct normative interpretations of U.S. history, challenge the enduring master narratives of American history, revise past interpretations within the profession, generate new ideas, and contribute to the humanizing of American culture.

In ending this book, the conclusion of Du Bois's review of Woodson's *The Education of the Negro Prior to 1861* in *The Crisis* (September 1915) is instructive: "Dr. Woodson's book ends abruptly and may on this account be criticized from a literary point of view. Nevertheless this very point of criticism may be held in favor of the author. It is an excellent habit to stop when you are through."

Notes

Preface

1. Julianne Malveaux and Cornel West, interview by Tavis Smiley, *Tavis Smiley Show*, PBS, August 28, 2008, http://www.pbs.org/kcet/tavissmiley/archive/200808_drsjuliannemalvea .html (accessed August 4, 2009).

2. Barack Obama, speech at the 99th Annual Convention of the NAACP, July 2008, http://www.naacp.org/events/convention/99th/speeches/obama/index.htm (accessed August 13, 2009).

3. Marable Manning, *Living Black History: How Reimagining the African-American Past Can Remake America's Racial Future* (New York: Basic, 2006).

Introduction

1. In dubbing the 1980s the golden age of African American history, I am not arguing that this decade was the most important period in the study of African American history, nor I am arguing that previous periods or decades could not also be called the golden age of the field. One could, for instance, substantially assert that the early black history movement from 1915 until about 1950 or the dynamic 1960s and 1970s represented a golden age of the discipline, especially when viewed within the broader context of the study of African American history. In calling the 1980s the golden age of African American history, I mean that during this decade of the post–civil rights era in the African American experience, the study of African American history not only garnered more serious attention from the American academy and historical profession—as evidenced by the sudden increase in articles dealing with African American subject matter in the *Journal of American History*, the *Journal of Southern History*, and the *American Historical Review* during the 1980s—but the discipline also underwent significant transformations in terms of historiographical developments. Simply put, during the 1980s a significant group of historians, especially African Americans, generated important scholarship that

elevated what Woodson and his contemporaries deemed the systematic, "scientific" study of African American history. At the same time, this golden age of African American history did not in many regards transcend the early black history movement in terms of the popularization of African American history. It could be argued that the golden age in the popularization of African American history spanned from the founding of "Negro History Week" in 1926 until approximately Woodson's death in 1950.

2. Earle E. Thorpe has arguably contributed the most to scholarship pertaining to the philosophy of black history. Today, there are very few books that delve into the philosophy of African American history. Chapter 1 of this study is important in addressing this void.

3. African American history has been "legitimate" in the eyes of African American historians since the antebellum era. The white American academy did not accept African American history until much later, during the Black Power era. William H. Harris posited that black history became a "legitimate and respected field" in 1974 and that the "legitimization" of black history was taking place during the mid-1980s. See William H. Harris, "Trends and Needs in Afro-American Historiography," in *The State of Afro-American History,* ed. by Darlene Clark Hine (Baton Rouge: Louisiana State University Press, 1986), 139.

4. Lawrence W. Levine, "The Unpredictable Past: Reflections on Recent American Historiography," *American Historical Review* 94 (June 1989): 673.

5. Robert L. Harris Jr., "Review: The Flowering of Afro-American History," *American Historical Review* 92 (December 1987): 1150–51.

6. William H. Harris, "Trends," 153; David Levering Lewis, "Radical History: Toward Inclusiveness," *Journal of American History* 76 (September 1989): 472.

7. A comprehensive roll call of all of the important studies in African American history published during the 1980s is not necessary. A perusal of the monographs published in the 1980s in African American history speaks to this assertion.

8. For a list of other key studies in black women's history published in the 1980s, see Wilma King, "African American Women," in *The African American Experience: An Historiographical and Bibliographical Guide,* ed. by Arvarh E. Strickland and Robert E. Weems Jr., 71–92 (Westport, Conn.: Greenwood, 2001).

9. John Hope Franklin, "Afro-American History: State of the Art," *Journal of American History* 75 (June, 1988): 162–73. Franklin did not acknowledge the work of Earl E. Thorpe in chronicling the lives and works of black historians before Meier and Rudwick. See Earl E. Thorpe, *Black Historians: A Critique* (New York: William Morrow, 1971), an updated version of his 1958 study *Negro Historians.*

10. Earle E. Thorpe, "Review," *Journal of Negro History* [hereinafter *JNH*] 78 (Spring 1993): 126.

11. For a discussion of the problems faced by black studies in terms of independence, see Noliwe M. Rooks, *White Money/Black Power: The Surprising History of African American Studies and the Crisis of Race in Higher Education* (Boston: Beacon, 2006).

12. Earl Lewis, "To Turn as on a Pivot: Writing African Americans into a History of Overlapping Diasporas," *American Historical Review* 100 (June 1995): 765–66.

13. August Meier and Elliott Rudwick, *Black History and the Historical Profession, 1915–1980* (Urbana: University of Illinois Press, 1986), 117.

14. In chronological order, the articles by black scholars in the *Journal of American*

History during the 1980s include David Levering Lewis, "Parallels and Divergences: Assimilationist Strategies of Afro-American and Jewish Elites from 1910 to the Early 1930s," 71 (December 1984): 543–64; Nell Irvin Painter, "Bias and Synthesis in History," 73 (March 1987): 109–12; Deborah Gray White, "Mining the Forgotten: Manuscript Sources for Black Women's History," 73 (March 1987): 237–42; Clayborne Carson, "Martin Luther King, Jr.: Charismatic Leadership in a Mass Struggle," 74 (September 1987): 448–54; James H. Cone, "Martin Luther King, Jr. and the Third World," 74 (September 1987): 455–67; Vincent Gordon Harding, "Beyond Amnesia: Martin Luther King, Jr. and the Future of America," 74 (September 1987): 468–76; Nathan Irvin Huggins, "Martin Luther King, Jr.: Charisma and Leadership," 74 (September 1987): 477–81; Vincent Gordon Harding, "Wrestling Toward the Dawn: The Afro-American Freedom Movement and the Changing Constitution," 74 (December 1987): 718–39; John Hope Franklin, "Afro-American History," 75 (June 1988): 163–73; Paul Buhle and Robin D. G. Kelley, "The Oral History of the Left in the United States: A Survey and Interpretation," 76 (September 1989): 537–50.

15. Benjamin Quarles, "Sources of Abolitionist Income," *Mississippi Valley Historical Review* 32 (June 1945): 63–76; Benjamin Quarles, "The Colonial Militia and Negro Manpower," *Mississippi Valley Historical Review* 45 (March 1959): 643–52; John Hope Franklin, "The North, the South, and the American Revolution," *Journal of American History* 62 (June 1975): 5–23.

16. My discussion of the numbers of black historians who published articles in the leading mainstream U.S. historical journals from the early twentieth century through the 1980s is based upon my examination of volumes of these journals that were available on JSTOR. I also focused on identifying the well-known, prolific black historians who published in these journals.

17. John Hope Franklin, *Mirror to America: The Autobiography of John Hope Franklin* (New York: Farrar, Straus and Giroux, 2005).

18. For Thorpe, Meier and Rudwick were "blind-sided" by "some of the negatives in the dominant culture." Thorpe indicted Meier and Rudwick for not including nonprofessionally trained black historians, ignoring key scholarship published on black historians, failing to investigate the "motivations" of black historians, and for overlooking the limitations of their "oral history technique." See Thorpe, "Review," 123–27. For another insightful critique of Meier and Rudwick's study, see John H. Stanfield, "Review," *Contemporary Sociology* 16 (September 1987): 612–14.

19. Lewis, "Radical History," 472.

20. Earl E. Thorpe, "Philosophy of History: Sources, Truths, and Limitations," *Quarterly Review of Higher Education Among Negroes* 25 (July 1957): 183; John Hope Franklin, "On the Evolution of Scholarship in Afro-American History," in Hine, *State of Afro-American History*, 13.

21. "In Selecting a Course Major Only a Tiny Percentage of African-American College Students Choose Black Studies," *Journal of Blacks in Higher Education* 49 (2005): 42–44; Robin Wilson, "Past Their Prime?" *Chronicle of Higher Education* 51 (April 22, 2005): A9–11.

22. Kelley's study was reviewed widely. The most extensive and strong review of Kelley's study was written by David Roediger, "Where Communism Was Black," *American Quarterly* 44 (March 1992): 123–28.

23. Robin D. G. Kelley, *Hammer and Hoe: Alabama Communists during the Great Depression* (Chapel Hill: University of North Carolina Press, 1990); Robin D. G. Kelley, *Race Rebels: Culture, Politics, and the Black Working Class* (New York: Free Press, 1994); Robin D. G. Kelley, *Yo' Mama's Disfunktional: Fighting the Culture Wars in Urban America* (Boston: Beacon, 1997). Kelley also deals with contemporary African American history in Robin D. G. Kelley and Earl Lewis, eds., *To Make Our World Anew: A History of African Americans* (New York: Oxford University Press, 2000).

24. William Jelani Cobb, *The Devil and Dave Chappelle and Other Essays* (New York: Thunder's Mouth, 2007), 255. Cobb makes reference to a host of historical personalities, organizations, movements, time periods, and events, including Tom Molineaux, Jack Johnson, W. E. B. Du Bois, Booker T. Washington, Ida B. Wells, the NACW, Paul Laurence Dunbar, Joe Louis, Paul Robeson, Martin Luther King Jr., Malcolm X, Muhammad Ali, *Brown v. Board of Education,* the civil rights movement, and slavery.

25. William Jelani Cobb, "I Am a Man," in *The Black Male Handbook: A Blueprint for Life,* ed. Kevin Powell, 189 (New York: Atria, 2008).

26. V. P. Franklin, "Jackanapes: Reflections on the Legacy of the Black Panther Party for the Hip Hop Generation," *Journal of African American History,* 92 (Fall 2007): 559.

27. Marable, *Living Black History,* xx, 21, 33.

28. Marable, *Living Black History,* 36–37.

29. Thorpe, *Black Historians,* 3.

30. Regan Toomer, "Decades in the Making," *Philadelphia Tribune,* May 23, 2006, 1A.

31. V. P. Franklin and Bettye Collier-Thomas, "Biography, Race Vindication, and African-American Intellectuals: Introductory Essay," *JNH* 81 (Winter—Autumn 1996): 1–16. In the same year the *JNH* called for a reinvestigation into African American intellectual history, William Banks published *Black Intellectuals: Race and Responsibility in American Life* (New York: Norton, 1996). While William Banks attempted to fill in what John Hope Franklin identified as a "void" in the "overall history of African American intellectuals," Banks did not propose a conceptualization of African American intellectual history.

32. John Hope Franklin, "Foreword," in Banks, *Black Intellectuals.*

33. Wilson Jeremiah Moses, *Creative Conflict in African American Thought: Frederick Douglass, Alexander Crummell, Booker T. Washington, W. E. B. Du Bois, and Marcus Garvey* (New York: Cambridge University Press, 2004), xii.

Chapter 1: Conceptualizing Black History, 1903–2006

1. William Jelani Cobb, ed., *The Essential Harold Cruse: A Reader* (New York: Palgrave, 2002), 209.

2. Thorpe, *Black Historians,* 3.

3. Earl Ofari Hutchinson, "Black History Is U.S. History: It's Time to Put the Role of Blacks on Center Stage," *San Francisco Chronicle,* February 8, 1999, A-21; Earl Ofari Hutchinson, "The Childish Debate over Black History Month," http://www.blackpower .com/arts-culture/the-childish-debate-over-black-history-month (accessed August 4, 2009).

4. Marable, *Living Black History,* 73, 79.

5. For discussions of the approaches of black historians from the antebellum era until

the founding of the ASNLH, see Thorpe, *Black Historians;* Elizabeth Rauh Bethel, *The Roots of African-American Identity: Memory and History in Antebellum Free Communities* (New York: St. Martin's, 1997); John Ernest, *Liberation Historiography: African American Writers and the Challenge of History, 1794–1861* (Chapel Hill: University of North Carolina Press, 2004); Ralph L. Crowder, *John Edward Bruce: Politician, Journalist, and Self-Trained Historian of the African Diaspora* (New York: New York University Press, 2004); Pero G. Dagbovie, *Black History: "Old School" Black Historians and the Hip Hop Generation* (Troy, Michigan: Bedford Publishers, 2006), 147–93; Stephen G. Hall, *A Faithful Account of the Race: African American Historical Writing in Nineteenth-Century America* (Chapel Hill: University of North Carolina Press, 2009).

6. W. E. B. Du Bois, *The Souls of Black Folk* (New York: Dover, 1995), 2–3.

7. Du Bois, *Souls of Black Folk,* 163 (emphasis added).

8. Du Bois, *Souls of Black Folk,* 3.

9. Du Bois, *Souls of Black Folk,* 4, 18.

10. Du Bois, *Souls of Black Folk,* 3.

11. Herbert Aptheker, ed., *Book Reviews by W .E. B. Du Bois* (Millwood, New York: KTO Press, 1977), 67–68. Du Bois's review of *The Negro Church* was originally published in the *Freeman,* October 4, 1922, 92–93.

12. Carter G. Woodson, "Negro History Week," *JNH* 13 (April 1928): 121–25; Carter G. Woodson, "Notes," *JNH* 13 (January 1928): 112.

13. Carter G. Woodson, "Negro History Week," *JNH* 11 (April 1926): 238–39.

14. Woodson, "Negro History Week," 11: 239.

15. Carter G. Woodson, "The Celebration of Negro History Week, 1927," *JNH* 12 (April 1927): 105.

16. Edward Hallett Carr, *What Is History?* (New York: Knopf, 1963), 15.

17. Carter G. Woodson, "The Annual Report of the Director," *JNH* 12 (October 1927): 573.

18. Thorpe, *Black Historians,* 4, 18; Nathan I. Huggins, "Integrating Afro-American History into American History," in Hine, ed., *State of Afro-American History,* 166–67.

19. Carter G. Woodson, "Timely Suggestions for Negro History Week," *Negro History Bulletin* 1 (February 1938): 11.

20. Arthur Schomburg, "The Negro Digs Up His Past," in *The New Negro,* ed. Alain Leroy Locke, 231–32 (New York: Atheneum, 1969).

21. Charles H. Wesley, "The Reconstruction of History," *JNH* 20 (October 1935): 411, 421–22.

22. L. D. Reddick, "A New Interpretation for Negro History," *JNH* 22 (January 1937): 17, 19, 21, 27.

23. Reddick, "New Interpretation," 19. See Robin D. G. Kelley, *Race Rebels: Culture, Politics, and the Black Working Class* (New York: Free Press, 1994), 1–13. Kelley dubbed "Black history from below" as being "Black history from way, way below."

24. Reddick, "New Interpretation," 27.

25. William T. Fontaine, "'Social Determination' in the Writings of Negro Scholars," *American Journal of Sociology* 49 (1944): 302, 303, 310, 313.

26. Fontaine, "'Social Determination,'" 306, 309; Thorpe, *Black Historians,* 18.

27. Ellen Wright and Michael Fabre, eds., *Richard Wright Reader* (New York: Harper, 1978), 240.

28. John Hope Franklin, "History—Weapon of War and Peace," *Phylon* 5 (1944): 249–50, 255–57, 259.

29. John Hope Franklin, "Whither Reconstruction Historiography?" *Journal of Negro Education* [hereinafter *JNE*] 17 (Autumn 1948): 448, 454.

30. John Hope Franklin, *From Slavery to Freedom: A History of Negro Americans* (New York: Vintage, 1969), xii.

31. Herbert Aptheker, *Negro Slave Revolts in the United States, 1526–1860* (New York: International Publishing, 1939), 69–70.

32. Herbert Aptheker, "Negro History: Arsenal for Liberation," *New Masses*, 11 February 1947, 12.

33. Benjamin Quarles, "Review: Memo's to Clio," *JNE* 26 (Autumn 1957): 478.

34. Herbert Aptheker, introduction to *A Documentary History of the Negro People in the United States,* vol. 1 (New York: Citadel, 1968). For Cruse's critique of Aptheker, see Harold Cruse, *The Crisis of the Negro Intellectual* (New York: Quill, 1984), 471–72, 505–8, 511–17. For Greene's description of Aptheker, see Harry Washington Greene, *Holders of Doctorates among American Negroes: An Educational Study of Negroes Who Have Earned Doctoral Degrees in Course, 1876–1943* (Boston: Meador, 1948).

35. Robin D. G. Kelley, "Afterword," *Journal of American History* (June 2000), http://www.historycooperative.org/journals/jah/87.1/afterword.html (accessed July 9, 2009). For more information about Herbert Aptheker, see Herbert Shapiro, ed., *African American History and Radical Historiography: Essays in Honor of Herbert Aptheker* (Minneapolis: MEP, 1998); Christopher Lehman-Haupt, "Herbert Aptheker, 87, Dies; Prolific Marxist Historian," *New York Times,* March 20, 2003, B8 (L); Robin D. G. Kelley, "Interview of Herbert Aptheker," *Journal of American History* (June 2000), http://www.historycooperative.org/journals/jah/87.1/interview.html (accessed July 9, 2009).

36. John Hope Franklin, "The New Negro History," *JNH* 42 (April 1957): 89–97.

37. Franklin, "New Negro History," 95.

38. Earl E. Thorpe, *Negro Historians in the United States* (Baton Rouge: Fraternal Press, 1958), 9, 151.

39. Samuel Du Bois Cook, "A Tragic Conception of Negro History," *JNH* 45 (October 1960): 219–40.

40. William Van Deburg, *New Day in Babylon: The Black Power Movement and American Culture, 1965–1975* (Chicago: University of Chicago Press, 1992), 280, 2–10.

41. Malcolm X, *The Autobiography of Malcolm X* (New York: Ballantine, 1965), 175, 180.

42. Benjamin Goodman, ed., *The End of White World Supremacy: Four Speeches* (New York: Monthly Review, 1971), 26–27.

43. Malcolm X, *Malcolm X on Afro-American History* (New York: Pathfinder, 1988), 4–5.

44. Van Deburg, *New Day in Babylon,* 2, 8.

45. Franklin, "Pioneer Negro Historians," 4.

46. Cruse, *Crisis,* 533, 564.

47. Cruse, *Crisis,* 565.

48. Vincent Harding, "The Uses of the Afro-American Past," *Negro Digest* 17 (February 1968): 5–6, 81.

49. Vincent Harding, *Beyond Chaos: Black History and the Search for the New Land* (Atlanta: Institute of the Black World, 1970), 7, 16, 26–27.

50. John Henrik Clarke, "The Meaning of Black History," *Black World* 20 (February 1971): 27, 34, 36.

51. Sterling Stuckey, "Twilight of Our Past: Reflections on the Origins of Black History," in *Amistad 2*, ed. John A. Williams and Charles F. Harris (New York: Vintage, 1971), 270–72.

52. Sterling Stuckey, "Twilight of Our Past," 290, 293; Meyer Weinberg, ed., *W. E. B. Du Bois: A Reader* (New York: Harper, 1970), 239.

53. I. A. Newby, "Historians and Negroes," *JNH* 54 (January 1969): 32–33.

54. Thorpe, *Black Historians*, 3–4.

55. Thorpe, *Black Historians*, 4.

56. Haki Madhubuti, *Enemies: Clash of Races* (Chicago: Third World, 1978), 14, 17.

57. For a detailed discussion of Quarles's "Black History's Diversified Clientele" (in Quarles, *Black Mosaic: Essays in Afro-American Historiography* [Amherst: University of Massachusetts Press, 1988, 202–13]), see Pero Gaglo Dagbovie, *The Early Black History Movement, Carter G. Woodson, and Lorenzo Johnston Greene* (Urbana: University of Illinois Press, 2007), 217–19.

58. Vincent Harding, *There Is a River: The Black Struggle for Freedom in America* (New York: Vintage Books, 1983), xix.

59. August Meier, "Whither the Black Perspective in Afro-American Historiography?" *Journal of American History* 70 (June 1983): 101–5.

60. Harris, "Trends," 153.

61. Nathaniel Norment Jr., ed., *The African American Studies Reader* (Durham: Carolina Academic Press, 2001), xxiii.

62. Maulana Karenga, *Introduction to Black Studies* (Los Angeles: University of Sankore Press, 1989), 31, 43.

63. Quarles, *Black Mosaic*, 181.

64. After a survey of *Ebony* magazines from the late 1950s through the 1990s, I located three major articles in which Bennett directly attempted to define black history as an ideology, a philosophy, a spiritual concept, and/or a field of study. He has published countless articles on many different aspects of black history in *Ebony*. Among some of his other articles that address the meaning of black history are: "Reading, 'Riting and Racism," *Ebony* 22 (March 1967): 130–38; "Guardian of the Truth of Black History," *Ebony* 35 (February 1980): 94–98; "The Ten Biggest Myths about Black History," *Ebony* 39 (February 1984): 25–32.

65. Lerone Bennett Jr., "Listen to the Blood: The Meaning of Black History," *Ebony* 36 (February 1981): 35–36.

66. Bennett, "Listen to the Blood," 36, 38, 42.

67. Lerone Bennett Jr., "Why Black History Is Important to You," *Ebony* 37 (February 1982): 61, 62, 66.

68. Lerone Bennett Jr., "Voices of the Past Speak to the Present," *Ebony* 40 (February 1985): 27–28.

69. V. P. Franklin, *Black Self-Determination: A Cultural History of the Faith of the Fa-*

thers (Westport: Lawrence Hill, 1984), 4. This book was later republished in 1992 as *Black Self-Determination: A Cultural History of African American Resistance.*

70. Ronald E. Butchart, "'Outthinking and Outflanking the Owners of the World': A Historiography of the African American Struggle for Education," *History of Education Quarterly* 28 (Autumn 1988): 333.

71. Harris, "Coming of Age," 116.

72. Robert L. Harris Jr., *Teaching African American History* (Washington, D.C.: American Historical Association, 1992), ix.

73. Darlene Clark Hine, preface to *Black Women in America: An Historical Encyclopedia*, ed. by Hine, Elsa Barkley Brown, and Rosalyn Terborg-Penn, xix (Bloomington: Indiana University Press, 1993).

74. For a brief review of the 1970s historiography in black women's history, see Rosalyn Terborg-Penn, "Teaching the History of Black Women: A Bibliographical Essay," *History Teacher* 13 (February 1980): 245–50. For definitions of black women's history that preceded Hine's from the 1990s, see Toni Cade, ed., *The Black Woman: An Anthology* (New York: A Mentor Book, 1970), 9; Angela Davis, "Reflections on the Black Woman's Role in the Community of Slaves," *Black Scholar* 3 (December 1971): 15; Gerda Lerner, *Black Women in White America: A Documentary History* (New York: Vintage Books, 1972), xix–xx; Sharon Harley and Rosalyn Terborg-Penn, eds., *The Afro-American Woman: Struggles and Images* (New York: Kennikat, 1978), ix; Michele Wallace, *Black Macho and the Myth of the Superwoman* (New York: Warner, 1978), 25, 248, 250; Paula Giddings, *When and Where I Enter: The Impact of Black Women on Race and Sex in America* (New York: Bantam, 1984), 6; White, *Ar'n't I a Woman*, 23.

75. Hine, preface to *Black Women in America*, xix.

76. Darlene Clark Hine, *Hinesight: Black Women and the Reconstruction of American History* (New York: Carlson, 1994), xxi.

77. Evelyn Brooks Higginbotham, "African-American Women's History and the Metalanguage of Race," *Signs* 17 (Winter 1992): 251, 274.

78. W. D. Wright, *Critical Reflections on Black History* (Westport, Conn.: Praeger, 2002), 19.

79. W. D. Wright, *Black History and Black Identity: A Call for a New Historiography* (Westport, Conn.: Praeger, 2002), 55.

80. Joe William Trotter, *The African American Experience* (New York: Houghton Mifflin, 2001); Clayborne Carson, Emma J. Lapsansky-Werner, and Gary B. Nash, *African American Lives: The Struggle for Freedom* (New York: Longman, 2005); Darlene Clark Hine, William C. Hine, and Stanley Harrold, *The African American Odyssey* (New Jersey: Prentice Hall, 2005); Nell Irvin Painter, *Creating Black Americans: African-American History and Its Meanings, 1619 to the Present* (New York: Oxford University Press, 2006).

81. Donald Spivey, *Fire from the Soul: A History of African American Struggle* (Durham: Carolina Academic Press, 2003), xiv.

82. Spivey, *Fire from the Soul*, x.

83. Marable, *Living Black History*, 36–37, 22, xiv–xv.

84. Marable, *Living Black History*, xx, 1, 20–21.

85. Marable, *Living Black History*, 14, 19.

86. Marable, *Living Black History*, xx.

Chapter 2: Approaches to Teaching and Learning African American History

1. Quarles, *Black Mosaic*, 185.

2. Carlos A. Brossard, "Classifying Black Studies Programs," in Norment, ed., *African American Studies Reader,* 65–67; Maulana Karenga, *Introduction to Black Studies* (Los Angeles: University of Sankore Press, 1982), 35–38; Molefi Kete Asante, "African American Studies: The Future of the Discipline," *Black Scholar* 22 (1992): 26; Hine, ed., *State of Afro-American History,* ix.

3. Nell Irvin Painter, *Creating Black Americans: African-American History and Its Meaning, 1619 to the Present* (New York: Oxford University Press, 2006), ix–x.

4. Mary Taylor Huber and Pat Hutchings, *The Advancement of Learning: Building the Teaching Commons* (San Francisco: Jossey-Bass, 2005).

5. Sam Wineburg, *Historical Thinking and Other Unnatural Acts: Charting the Future of Teaching the Past* (Philadelphia: Temple University Press, 2001), viii–ix.

6. James H. Cones III and Joseph L. White, *Black Man Emerging: Facing the Past and Seizing a Future in America* (New York: Routledge, 1999), 49.

7. Asante, "African American Studies," 24; C. Tsehloane Keto, *The African-Centered Perspective of History* (Blackwood, N.J.: K & A Publishers, 1991).

8. James D. Anderson, "How We Learn About Race through History," in *Learning History in America: Schools, Culture, and Politics,* ed. William L. Barney, Lloyd S. Kramer, and Donald Reid, 102–3 (Minneapolis: University of Minnesota Press, 1994).

9. Darlene Clark Hine, William C. Hine, and Stanley Harrold, *The African American Odyssey: Combined Volume,* 2nd ed. (New Jersey: Prentice Hall, 2005), 125, 148–49; John Hope Franklin, *The Free Negro in North Carolina, 1790–1860* (Chapel Hill: University of North Carolina Press, 1943); Ira Berlin, *Slaves without Masters: The Free Negro in the Antebellum South* (New York: Oxford University Press, 1974), iii. For a discussion of the life-threatening challenges faced by free blacks in the North, see Leonard P. Curry, *The Free Black in Urban America, 1800–1850: The Shadow of the Dream* (Chicago: University of Chicago Press, 1981).

10. Douglas A. Blackmon, *Slavery by Another Name: The Re-Enslavement of Black Americans from the Civil War to World War II* (New York: Doubleday, 2008), 5.

11. Darlene Clark Hine, "Black Professionals and Race Consciousness: Origins of the Civil Rights Movement, 1890–1950," *Journal of American History* 89 (March 2003): 1294; Gilmore, *Defying Dixie*, 1–12.

12. Peter C. Seixas, Peter N. Stearns, and Samuel S. Wineberg, eds., *Knowing, Teaching, and Learning History: National and International Perspectives* (New York: New York University Press, 2000), 8–9.

13. Diana Oblinger, "Boomers, Gen-Exers, and Millenials: Understanding the New Students," *Educause Review* 38.4 (July/August 2003): 40.

14. Meier taught at Tougaloo. See August Meier, *A White Scholar and the Black Community, 1945–1965* (Amherst: University of Massachusetts Press, 1992), 8–10.

15. Carter G. Woodson, "Negro Life and History in Our Schools," *JNH* 4 (July 1919): 278; Meier and Rudwick, *Black History and the Historical Profession*, 109, 134, 127.

16. For a discussion of Johnson's work, see Thorpe, *Black Historians,* 149–50. For a discussion of Durham, see William Toll, "Free Men, Freedmen, and Race: Black Social Theory in the Gilded Age," *Journal of Southern History* 44 (November 1978): 571–96. Toll asserted that Durham influenced the thought of black intellectuals during "the nadir," as did Du Bois.

17. See, for example, L. V. Williams, "Teaching Negro Life and History in Texas High Schools," *JNH* 20 (January 1935): 13–18; William Loren Katz, "Black History in Secondary Schools," *JNE* 38 (Autumn 1969): 430–34; Richard M. Merelman, "Black History and Cultural Empowerment: A Case Study," *American Journal of Education* 101 (August 1993): 331–58; Jacqui Grice and Evelyn Sweerts, "Hitting the Right Note: How Useful Is the Music of African-Americans to Historians?" *Teaching History* (September 2002): 36–41.

18. Seixas, Stearns, and Wineberg, eds., *Knowing, Teaching, and Learning History,* 2.

19. Woodson, "Annual Report of the Director," *JNH* 14 (October 1929): 367.

20. J. W. Bell, "The Teaching of Negro History," *JNH* 8 (April 1923): 123; J. A. Bailey, "Perspective in the Teaching of Negro History," *JNH* 20 (January 1935): 26.

21. Samuel E. Warren, "A Partial Background for the Study and Development of Negro Labor: An Adventure in Teaching Certain Aspects of American Labor History," *JNH* 25 (January 1940): 47.

22. Wiliam M. Brewer, "The Teaching of Negro History in Secondary Schools," *JNH* 36 (January 1951): 71.

23. R. O. Johnson, "Teaching Negro History to Adults," *JNH* 36 (April 1951): 197.

24. Rita M. Cassidy, "Black History: Some Basic Reading," *History Teacher* 2 (May 1969): 36–39; Leroy F. Psencik, "Teaching Black History in Secondary Schools: A Bibliography," *History Teacher* 6 (May 1973): 375–82; James M. Sears, "Black Americans and the New Deal," *History Teacher* 10 (November 1976): 89–105; Rosalyn Terborg-Penn, "Teaching the History of Black Women: A Bibliographic Essay," *History Teacher* 13 (February 1980): 245–50.

25. Davis D. Joyce and Michael W. Whalon, "An Experimental Course in Black History," *History Teacher* 4 (November 1970): 34.

26. Dominic Candeloro, "Undergraduates as Historians: Recovering the History of a Black Community," *History Teacher* 7 (November 1973): 25, 27.

27. Melvin Drimmer, "Teaching Black History in America: What Are the Problems?" *JNE* 38 (Autumn 1969): 440, 442.

28. Drimmer, "Teaching Black History in America," 442.

29. Edwin S. Redkey, "On Teaching and Learning Black History in the Secondary Schools," in *Black Studies in the University: A Symposium,* ed. Armstead L. Robinson, Craig C. Foster, Donald H. Ogilvie, and Black Student Alliance at Yale, 182 (New Haven: Yale University Press, 1969).

30. Nathan Hare, "The Teaching of Black History and Culture," *Social Education* 33 (1969): 386–87, 388.

31. Louis R. Harlan, "Tell It Like It Was: Suggestions on Black History," *Social Education* 33 (1969): 390–95. For those who share Harlan's questioning of the black nationalist view of teaching black history, see Letitia W. Brown, "Why and How the Negro in History," *JNE* 38 (Autumn 1969): 447–52; Mark M. Krug, "On Teaching Negro History," *School Review* 77 (March 1969): 1–17; William Bruce Wheeler, "Teaching Negro History in the Public Schools: Let's Not Repeat Our Mistakes," *JNE* (Winter 1970): 91–95.

32. John W. Blassingame, "Black Studies and the Role of the Black Historian," in *New Perspectives on Black Studies,* ed. Blassingame, 224 (Urbana: University of Illinois Press, 1971); Blassingame, "Black Studies: An Intellectual Crisis," in *New Perspectives on Black Studies,* 149–68.

33. B. Lee Cooper, "Popular Music: An Untapped Resource for Teaching Contemporary Black History," *JNE* 48 (Winter 1979): 20, 22, 36, 33–35.

34. Bettye J. Gardner, "The Teaching of Afro-American History in Schools and Colleges," in Hine, ed., *State of Afro-American History,* 177.

35. Harris, *Teaching African-American History,* x.

36. Rhonda Y. Williams, "Raising the Curtain: Performance, History, and Pedagogy," in *Teaching the American Civil Rights Movement: Freedom's Bittersweet Song,* ed. Julie Buckner Armstrong, Susan Hult Edwards, Houston Bryan Roberson, and Rhonda Y. Williams, 76 (New York: Routledge, 2002).

37. Beverly A. Bunch-Lyons, "A Novel Approach: Using Fiction by African American Women to Teach Black Women's History," *Journal of American History* 86 (March 2000): 1708. While this is the first article on the teaching of African American history in colleges and universities in the twenty-first century, Bunch-Lyons piece is not the most recent study on this topic; that is, rather, "Strategies for Teaching African American History: Musings from the Past, Ruminations for the Future," *JNE* 75 (Fall 2006): 635–48, by Pero Gaglo Dagbovie, which lays the foundation for this chapter.

38. Daina Ramey Berry, "Teaching *Ar'n't I a Woman?*" *Journal of Women's History* 19 (Summer 2007): 139–45.

39. Brossard, "Classifying Black Studies Programs," in Norment, ed., *African American Studies Reader,* 67.

40. Stephen Brookfield, "Critically Reflective Practice," *Journal of Continuing Education in the Health Professions* 18 (Fall 1998): 197–205.

41. "African Americans Continue to Make Solid Gains in Bachelor and Master Degree Awards: But Professional and Doctoral Degrees Show Declines," *Journal of Blacks in Higher Education* 60 (Summer 2008): 56–61.

42. Gloria Ladson-Billings, "Toward a Theory of Culturally Relevant Pedagogy," *American Educational Research Journal* 32 (Autumn 1995): 476.

43. Heather E. Bruce and Bryan Dexter Davis, "Slam: Hip-hop Meets Poetry—A Strategy for Violence Intervention," *English Journal* 89 (May 2000): 122.

44. Derrick P. Alridge, "Teaching Martin Luther King, Jr. and the Civil Rights Movement in High School History Courses: Rethinking Content and Pedagogy," in Armstrong, Edwards, Roberson, and Williams, eds., *Teaching the American Civil Rights Movement: Freedom's Bittersweet Song,* 13.

45. Blake Harrison and Alexander Rappaport, *Hip-Hop U.S. History: The New and Innovative Approach to Learning American History* (Maine: Cedar Mill, 2006), 4–5.

46. For a detailed discussion of the scholarship on hip hop, see Derrick Alridge's, "From Civil Rights to Hip Hop: Toward a Nexus of Ideas," *Journal of African American History* 90 (Summer 2005): 226–52. For an extensive analysis of hip hop's historicism, see Pero Gaglo Dagbovie, "'Of All Our Studies, History is Best Qualified to Reward Our Research': Black History's Relevance to the Hip Hop Generation," *Journal of African American History* 90 (Summer 2005): 299–323.

47. Tricia Rose, *Black Noise: Rap Music and Black Culture in Contemporary America* (Middletown, Conn.: Wesleyan University Press, 1994), 2–3.

48. Molefi Kete Asante, *The Afrocentric Idea* (Philadelphia: Temple University Press, 1998), 50.

49. James B. Stewart, "Will the Revolution Be Digitized? Using Digitized Resources in Undergraduate Africana Studies Courses," *Western Journal of Black Studies* 27 (Fall 2003): 194. For a discussion of the "racial digital divide," see Tyrone D. Taborn, "Closing the Racial Digital Divide," in *The Covenant,* ed. Tavis Smiley, 215–21 (Chicago: Third World Press, 2006).

50. Smiley, ed., *Covenant,* 222.

51. Marable, *Living Black History,* 22.

52. James A. Banks, "Teaching Black History with a Focus on Decision Making," *Social Education* 35 (1971): 741.

53. Bakari Kitwana, *The Hip Hop Generation: Young Blacks and the Crisis in African American Culture* (New York: Basic, 2003); Todd Boyd, *The New H.N.I.C.: The Death of Civil Rights and the Reign of Hip Hop* (New York: New York University Press, 2002).

54. Thad Sitton, "Black History from the Community: The Strategies of Fieldwork," *JNE* 50 (Spring 1981): 181.

55. See James W. Loewen, *Lies My Teacher Told Me: Everything Your American History Textbook Got Wrong* (New York: Simon and Schuster, 2007); Sam Wineburg, *Historical Thinking and Other Unnatural Acts: Charting the Future of Teaching the Past* (Philadelphia: Temple University Press, 2001).

56. Peter Kolchin, "Slavery in United States Survey Textbooks," *Journal of American History* 84 (March 1998): 1425.

57. James D. Anderson, "Secondary School History Textbooks and the Treatment of Black History," in Hine, ed., *The State of Afro-American History,* 273.

58. Derrick P. Alridge, "The Limits of Master Narratives in History Textbooks: An Analysis of Representations of Martin Luther King, Jr.," *Teachers College Record* 108 (April 2006): 663–64.

59. See, for example, "John Hope Franklin: Historian of the Century," *Journal of Blacks in Higher Education* (December 31, 1996), 84; *JNH* 85 (Winter 2000). Also see Beverly Jarrett, ed., *Tributes to John Hope Franklin: Scholar, Mentor, Father, Friend* (Columbia: University of Missouri Press, 2003).

60. Charles Pete Banner-Haley, "Book Reviews," *Journal of Southern History* 68 (August 2002): 669.

61. Robin D. G. Kelley and Earl Lewis, eds., *To Make Our World Anew: A History of African Americans* (New York: Oxford University Press, 2000), ix.

62. Joe William Trotter, *The African American Experience* (Boston: Houghton Mifflin, 2001), xiii.

63. Hine, Hine, and Harrold, *The African-American Odyssey,* xxv.

64. Clayborne Carson, Emma J. Lapsansky-Werner, and Gary B. Nash, *African American Lives: The Struggle for Freedom* (New York: Pearson Longman, 2004), xvii–xviii.

65. Painter, *Creating Black Americans,* xiii.

66. John E. Fleming, "African-American Museums, History, and the American Ideal," *Journal of American History* 81 (December 1994): 1021, 1026.

67. Thomas Bender, Philip M. Katz, Colin A. Palmer, and the Committee on Graduate Education in the American Historical Association, *The Education of Historians for the Twenty-First Century* (Urbana: University of Illinois Press, 2004), 24.

Chapter 3: Carter G. Woodson's Appeal, *Black History, and Black Radical Thought*

1. For a recent assessment of Carter G. Woodson, see Dagbovie, *The Early Black History Movement, Carter G. Woodson, and Lorenzo Johnston Greene.*

2. See http://www.images.nicekicks.com/images/black-history-month-air-force-ones-dr-woodson-3.jpg. (accessed on November 21, 2008).

3. Cedric J. Robinson, *Black Marxism: The Making of the Black Radical Tradition* (London: Zed, 1983), 259.

4. Adolph Reed Jr. argues that decades after the decline of the Black Power era, black radicalism was appropriated and commercialized by, among others, black public intellectuals. See Adolph Reed Jr., *Class Notes: Posing as Politics and Other Thoughts on the American Scene* (New York: New Press, 2000).

5. Jacqueline Goggin, *Carter G. Woodson: A Life in Black History* (Baton Rouge: Louisiana State University Press, 1993), 140, 145–53. Goggin provides a fascinating narrative of Woodson's early political activism. For instance, while Goggin posits that Woodson "became more radical as he grew older," she chronicles his early expressions of radical activism with much of its nuances. While he supported A. Philip Randolph and Chandler Owen by joining the Friends of Negro Freedom in 1920 and even called Randolph a "twentieth-century prophet," he did not agree with Randolph's and Owen's critiques of Marcus Garvey.

6. For intriguing discussions of the relationship between conservatism and radicalism in African American thought and leadership approaches, see the introduction to and various chapters in *Black Conservatism: Essays in Intellectual and Political History,* ed. by Peter Eisenstadt (New York: Garland, 1999). Also see Christopher Alan Bracey, *Saviors or Sellouts: The Promise and Peril of Black Conservatism, from Booker T. Washington to Condoleezza Rice* (Boston: Beacon, 2008).

7. For discussions of racism in the academy and the historical profession during the late nineteenth century and the early twentieth century, see Peter Novick, *That Noble Dream: The "Objectivity Question" and the American Historical Profession* (Cambridge: Cambridge University Press, 1988); Meier and Rudwick, *Black History and the Historical Profession;* Lewis, "To Turn as on a Pivot," 765–87; Michael R. Winston, "Through the Back Door: Academic Racism and the Negro Scholar in Historical Perspective," *Daedalus* 100 (Summer 1971): 678–719.

8. For a discussion of heretical black radical thought, see Anthony Bogues, *Black Heretics, Black Prophets: Radical Political Intellectuals* (New York: Routledge, 2003).

9. Daryl Michael Scott, ed., *Carter G. Woodson's Appeal* (Washington, D.C.: ASALH Press, 2008), xii.

10. Scott, ed., *Woodson's Appeal,* xiv.

11. Goggin, *Carter G. Woodson,* 94.

12. Jonathan Silverman, "A 'Dove with Claws'? Johnny Cash as Radical," *Journal for the Study of Radicalism* 1.2 (2007): 92–93.

13. Herbert H. Haines, *Black Radicals and the Civil Rights Mainstream, 1954–1970* (Knoxville: University of Tennessee Press, 1988), 7.

14. See Glenda Gilmore, *Defying Dixie: The Radical Roots of Civil Rights* (New York: Norton, 2008). Highlighting the contributions of Lovett Fort-Whiteman and Pauli Murray, Gilmore argues that there existed a radical group of important black communists, socialists, and activists who laid the foundations for the modern civil rights movement in the South by contributing to the dismantling of Jim Crow segregation.

15. Professionally trained, black doctoral scholars during the early twentieth century have not traditionally been heralded for their radicalism. For studies that have identified professionally trained black scholars as being radical, see Jonathan Scott Holloway, *Confronting the Veil: Abram Harris Jr., E. Franklin Frazier, and Ralph Bunche, 1919–1941* (Chapel Hill: University of North Carolina Press, 2002); Anthony Platt, *E. Franklin Frazier Reconsidered* (New Brunswick: Rutgers University Press, 1991); Kenneth Robert Janken, *Rayford W. Logan and the Dilemma of the African-American Intellectual* (Amherst: University of Massachusetts Press, 1993). Most of the scholars who have written on Du Bois have acknowledged his radicalism. Though he does not explicitly theorize him within the context of black radicalism, the title of Manning Marable's study assumes Du Bois's connection with black radicalism. See Marable, *W. E. B. Du Bois: Black Radical Democrat* (Boston: Twayne, 1986). Among non–Du Bois biographers, Du Bois is often considered a leading black radical thinker.

16. Harris, "Trends and Needs," 152.

17. Herbert Aptheker, "The Nature of African-American History," *Souls: A Critical Journal of Black Politics, Culture, and Society* 1 (Fall 1999): 42.

18. W. E. B. Du Bois, *The Souls of Black Folk: Essays and Sketches* (Chicago: McClurg, 1903), 203.

19. Kelly Miller, "Radicals and Conservatives," in *Radicals and Conservatives, and Other Essays on the Negro in America* (New York: Schoken, 1968), 25, 31, 37, 38.

20. On the covers of *The Messenger,* Randolph and Owen advertised the magazine in different ways. On several covers, they hailed their magazine being the "only radical negro magazine in America."

21. A. Philip Randolph and Chandler Owen, "The Negro—A Menace to Radicalism," *Messenger* (March 1919): 20.

22. A. Philip Randolph and Chandler Owen, "The Negro Radicals," *Messenger* 2 (October 1919): 20, 17, 18.

23. Ralph J. Bunche, *A Brief and Tentative Analysis of Negro Leadership* (New York: New York University Press, 2005).

24. Gunnar Myrdal, *An American Dilemma: The Negro Problem and Modern Democracy,* vol. 1 (New York: Harper, 1962), 752, 720.

25. August Meier, *Negro Thought in America, 1880–1915: Racial Ideologies in the Age of Booker T. Washington* (Ann Arbor: University of Michigan Press, 1963), 74, 77, 78, 168–69.

26. For a discussion of the varieties of black nationalism, see August Meier, Elliott Rudwick, and John Bracey Jr., *Black Nationalism in America* (Indianapolis: Bobbs-Merrill,

1970); Wilson Jeremiah Moses, *The Golden Age of Black Nationalism, 1850–1925* (New York: Oxford University Press, 1978).

27. Robinson, *Black Marxism*, 97, 273, 285, 287, 323.

28. Gayraud Wilmore, *Black Religion and Black Radicalism: An Interpretation of the Religious History of African Americans* (New York: Orbis, 1998), xiii, ix.

29. During the 1960s and 1970s black activists were routinely referred to as being radical and militant, and radicalism is often associated with the Black Power era. For some recent examples, see Cedric Johnson, *Revolutionaries to Race Leaders: Black Power and the Making of African American Politics* (Minneapolis: University of Minnesota Press, 2007); Curtis J. Austin, *Up against the Wall: Violence in the Making and Unmaking of the Black Panther Party* (Fayetteville: University of Arkansas Press, 2006); Jama Lazerow and Yohuru Williams, eds., *In Search of the Black Panther Party: New Perspectives on a Revolutionary Movement* (Durham: Duke University Press, 2006); Peniel E. Joseph, *Waiting 'til the Midnight Hour: A Narrative History of Black Power in America* (New York: Henry Holt, 2006); Peniel E. Joseph, ed., *The Black Power Movement: Rethinking the Civil Rights–Black Power Era* (New York: Routledge, 2006); James Tyner, *The Geography of Malcolm X: Black Radicalism and the Remaking of American Space* (New York: Routledge, 2006); Jeffrey Ogbonna Green Ogbar, *Black Power: Politics and African American Identity* (Baltimore: Johns Hopkins University Press, 2004); Scot Brown, *Fighting for US: Maulana Karenga, the US Organization, and Black Cultural Nationalism* (New York: New York University Press, 2003); Komozi Woodward, editorial advisor, and Randolph H. Boehm, *The Black Power Movement: Part I, Amiri Baraka from Black Arts to Black Radicalism* (Bethesda, Md.: University Publishers of America, 2000); Komozi Woodward, *A Nation within a Nation: Amiri Baraka (LeRoi Jones) and Black Politics* (Chapel Hill: University of North Carolina Press, 1999). Throughout African American historiography, black communists are referred to as being radical. See, for instance, Gilmore, *Defying Dixie;* Walter T. Howard, ed., *Black Communists Speak on Scottsboro: A Documentary History* (Philadelphia: Temple University Press, 2008); Carole Boyce Davies, *Left of Marx: The Political Life of Black Communist Claudia Jones* (Durham: Duke University Press, 2007); Mark Solomon, *The Cry Was Unity: Communists and African Americans, 1917–36* (Jackson: University of Mississippi Press, 1998); Kelley, *Hammer and Hoe;* Mark Naison, *Communists in Harlem During the Depression* (Urbana: University of Illinois Press, 1983); Nell Irvin Painter, *The Narrative of Hosea Hudson: His Life as a Negro Communist in the South* (Cambridge: Harvard University Press, 1979). For black radicals in the context of socialism, see Winston James, "Being Red and Black in Jim Crow America: On the Ideology and Travails of Afro-America's Socialist Pioneers, 1877–1930," in *Time Longer than Rope: A Century of African American Activism, 1850–1950,* ed. Charles M. Payne and Adam Green, 336–99 (New York: New York University Press, 2003).

30. Winston James, *Holding Aloft the Banner of Ethiopia: Caribbean Radicalism in Early Twentieth-Century America* (New York: Verso, 1998), 292.

31. Robin D. G. Kelley, *Race Rebels: Culture, Politics, and the Black Working Class* (New York: Free Press, 1994).

32. Robin D. G. Kelley, *Freedom Dreams: The Black Radical Imagination* (Boston: Beacon Press, 2002), 6.

33. Bogues, *Black Heretics, Black Prophets;* Tyner, *The Geography of Malcolm X,* 8, 9, 13.

34. Erik S. McDuffie, "'[She] devoted twenty minutes to condemning all other forms of government but the Soviet': Black Women Radicals in the Garvey Movement and the Left during the 1920s," in *Diasporic Africa: A Reader,* ed. Michael A. Gomez, 339 (New York: New York University Press, 2006).

35. For a basic discussion of the black promoters of the Harlem renaissance, see Cary D. Wintz, *Black Culture and the Harlem Renaissance* (Houston: Rice University Press, 1988).

36. Scott, ed., *Woodson's Appeal,* 96–97.

37. Scott, ed., *Woodson's Appeal,* 99, 101.

38. Scott, ed., *Woodson's Appeal,* 101–8.

39. Scott, ed., *Woodson's Appeal,* 103–9.

40. For discussions of race vindication in African American history, see V. P. Franklin, *Living Our Stories, Telling Our Truths: Autobiography and the Making of the Black Intellectual Tradition* (New York: Scribners, 1995); V. P. Franklin and Bettye Collier-Thomas, "Biography, Race Vindication, and African-American Intellectuals: Introductory Essay," *JNH* 81 (Winter—Autumn 1996): 1–14; and Pero G. Dagbovie, "Inspiring, Historicizing, and Defending the Race: African American Historians during the 'Nadir,' 1890–1920," *Contours: A Journal of the African Diaspora* 3 (Fall 2005): 113–38.

41. Scott, ed., *Woodson's Appeal,* 2.

42. Maghan Keita, *Race and the Writing of History: Riddling the Sphinx* (New York: Oxford University Press, 2000), 57, 61.

43. Scott, ed., *Woodson's Appeal,* 21.

44. Scott, ed., *Woodson's Appeal,* 20.

45. Scott, ed., *Woodson's Appeal,* 2.

46. Scott, ed., *Woodson's Appeal,* 3.

47. Earl Ofari Hutchinson, *"Let Your Motto Be Resistance": The Life and Thought of Henry Highland Garnet* (Boston: Beacon Press, 1972), 161, 162, 166. For Garnet as a radical, see Joel Schor, *Henry Highland Garnet: A Voice of Black Radicalism in the Nineteenth Century: His Anti-Slavery and Civil Rights Role to 1865* (Westport, Conn.: Greenwood, 1977).

48. Scott, ed., *Woodson's Appeal,* 42.

49. For the phrase "Speak truth to power," see Darlene Clark Hine, *Speak Truth to Power: Black Professional Class in United States History* (New York: Carlson, 1996).

50. Scott, ed., *Woodson's Appeal,* 129.

51. Scott, ed., *Woodson's Appeal,* 69.

52. Scott, ed., *Woodson's Appeal,* 109–13, 116.

53. Scott, ed., *Woodson's Appeal,* 119.

54. Scott, ed. *Woodson's Appeal,* 143, 144, 145, 151.

55. Scott, ed., *Woodson's Appeal,* 167.

56. Scott, ed., *Woodson's Appeal,* 147.

57. For an analysis of Woodson's *The Mis-Education of the Negro,* see Dagbovie, *The Early Black History Movement,* 68–73.

58. Scott, ed., *Woodson's Appeal,* 76.

59. Scott, ed., *Woodson's Appeal,* 83.

60. Scott, ed., *Woodson's Appeal*, 91.

61. Booker T. Washington, "The Case of the Negro," *Atlantic Monthly* 84 (1899): 577–87.

Chapter 4: *"Ample Proof of This May Be Found"*: Early Black Women Historians

1. Pauline Hopkins, *Contending Forces: A Romance Illustrative of Negro Life in the North and South* (New York: Oxford University Press, 1988), 14.

2. Deborah Gray White, ed., *Telling Histories: Black Women Historians in the Ivory Tower* (Chapel Hill: University of North Carolina Press, 2008). In "Introduction: A Telling Story," White dubs the black women historians featured in this volume the "spiritual descendants" of black clubwomen like Fannie Barrier Williams. White also offers a compelling explanation for black women's late entry into the U.S. historical profession. Her discussion of "could-be black women historians" is especially intriguing. See pp. 1–27.

3. Rayford W. Logan, *The Negro in American Life and Thought: The Nadir, 1877–1901* (New York: Dial Press, 1954); William M. Banks, *Black Intellectuals: Race and Responsibility in American Life* (New York: Norton, 1996). For discussions of Progressive Era black male leaders' opposition to their female counterparts, see Beverly Guy-Sheftall, *Daughters of Sorrow: Attitudes toward Black Women, 1880–1920* (New York: Carlson Publishing, 1990); Patricia Morton, *Disfigured Images: The Historical Assault on Afro-American Women* (New York: Greenwood, 1991), 37–50, 55–85, 99–102; Deborah Gray White, *Too Heavy a Load: Black Women in Defense of Themselves, 1894–1994* (New York: Norton, 1999), 56–68; Alfred A. Moss Jr., *The American Negro Academy: Voice of the Talented Tenth* (Baton Rouge: Louisiana State University Press, 1981), 78. For a different discussion, see Rosalyn Terborg-Penn, "Black Male Perspectives on the Nineteenth-Century Woman," in *The Afro-American Woman: Struggles and Images,* ed. Sharon Harley and Terborg-Penn, 28–42 (New York: National University Publications, 1978).

4. Stephanie Shaw, *What a Woman Ought to Be and Do: Black Professional Women Workers during the Jim Crow Era* (Chicago: University of Chicago Press, 1996), 3.

5. Giddings, *When and Where I Enter*, 7.

6. In 1891, Anna J. Cooper noted in *The Southland* that only twenty-nine black women earned bachelor's degrees. See Anna Julia Cooper, "The Higher Education of Women," in *Black Women in Higher Education: An Anthology of Essays, Studies, and Documents*, ed. Elizabeth L. Ihle, 58 (New York: Garland, 1992). In the 1920s, the first four black women earned doctorates. In addition to Cooper, the fourth black woman to earn a PhD, this pioneering group included Georgiana R. Simpson, Eva B. Dykes, and Sadie T. M. Alexander. During the first half of the twentieth century, the presence of black women doctorates in all fields combined was very limited. According to Harry Washington Greene's research, forty-six to forty-eight black women received PhDs by 1943. The vast majority of these women were engaged in education in some manner. See, Greene, *Holders of Doctorates*, 22–29.

7. White, ed., *Telling Histories*, 13.

8. For a discussion of black professionals' "parallel institutions" and the concept of "parallelism" during the era of segregation, see Hine, "Black Professionals and Race Consciousness," 1279–94.

9. In 1979, black women historians created the still-active Association of Black Women Historians, Inc. (ABWH), the first professional organization for black women historians. See Darlene Clark Hine, "Black Women's History at the Intersection of Knowledge," in *Black Women's History and the Intersection of Knowledge and Power: ABWH's Twentieth Anniversary Anthology*, ed. Rosalyn Terborg-Penn and Janice Sumler-Edmond, 3–12 (Acton, Mass.: Tapestry, 2000); Francille Rusan Wilson, "Our Foremothers' Keepers: The Association of Black Women Historians and Black Women's History," in Terborg-Penn and Sumler Edmond, eds., *Black Women's History*, 13–24.

10. Francille Rusan Wilson, "Our Foremothers' Keepers," 13; Darlene Clark Hine, "Black Women's History," 4.

11. Meier and Rudwick, *Black History and the Historical Profession*, xii.

12. Carter G. Woodson, "Negro Historians of Our Times," *Negro History Bulletin* 8 (April 1945): 155–59, 166; see also Thorpe, *Negro Historians in the United States*; Thorpe, *Black Historians*; Benjamin Quarles, "Black History's Antebellum Origins," *American Antiquarian Society* 89 (1979): 89–122; Franklin, "On the Evolution of Scholarship in Afro-American History"; John Hope Franklin, *George Washington Williams: A Biography* (Chicago: University of Chicago Press, 1985); Wilson J. Moses, *Afrotopia: The Roots of African American Popular History* (Cambridge: University of Oxford Press, 1998); Julie Des Jardins, *Women and the Historical Enterprise in America: Gender, Race, and Politics of Memory, 1880–1945* (Chapel Hill: University of North Carolina Press, 2003); Hall, *A Faithful Account of the Race*.

13. Moses, *Afrotopia*, 1.

14. Claudia Tate, *Domestic Allegories of Political Desire: The Black Heroine's Text at the Turn of the Century* (New York: Oxford University Press, 1992), 5.

15. Tate, *Domestic Allegories of Political Desire*, 19.

16. Thorpe, *Black Historians*, 144. Thorpe's "historians without portfolio" include Arthur Schomburg, John Wesley Cromwell, John R. Lynch, Henry A. Wallace, John Edward Bruce, Edward Austin Johnson, Laura Eliza Wilkes, Theophilus Gould Steward, William Henry Crogman Sr., Kelly Miller, and J. A. Rogers.

17. Des Jardins, *Women and the Historical Enterprise*, 8. For her detailed discussions of black women historians, see 118–42, 145–76.

18. This represents only a handful of the total number of black women "historians without portfolio" during the era of segregation. This chapter does not address the many black women "historians without portfolio" within the ASNLH during Woodson's years. This has already been extensively treated. See Pero Gaglo Dagbovie, "Black Women, Carter G. Woodson, and the Association for the Study of Negro Life and History, 1915–1950," *Journal of African American History* 88 (Winter 2003): 21–41

19. There were other women besides Merze Tate who received doctorates during the 1930s and 1940s whose dissertations dealt with historical subject matter. This larger group included scholars like Marie Carpenter, Jean Hamilton Walls, Nancy Wooldridge, Hilda Lawson, and Irene Caldwell Malvan Hypps.

20. Bettye Collier-Thomas, "F. E. W. Harper: Abolitionist and Feminist Reformer, 1825–1911," in *African American Women and the Vote, 1837–1965*, ed. Ann D. Gordon with Bettye Collier-Thomas, et al., 41 (Amherst: University of Massachusetts Press, 1997).

21. Frances Smith Foster, introduction to *Iola Leroy, or Shadows Uplifted* by Frances E. W. Harper (New York: Oxford University Press, 1988), xxvii; Hazel V. Carby, *Reconstructing*

Womanhood: The Emergence of the Afro-American Woman Novelist (New York: Oxford University Press, 1987), 63–64.

22. Melba Joyce Boyd, *Discarded Legacy: Politics and Poetics in the Life of Frances E. W. Harper, 1825–1911* (Detroit: Wayne State University Press, 1994), 172, 174, 175, 176, 177.

23. Harper, *Iola Leroy*, 199, 57, 219, 235, 246.

24. Carby, *Reconstructing Womanhood*, 92.

25. Hopkins, *Contending Forces*, 13.

26. Hopkins, *Contending Forces*, xxviii; John Cullen Gruesser, preface to *The Unruly Voice: Rediscovering Pauline Elizabeth Hopkins*, ed. Gruesser (Urbana: University of Illinois Press, 1996), ix.

27. Hopkins, *Contending Forces*, 14.

28. Hopkins, *Contending Forces*, 14–15.

29. Martha H. Patterson, "'Kin' o' Rough Jestice Fer a Parson'": Pauline Hopkins's *Winona* and the Politics of Reconstructing History," *African American Review* 32.3 (Autumn 1998): 445. In discussing John Brown, she relied on Franklin B. Sanborn's *Life and Times of John Brown* (1885).

30. C. K. Doreski, "Inherited Rhetoric and Authentic History: Pauline Hopkins at the Colored American Magazine," in Gruesser, ed. *The Unruly Voice*, 72, 74, 82.

31. Ira Dworkin, ed., introduction to *Daughter of the Revolution: The Major Nonfiction Works of Pauline E. Hopkins* (New Brunswick: Rutgers University Press, 2007), xix–xlii.

32. According to Martha H. Patterson, of a total circulation of 15,000–16,000 per month, about 5,000 issues of the Colored American Magazine were purchased by whites. See Patterson, "Kin' o' Rough Jestice," 458.

33. Dworkin, ed., *Daughter of the Revolution*, 115, 344.

34. Joanne Braxton, introduction to Mrs. N. F. Mossell, *The Work of the Afro-American Woman* (New York: Oxford University Press, 1988), xxvii, xxix; Mossell, *Work of the Afro-American Woman*, 9.

35. Mossell, *Work of the Afro-American Woman*, 26.

36. Mossell, *Work of the Afro-American Woman*, 48–49.

37. Patricia Romero, ed., *Susie King Taylor, Reminiscences of My Life in Camp with the 33rd U.S. Colored Troops, Late 1st South Carolina Volunteers* (New York: M. Wiener Publishing, 1988), 7–17.

38. Thomas Wentworth Higginson, introduction to Romero, ed., *Susie King Taylor*, 23.

39. Romero, ed., *Susie King Taylor*, 107–8, 141–42.

40. Romero, ed., *Susie King Taylor*, 119–20.

41. See Laura Wilkes, *The Story of Frederick Douglass, with Quotations and Extracts* (Washington, D.C., 1899).

42. Laura Wilkes to Carter G. Woodson, July 22, 1921, quoted as it appears in Des Jardins, *Women and the Historical Enterprise*, 150.

43. Des Jardins, *Women and the Historical Enterprise*, 150.

44. Laura E. Wilkes, foreword to *Missing Pages in American History, Revealing the Services of Negroes in the Early Wars in the United States of America, 1641–1815* (Washington, D.C.: R. L. Pendleton, 1919). In addition to various state archives and state histories, this work includes Nell's scholarship, Bancroft's *History of the United States*, Wilson's *Camp*

Fires of Afro-Americans, and several state studies on slavery. Wilkes drew from a wide range of sources and provided her reader with a helpful index.

45. Wilkes, foreword to *Missing Pages in American History.*

46. Leila Amos Pendleton, *A Narrative of the Negro,* electronic edition (Chapel Hill: University Library, University of North Carolina at Chapel Hill, 2004), 3.

47. W. E. B. Du Bois, *The Negro* (New York: Oxford University Press, 1970), 3.

48. Pendleton, *Narrative of the Negro,* 46, 59, 90, 93.

49. Jessie Fauset, "What to Read," *The Crisis,* August 1912, 183.

50. See Leila Amos Pendleton, "Our New Possessions—The Danish West Indies," *JNH* 2 (1917): 267–88. Pendleton wrote several short stories in *The Crisis* in the early 1920s. See Marcy Knopf, *The Sleeper Wakes: Harlem Renaissance Stories by Women* (New Brunswick: Rutgers University Press, 1993), 159–69.

51. Delilah L. Beasley, foreword to *The Negro Trail Blazers of California* (Los Angeles, 1919).

52. Beasley, *Negro Trail Blazers,* 121–22.

53. "Book Reviews," *JNH* 5 (January 1920): 129.

54. Elizabeth Ross Haynes, foreword to *Unsung Heroes* (New York: Du Bois and Dill, 1921); Francille Rusan Wilson, introduction to *Unsung Heroes; The Black Boy of Atlanta; "Negroes in Domestic Service in the United States,"* by Elizabeth Ross Haynes (New York: G. K. Hall, 1997), xx, xxii. For a further discussion of Haynes as a social scientist, see Francille Rusan Wilson, *The Segregated Scholars: Black Social Scientists and the Creation of Black Labor Studies, 1890–1950* (Charlottesville: University of Virginia Press, 2006), 6–7, 107–13, 203–8.

55. Elizabeth Ross Haynes, "Negroes in Domestic Service in the U.S.," *JNH* 8 (October 1923): 384–442.

56. Elizabeth Lindsay Davis, foreword to *The Story of the Illinois Federation of Colored Women's Clubs* (New York: G. K. Hall, 1997).

57. Wanda Hendricks has posited that much of what were currently know about the efforts of black club women is "due to the commitment" of Davis. See Wanda Hendricks, "Davis, Elizabeth Lindsay," in *Black Women in America: An Historical Encyclopedia,* volume 1, *A–L,* ed. Darlene Clark Hine, Elsa Barkley Brown, and Rosalyn Terborg-Penn, 306 (Bloomington: Indiana University Press, 1993).

58. W. Paul Coates, "Drusilla Dunjee Houston: An Introductory Note about the Author and Her Work," in *Wonderful Ethiopians of the Ancient Cushite Empire,* Book 1, Drusilla Dunjee Houston, i–v (Baltimore: Black Classic, 1985); Houston, *Wonderful Ethiopians of the Ancient Cushite Empire,* 8, 9.

59. Houston, *Wonderful Ethiopians,* 11–12.

60. Arvil Johnson Madison and Dorothy Porter Wesley, "Dorothy Porter Wesley: Enterprising Steward of Black Culture," *Public Historian* 17 (Winter 1995): 22. This article is invaluable. It is an oral history interview conducted in three sessions between Madison and Porter Wesley from January 28, 1993, to February 10, 1994. Ms. Madison, director for the Voting Rights Act: Oral History and Documentation Project at Moorland-Spingarn Research Center, posed open-ended questions to Wesley.

61. Madison and Wesley, "Dorothy Porter Wesley," 22, 28, 33

62. Madison and Wesley, "Dorothy Porter Wesley," 33.

63. Madison and Wesley, "Dorothy Porter Wesley," 18.

64. Henry Louis Gates Jr., ed., *The Bondwoman's Narrative* (New York: Time Warner, 2002), xi.

65. For a sampling of Porter Wesley's scholarship before the modern civil rights movement, see "The Negro in the Brazilian Abolition Movement," *JNH* 37 (January 1952), 54–80; "Padre Domingo Caldas Barbosa, Afro-Brazilian Poet," *Phylon* 12 (1951): 264–71; "Negro Women in Our Wars," *NHB* 7 (June 1944): 195–96, 215; "David Ruggles, an Apostle of Human Rights," *JNH* 28 (January 1943): 23–50; "Sarah Parker Remond, Abolitionist and Physician," *JNH* 20 (July 1935): 287-93.

66. Gerald Horne, *Race Woman: The Lives of Shirley Graham Du Bois* (New York: New York University Press, 2000), 10, 11.

67. Horne, *Race Woman*, 1.

68. Graham Du Bois's biographies between 1944 and 1955, including one that does not deal with black history, are: *Dr. George Washington Carver: Scientist* (New York: Messner, 1944); *Paul Robeson: Citizen of the World* (New York: Messner, 1946); *There Once Was a Slave. . .: The Heroic Story of Frederick Douglass* (New York: Messner, 1947); *Your Most Humble Servant* (New York: Messner, 1949); *The Story of Phillis Wheatley* (New York: Messner, 1949); *Jean Baptist Pointe de Sable: Founder of Chicago* (New York: Messner, 1953); *The Story of Pocahontas* (New York: Messner, 1953); *Booker T. Washington: Educator of Hand, Head, and Heart* (New York: Messner, 1955).

69. Graham, *There Once Was a Slave*.

70. Elizabeth Brown-Guillory, "Du Bois, Shirley Graham," in Hine, Brown, and Terborg-Penn, eds., *Black Women in America*, vol. 1, 357.

71. Stephanie Y. Evans, *Black Women in the Ivory Tower, 1850–1954: An Intellectual History* (Gainesville: University of Florida Press, 2007), 134–37.

72. Hutchinson, *Anna Julia Cooper: A Voice from the South* (Washington D.C.: Smithsonian Institution Press, 1987), 138–43; Frances Richardson Keller, introduction to *Slavery and the French Revolutionists (1788–1805)* by Anna Julia Cooper (New York: Mellen, 1988), 11.

73. Cooper, *Voice from the South*, 31.

74. Hutchinson, *Anna Julia Cooper*, 134.

75. Keller, introduction to Cooper, *Slavery and the French Revolutionists*, 12.

76. Cooper, *Slavery and the French Revolutionists*, 31.

77. To understand the connections between Rodney and Cooper, see Walter Rodney, *How Europe Underdeveloped Africa* (Washington, D.C.: Howard University, 1981).

78. Evans, *Black Women in the Ivory Tower*, 120–27. Evans points out that previous scholarship on black doctorates has provided inaccurate statistics.

79. Margaret E. Hayes and Doris B. Armstrong, "Marion Manola Thompson Wright, 1902- 1962," in *Past and Promise: Lives of New Jersey Women*, ed. Joan N. Burstyn, 436 (Syracuse: Syracuse University Press, 1997).

80. Marion Thompson Wright, *The Education of Negroes in New Jersey* (New York: Teachers College Columbia University, 1941), 205–6.

81. Wright, *Education of Negroes in New Jersey*, 209.

82. Wright, *Education of Negroes in New Jersey*, 211.

83. "Proceedings of the Twenty-Eighth Annual Meeting of the Association for the

Study of Negro Life and History, Held at Detroit, Michigan, October 29–3 1, 1943," *JNH* 29 (January 1944): 6.

84. Horace Mann Bond, "It's All Happened Before," *JNE* 11 (January 1942): 64–65.

85. Margaret Smith Crocco, "Shaping Inclusive Social Education: Mary Ritter Beard and Marion Thompson Wright," in *"Bending the Future to Their Will": Civic Women, Social Education, and Democracy,* ed. Margaret Smith Crocco and O. L. Davis Jr., 110–11 (New York: Rowman and Littlefield, 1999).

86. Hayes and Armstrong, "Marion Manola Thompson Wright, 1902–1962," in Burstyn, ed., *Past and Promise,* 437.

87. While at Howard, Wright was an active member of the Urban League, the NAACP, Bethune's National Council of Negro Women, Delta Sigma Theta sorority, the ASNLH, the National Association of College Women, the NEA, and the American Teachers Association. See Margaret Smith Crocco, Petra Munro, and Kathleen Weiler, *Pedagogies of Resistance: Women Educator Activists, 1880–1960* (New York: Teachers College Press, 1999), 73.

88. Crocco, Munro, and Weiler, *Pedagogies of Resistance,* 70, 73, 74, 75. Crocco has suggested that Wright's death, declared a suicide by many, was in part the result of her failure to gain recognition and respect at Howard. Unlike some of her other female contemporaries and colleagues, Wright may not have had the support network necessary to help her overcome the prevalent gender discrimination within pre–civil rights era black American and U.S. society in general.

89. Greene, *Holders of Doctorates,* 63.

90. Rosalyn Terborg-Penn, "Tate, Merze," in *Black Women in America: An Historical Encyclopedia:* vol. 2, M–Z, ed. Hine, Brown, and Terborg-Penn, 1142 (Bloomington: Indiana University Press, 1993).

91. Greene, *Holders of Doctorates,* 64.

92. According to Meier and Rudwick, "The first article by a Negro to appear in the *JSH*" was Robert L. Clarke's 1953 essay, "The Florida Railroad Company in the Civil War." See Meier and Rudwick, *Black History and the Historical Profession,* 130.

93. Elsie M. Lewis, "The Political Mind of the Negro, 1865–1900," *Journal of Southern History* 21 (May 1955): 190, 193, 189–202.

94. Lewis, "The Political Mind of the Negro, 1865–1900," 189.

95. For a brief discussion of Lewis, see Meier and Rudwick, *Black History and the Historical Profession,* 128–30, 133, 151, 152, 154, 157, 174, 175, 187, 223.

96. Helen G. Edmonds, "A Republican President Needs a Republican Congress to Support Him," Papers of Helen G. Edmonds, box 1, Duke University Rare Book, Manuscript, and Special Collections Library.

97. "Dr. Helen G. Edmonds to Launch Education Week: World Renowned Lecturer to Speak at NNTA Public Meeting," Papers of Helen G. Edmonds, Box 1, Duke University Rare Book, Manuscript, and Special Collections Library.

98. See, for instance, John L. Clark, "Dr. Helen Edmonds 'Seconds' Ike," *Pittsburgh Courier,* August 25, 1956, 1; "Dr. Helen Edmonds to Speak Oct. 19," *Pittsburgh Courier,* October 13, 1956, A1; "Dr. Helen G. Edmonds Will Address GOP Women Here," *Pittsburgh Courier,* November 22, 1958, 1.

99. Helen G. Edmonds, "Vita (updated as of June 1, 1975)," Papers of Helen G. Edmonds, box 1, Duke University Rare Book, Manuscript, and Special Collections Library.

100. Arthur S. Link, "A Shock and a Revelation," *Phylon* 12 (4th Quarter 1951): 389.

101. Rosser H. Taylor, "Book Reviews," *Journal of Southern History* 17 (1951): 567; Rayford W. Logan, "Book Reviews," *JNH* 36 (October 1951): 456. Other positive reviews include Williston H. Lofton, "Current Literature," *JNE* 23 (Winter 1954): 66–67; A. D. Kirwan, "Book Reviews," *Mississippi Valley Historical Review* 38 (December 1951): 528–29; G. S., "Short Notices," *English Historical Review* 67 (July 1952): 460–61.

102. Helen G. Edmonds, "Biographic Sketch of Helen G. Edmonds," Papers of Helen G. Edmonds, Box 1, Duke University Rare Book, Manuscript, and Special Collections Library.

103. Gale Hodkinson, "Negro Leader Says: Sex, Not Race, Is Big Barrier to Succeeding," *Richmond News Leader,* July 26, 1967, 14.

104. Helen G. Edmonds, "The American Negro Woman," Papers of Helen G. Edmonds, box 1, Duke University Rare Book, Manuscript, and Special Collections Library.

105. See Meier and Rudwick, *Black History and the Historical Profession,* 130–31. Meier and Rudwick note that Rowley wanted to do a study of the NAACP for her dissertation, but was "deflected by several considerations."

106. J. E. Geshwiler, "Obituaries: Atlanta: Margaret Rowley, History Professor," *Atlanta Journal and Constitution,* December 12, 2003, 5G.

107. For some information on Williams, see "In Memoriam and Tribute: Dr. Lorraine A. Williams, 1923–1996," *JNH* 82 (Winter 1997): 182, 183, 198.

108. A landmark anthology in black women's history bears the title of this saying. See Darlene Clark Hine, Wilma King, and Linda Reed, eds., *"We Specialize in the Wholly Impossible": A Reader in Black Women's History* (New York: Carlson, 1995).

Chapter 5: *"Shadow vs. Substance": Deconstructing Booker T. Washington*

1. Du Bois, *Souls of Black Folk,* 44–45.

2. W. E. B. Du Bois, "The Late Booker T. Washington," *The Crisis* 11 (November 1915): 82.

3. For a critical assessment of "the hagiographical sanitizing impulse" that "prevails in Du Bois scholarship," see Adolph Reed Jr., *W. E. B. Du Bois and American Political Thought: Fabianism and the Color Line* (New York: Oxford University Press, 1997), 4–7.

4. Louis R. Harlan, *Booker T. Washington: The Wizard of Tuskegee, 1901–1915* (New York: Oxford University Press, 1983), xi. Scholars of U.S. history almost universally welcomed Harlan's biographies on Washington. James D. Anderson and V. P. Franklin were among the few scholars to offer insightful critiques of Harlan's study. See James Douglas Anderson, review of *Booker T. Washington: The Wizard of Tuskegee, 1901–1915,* by Louis R. Harlan, *Journal of American History* 70 (March 1984): 903–4; V. P. Franklin, review of *Booker T. Washington in Perspective: Essays of Louis R. Harlan,* ed. Raymond W. Smock, *Journal of Southern History* 56 (November 1990): 772–74. On the other hand, historians including Arvarh E. Strickland, Emma Lou Thornbrough, Elliott Rudwick, Lester Lamon,

Jacqueline A. Rouse, Willard B. Gatewood Jr., William Cheek, and I. A. Newby welcomed Harlan's scholarship without any significant criticisms.

5. Raymond Hedin, "Paternal at Last: Booker T. Washington and the Slave Narrative Tradition," *Callaloo* 7 (October 1979): 95.

6. Donald Cunnigen, Rutledge M. Dennis, and Myrtle Gonza Glascoe, introduction to *The Racial Politics of Booker T. Washington,* ed. Cunnigen, Dennis, and Glascoe, xvi (Amsterdam: JAI Press, 2006).

7. One partial exception is the recently published study *Uncle Tom or New Negro? African Americans Reflect on Booker T. Washington and "Up from Slavery" One Hundred Years Later,* edited by Rebecca Carroll. Challenging especially coming generations of younger African Americans to contextualize Washington more precisely, Carroll and a few of her colleagues reject the notion that Washington was simply an "Uncle Tom," "passive," a "house nigger," "spineless," or a "sellout." Carroll's study includes largely unscholarly reflections on Washington and *Up from Slavery* by twenty "contemporary black figures." The more sophisticated essays in this volume are by Ronald Walters and Earl Ofari Hutchinson. See Rebecca Carroll, ed., *Uncle Tom or New Negro? African Americans Reflect on Booker T. Washington and "Up from Slavery" One Hundred Years Later* (New York: Harlem Moon, 2006), 25–31, 106–14. For the most recent celebration of Washington by a group of black social critics, see Diane Bast and S. T. Karnick, eds., *Booker T. Washington: A Re-examination* (Chicago: The Heartland Institute, 2008).

8. Manning Marable, "Booker T. Washington and the Political Economy of Black Accommodation," in *The Souls of Black Folk: Centennial Reflections,* ed. The Association for the Study of African American Life and History, 227 (New Jersey: African World Press, 2004).

9. Adolph Reed Jr., "What Are the Drums Saying, Booker? The Current Crisis of the Black Intellectual," *Village Voice,* April 11, 1995, 32.

10. Julianne Malveaux, "The Niagara Movement's Powerful Fruit—100 Years of Protest," *Black Issues in Higher Education* 21 (February 10, 2005): 37. For Malveaux on Washington, see Carroll, ed., *Uncle Tom or New Negro?* 69–70. For information on the cause of Washington's death, see "Study Clarifies Death of a Black Pioneer," *New York Times,* May 7, 2006, 20.

11. Kevern Verney, *The Art of the Possible: Booker T. Washington and Black Leadership in the Untied States, 1881–1925* (New York: Routledge, 2001), 60, 44, 46, 63, 68.

12. See W. Fitzhugh Brundage, ed., *"Up from Slavery" by Booker T. Washington, with Related Documents* (Boston: Bedford/St. Martin's, 2003); Jacqueline M. Moore, *Booker T. Washington, W. E. B. Du Bois, and the Struggle for Racial Uplift* (Wilmington, Del.: SR Books, 2003). Brundage's introductory comments about Washington are very basic and are designed primarily for undergraduate students. Moore conforms largely to Harlan's approach, noting in her acknowledgements that "there have been attempts to challenge his interpretation of Washington; none has succeeded."

13. Linda Martin Alcoff, *Epistemology: The Big Questions* (Malden, Mass.: Blackwell, 1998), viii.

14. There are four works that address the historiography on Washington in detail. See Hugh Hawkins, ed., *Booker T. Washington and His Critics: The Problem of Negro Leadership* (Boston: Heath, 1962); Emma Lou Thornbrough, ed., *Booker T. Washington* (New Jersey:

Prentice Hall, 1969); Virginia Lantz Denton, *Booker T. Washington and the Adult Education Movement* (Gainesville: University of Florida Press, 1993), 154–88; Harvey G. Hudspeth, "Up from Disrepute: The Historiographical Accommodation of Booker T. Washington, 1901–1991," in *Booker T. Washington: Interpretive Essays*, ed. Tunde Adeleke (New York: Edwin Mellen, 1998). Kevern Verney and Jacqueline M. Moore also provide brief comments on the historiography on Washington, and more than a few scholars commented upon the state of Washingtonian scholarship in the 1970s. See, for instance, Lawrence J. Friedman, "Life 'In the Lion's Mouth'": Another Look at Booker T. Washington," *JNH* 59 (October 1974): 337–51; Booker T. Gardner, "The Educational Contributions of Booker T. Washington," *JNE* 44 (Autumn 1975): 502–18; Alfred Young, "The Educational Philosophy of Booker T. Washington: A Perspective for Black Liberation," *Phylon* 37 (3rd Quarter 1976): 224–35; Don Quinn Kelley, "The Political Economy of Booker T. Washington: A Bibliographic Essay," *JNE* 46 (Autumn 1977): 403–18.

15. The term "millennials" used in this chapter refers to those college and university students who were born during the early to mid-1980s and who share a range of group characteristics. For instance, influenced by an unprecedented wave of new information technology, Diana Oblinger has argued that for these students, historical knowledge "is no longer perceived to be the ultimate goal, particularly in light of the fact that the half-life of information is so short. Results and actions are considered more important than the accumulation of facts" (40). See Oblinger, "Boomers, Gen-Xers, Millennials," 37–47.

16. Frederick E. Drinker, *Booker T. Washington: The Master Mind of a Child of Slavery* (Chicago: Howard Chandler and Company, 1915).

17. Carter G. Woodson, review of *The Life and Times of Booker T. Washington*, by B. F. Riley, *JNH* 2 (January 1917): 97. See B. F. Riley, *The Life and Times of Booker T. Washington* (New York: Fleming H. Revelly, 1916). For examples of how Woodson praised Washington, see Carter G. Woodson, *The Negro in Our History* (Washington, D.C.: Associated Publishers, 1922), 274–79; Carter G. Woodson, "Honor to Booker T. Washington," *Negro History Bulletin* 10 (March 1947): 126–28.

18. *The Crisis* 13 (January 1917): 151.

19. Carter G. Woodson, review of *Booker T. Washington: Builder of Civilization*, by Emmett J. Scott and Lyman B. Stowe, *JNH* 2 (January 1917): 97.

20. Emmett J. Scott and Lyman B. Stowe, *Booker T. Washington: Builder of Civilization* (New York: Doubleday, 1918), 26.

21. See Emmett J. Scott, "Twenty Years Later: An Appraisal of Booker T. Washington," *JNE* 5 (October 1936): 543–54.

22. The last major biographical sketch of Washington within five years of his death is the first annual Founder's Day address, delivered at Tuskegee Institute on April 5, 1917, by William G. Willcox, chairman of the Board Trustees of Tuskegee Institute as well as the president of the Board of Educators in New York City. This twenty-seven-page tribute to Washington basically reiterates Washington's *Up from Slavery*. Also see, W. C. Jackson's *The Boy's Life of Booker T. Washington* (New York: Macmillan, 1922); Arthur Huff Fauset, *Booker T. Washington* (Philadelphia, 1924); Anson Phelps Stokes, *A Brief Biography of Booker Washington* (Hampton, Va.: Hampton Institute Press, 1936); Theodore S. Boone *The Philosophy of Booker T. Washington: The Apostle of Progress, the Pioneer of the New Deal* (Texas: Manney, 1939).

23. E. Davidson Washington, ed., *Selected Speeches of Booker T. Washington* (New York: Doubleday, 1932).

24. Lyman Abbott, *Silhouettes of My Contemporaries* (New York: Doubleday, 1922); M. A. De Wolfe, *Causes and Their Champions* (Boston: Little, Brown, 1926); Mildred Sandison Fenner and Eleanor C. Fishburn, *Pioneer American Educators* (New York: Kennikat, 1968).

25. Merle Curti, *The Social Ideas of American Educators* (New Jersey: Pageant, 1959), 292–93, 308.

26. Curti, *Social Ideas*, 303.

27. See W. E. B. Du Bois, *Darkwater: Voices from within the Veil* (New York: Harcourt, 1920); Du Bois, *Dusk of Dawn: An Autobiography of a Race Concept* (New York: Harcourt, 1940).

28. Alfreda M. Duster, ed., *Crusade for Justice: The Autobiography of Ida B. Wells* (Chicago: University of Chicago Press, 1970), 280–81.

29. For a discussion of the relationship between Fortune and Washington, see Emma Lou Thornbrough, *T. Thomas Fortune: Militant Journalist* (Chicago: University of Chicago Press, 1972); Thornbrough, "T. Thomas Fortune: Militant Editor in the Age of Accommodation," in *Black Leaders of the Twentieth Century*, ed. John Hope Franklin and August Meier, 19–37 (Urbana: University of Illinois Press, 1982). Fortune praised Washington in an article in the *New York Sun* in April 1916 yet critiqued him in an article in the *A.M.E. Church Review*. For Fortune's views of Washington, see Thornbrough, ed., *Booker T. Washington*, 109–14.

30. Kelly Miller, *Booker T. Washington: Five Years Later* (Washington, D.C.: Howard University, 1921), 16.

31. Monroe N. Work, "Booker T. Washington, Pioneer," *Journal of Social Forces* 3 (January 1925): 310–15. While Work's essay is a conventional praise song, he does quote extensively from Washington's "Sunday evening talks," sources that, until recently, have been overlooked.

32. Charles S. Johnson, "The Social Philosophy of Booker T. Washington," *Opportunity* 6 (April 1928): 104. According to August Meier, Johnson was an admirer of Washington, and there were many similarities between the two. See Meier, *White Scholar*, 16–17.

33. Johnson, "Social Philosophy," 115.

34. Horace Mann Bond, "Negro Leadership Since Washington," *South Atlantic Quarterly* 24 (April 1925): 122.

35. Horace Mann Bond, *The Education of the Negro in the American Social Order* (New York: Octagon, 1969), 121.

36. Horace Mann Bond, *Negro Education in Alabama: A Study in Cotton and Steel* (New York: Atheneum, 1969), 224–25.

37. Bond, *Negro Education in Alabama*, 216.

38. Bond, *Negro Education in Alabama*, 219.

39. See Charles S. Johnson, *Shadow of the Plantation* (Chicago: University of Chicago Press, 1934) for the approach that Bond critiqued.

40. Bond, *Negro Education in Alabama*, 233.

41. Gunnar Myrdal, *An American Dilemma: The Negro Problem and Modern Democracy* (New York: Harper, 1944), 640–41, 739.

42. U.S. Library of Congress, *Annual Report of the Librarian of Congress: For the Fiscal Year Ending June 30, 1943* (Washington, D.C.: United States GPO, 1944), 119.

43. U.S. Library of Congress, *Annual Report of the Librarian of Congress: For the Fiscal Year Ending June 30, 1942* (Washington: United States GPO, 1943), 24.

44. U.S. Library of Congress, *Annual Report of the Librarian of Congress: For the Fiscal Year Ending June 30, 1942*, 4.

45. U.S. Library of Congress, *Annual Report of the Librarian of Congress: For the Fiscal Year Ending June 30, 1942*, 8.

46. E. Franklin Frazier, "The Booker T. Washington Papers," *Library of Congress Quarterly Journal of Current Acquisitions* 2 (October/November/December 1944): 24.

47. Frazier, "Booker T. Washington Papers," 25.

48. Basil Mathews, *Booker T. Washington: Educator and Inter-Racial Interpreter* (London: SCM Press, 1949), 96–105.

49. Samuel R. Spencer Jr., *Booker T. Washington and the Negro's Place in American Life* (Boston: Little, Brown, 1955), 178.

50. Spencer, *Booker T. Washington,* 204–5.

51. Shirley Graham, *Booker T. Washington: Educator of Hand, Head, and Heart* (New York: Juilan Messner, 1955). Graham's book is a juvenile book predating Bontemps's *Young Booker.*

52. Rayford W. Logan, *The American Negro in American Life and Thought: The Nadir, 1877–1901* (New York: Dial, 1954), 80, 275, 276.

53. August Meier and Elliott Rudwick, *Along the Color Line: Exploration in the Black Experience* (Urbana: University of Illinois Press, 1976), 56.

54. Meier and Rudwick, *Along the Color Line,* 63.

55. August Meier, "Booker T. Washington and the Town of Mound Bayou," *Phylon* 15 (4th Quarter 1954): 396–401.

56. August Meier, "Booker T. Washington and the Rise of the NAACP," *The Crisis* 61 (February 1954): 117–23.

57. August Meier, "Towards a Reinterpretation of Booker T. Washington," *Journal of Southern History* 23 (May 1957): 227.

58. Mercer Cook, "Booker T. Washington and the French," *JNH* 40 (October 1955): 325.

59. Emma Lou Thornbrough, "More Light on Booker T. Washington and the New York Age," *JNH* 43 (January 1958): 35–36.

60. Elliott Rudwick, "Booker T. Washington's Relations with the National Association for the Advancement of Colored People," *JNE* 29 (Spring 1960): 134–44.

61. Emma Lou Thornbrough, "Booker T. Washington as Seen By His White Contemporaries," *JNH* 53 (April 1968): 161–82.

62. John P. Flynn, "Booker T. Washington: Uncle Tom or Wooden Horse," *JNH* 54 (July 1969): 271.

63. Willard Gatewood, "Booker T. Washington and the Ulrich Affair," *JNH* 55 (January 1970): 29–44.

64. Louis R. Harlan, "Booker T. Washington and the White Man's Burden," *American Historical Review* 61 (January 1966): 441.

65. J. Congress Mbata, "Booker T. Washington and John Tengo Jabavu: A Comparison," *Afro-American Studies* 2 (1971): 186.

66. Manning W. Marable, "Booker T. Washington and African Nationalism," *Phylon* 35 (4th Quarter 1974): 400, 405–6.

67. Sylvia M. Jacobs, *The African Nexus: Black American Perspectives on the European Partitioning of Africa, 1880–1920* (Westport, Conn.: Greenwood, 1981), 49.

68. Donald Spivey, *The Politics of Miseducation: The Booker T. Washington Institute of Liberia, 1929–1984* (Lexington: University of Kentucky Press, 1986).

69. Michael O. West, "The Tuskegee Model of Development in Africa: Another Dimension of the African/African-American Connection," *Diplomatic History: The Journal of the Society for Historians of American Foreign Relations* 16 (Summer 1992): 372. An earlier study that considered Washington within the context of pan-Africanism is Kenneth James King, *Pan-Africanism and Education: A Study of Race and Philanthropy in the Southern States of America and East Africa* (London: Clarendon, 1971).

70. Mildred C. Fierce, *The Pan-African Idea in the United States, 1900–1910: African-American Interest in Africa and Interactions with West Africa* (New York: Garland, 1993), 176.

71. Edward O. Erhagbe, "African-Americans and the Defense of African States against European Imperial Conquest: Booker T. Washington's Diplomatic Efforts to Guarantee Liberia's Independence, 1907–1911," *African Studies Review* 39 (April 1996): 56, 61.

72. See Arna Bontemps, *Young Booker: Booker T. Washington's Early Days* (New York: Dodd, Mead, 1972); Bernard Weisberger, *Booker T. Washington* (New York: New American Library, 1972); Barry Mackintosh, *Booker T. Washington: An Appreciation of the Man and His Times* (Washington, D.C.: National Park Service, 1972); Harlan, *Booker T. Washington: The Making of a Black Leader, 1856–1901.*

73. Joseph F. Citro, "Booker T. Washington's Tuskegee Institute: Black School Community, 1900–1915" (PhD diss., University of Rochester, 1973), 4.

74. Citro, "Booker T. Washington's Tuskegee Institute," 435.

75. Donald Spivey, *Schooling for the New Slavery: Black Industrial Education, 1868–1915* (Westport, Conn.: Greenwood, 1978), 45, 47.

76. Spivey, *Schooling*, 54, 55.

77. James D. Anderson, *The Education of Blacks in the South, 1860–1935* (Chapel Hill: University of North Carolina Press, 1988), 73–74.

78. Spivey, *Schooling*, 66.

79. Donald Generals, "Booker T. Washington and Progressive Education: An Experimentalist Approach to Curriculum Development and Reform," *JNE* 69 (Summer 2000): 215–34.

80. Allen W. Jones, "The Role of Tuskegee Institute in the Education of Black Farmers," *JNH* 60 (April 1975): 252–67. Allen laid the foundations for La Verne Gyant, "Contributions to Adult Education: Booker T. Washington, George Washington Carver, Alain L. Locke, and Ambrose Caliver," *Journal of Black Studies* 19 (September 1988): 97–110; Denton, *Booker T. Washington and the Adult Education Movement.*

81. Friedman, "Life 'In the Lion's Mouth,'" 342.

82. Friedman, "Life 'In the Lion's Mouth,'" 337–51.

83. Louis R. Harlan, "Sympathy and Detachment: Dilemmas of a Biographer," in *Booker T. Washington in Perspective: Essays of Louis R. Harlan*, ed. Raymond W. Smock, 186 (Jackson: University of Mississippi Press, 1988).

84. See Louis R. Harlan, *Separate and Unequal: Public School Campaigns and Racism in the South Seaboard States, 1901–1915* (Chapel Hill: University of South Carolina Press, 1958).

85. Louis R. Harlan, *The Negro in American History* (Washington, D.C.: American Historical Association, 1965), 21–22.

86. Harlan, *Booker T. Washington: The Making of a Black Leader, 1856–1901*, 204.

87. Harlan, *Booker T. Washington: The Making of a Black Leader, 1856–1901*, 92.

88. Smock, ed., *Booker T. Washington in Perspective*, 181.

89. Daniel T. Williams, *Booker T. Washington: A Register of His Papers in the Tuskegee Institute Archives* (Tuskegee, Alabama, 1974).

90. Harlan, *Booker T. Washington: The Wizard of Tuskegee, 1901–1915*, ix.

91. Harlan, *Booker T. Washington: The Wizard of Tuskegee, 1901–1915*, xi.

92. Du Bois, *Souls of Black Folk*; Meier, "Booker T. Washington and the Rise of the NAACP"; Thornbrough, "More Light on Booker T. Washington and the New York Age"; Rudwick, "Booker T. Washington's Relations with the National Association for the Advancement of Colored People"; Robert G. Sherer, *Subordination or Liberation? The Development and Conflicting Theories of Black Education in Nineteenth Century Alabama* (Alabama: University of Alabama Press, 1977), 52–58; June O. Patton, "The Black Community of Augusta and the Struggle for Ware High School, 1880–1899," in *New Perspectives on Black Educational History*, ed. Vincent P. Franklin and James D. Anderson, 45–60 (Boston: G. K. Hall, 1978); June O. Patton, " Major Richard Robert Wright, Sr. and Black Higher Education in Georgia, 1880–1920" (PhD diss., University of Chicago, 1980); V. P. Franklin, review of *Booker T. Washington: The Wizard of Tuskegee, 1901–1915*, by Louis R. Harlan, *Educational Studies: A Journal in the Foundations of Education* 15 (Winter 1984): 396–98.

93. See Anderson, review of *Booker T. Washington: The Wizard of Tuskegee, 1901–1915*, by Louis R. Harlan; V. P. Franklin, review of *Booker T. Washington in Perspective: Essays of Louis R. Harlan*, ed. Raymond W. Smock.

94. Moore, *Booker T. Washington, W. E. B. Du Bois, and the Struggle for Racial Uplift*, "Acknowledgements."

95. Louis R. Harlan, "A Black Leader in the Age of Jim Crow," in Cunnigen, Dennis, and Glascoe, eds., *Racial Politics of Booker T. Washington*, 24.

96. Since 1998, there have also been several studies on Washington that have not challenged Harlan's thesis, including Adeleke, *Booker T. Washington*; John Perry, *Unshakable Faith: Booker T. Washington and George Washington Carver* (Oregon: Multnomah, 1999); W. Fitzhugh Brundage, ed., *Booker T. Washington and Black Progress: Up from Slavery 100 Years Later* (Gainesville: University of Florida Press, 2003); Wilson Jeremiah Moses, *Creative Conflict in African American Thought: Frederick Douglass, Alexander Crummell, Booker T. Washington, W. E. B. Du Bois, and Marcus Garvey* (New York: Cambridge University Press, 2004).

97. Denton, *Booker T. Washington and the Adult Education Movement*, 165–67.

98. Denton, *Booker T. Washington and the Adult Education Movement*, 87, 106, 106–53. For discussions similar to Denton's, see Felix James, "The Tuskegee Institute Movable School, 1906–1923," *Agricultural History* 45 (July 1971): 201–9; Jones, "The Role of Tuskegee Institute in the Education of Black Farmers."

99. Karen J. Ferguson, "Caught in 'No Man's Land': The Negro Cooperative Demonstra-

tion Service and the Ideology of Booker T. Washington, 1900–1918," *Agricultural History* 72 (Winter 1998): 34, 48.

100. Brundage, ed., *Booker T. Washington and Black Progress*, 4, 11, 12. Brundage suggests that Washington scholarship can be expanded by exploring a range of issues, including Washington's economic thought, his attitudes about religion, his educational philosophy, his "performative strategies," his international influence, and his status as a popular culture icon.

101. Michael Rudolph West, *The Education of Booker T. Washington: American Democracy and the Idea of Race Relations* (New York: Columbia University Press, 2006), 54.

102. West, *Education of Booker T. Washington*, 4.

103. Cunnigen, Dennis, and Glascoe, eds., *Racial Politics of Booker T. Washington*. In the introduction the editors indicate that the essays in their volume call upon scholars to revisit the relevancy of Washington's strategies to the present. In the epilogue, Dennis briefly addresses how Washington's programs can be useful in addressing African American life in the twenty-first century. However, the only recent study to really argue that Washington's strategies can be applied to the present is Bast and Karnick, eds., *Booker T. Washington: A Re-examination*.

104. Lee H. Walker, introduction to Bast and Karnick, eds., *Booker T. Washington: A Re-examination*, 6–7. Three historians contributed to this volume, Robert J. Norrell, Christopher R. Reed, and Daryl Scott.

105. Michael Bieze, *Booker T. Washington and the Art of Self-Representation* (New York: Peter Lang, 2008), 132, 13, 2, 4. Bieze's study is especially refreshing because most scholars stress the importance of photography and the media when dealing with the civil rights and Black Power movements. See, for instance, Iris Schneisser, "Liberating Views/Views of Liberation: The Photographic Side of the Black Consciousness Movement," in *Black Liberation in the Americas*, ed. Fritz Gysin and Christopher Mulvey, 221–40 (New Brunswick: Transaction, 2001).

106. Bieze, *Booker T. Washington and the Art of Self-Representation*, 34.

107. Bieze, *Booker T. Washington and the Art of Self-Representation*, 111.

108. David H. Jackson, *Booker T. Washington and the Struggle against White Supremacy: The Southern Educational Tours, 1908–1912* (New York: Palgrave Macmillan, 2008), 4, 10.

109. Robert J. Norrell, *Up from History: The Life of Booker T. Washington* (Cambridge: Harvard University Press, 2009), 16.

110. Norrell, *Up from History*, 439.

111. Reed, *W. E. B. Du Bois and American Political Thought*, 7.

112. See Wilson Jeremiah Moses, *The Golden Age of Black Nationalism, 1859–1925* (New York: Oxford University Press, 1978); Kevin K. Gaines, *Uplifting the Race: Black Leadership, Politics, and Culture in the Twentieth Century* (Chapel Hill: University of North Carolina Press, 1996).

113. Houston A. Baker Jr., *Long Black Song: Essays in Black American Literature* (Charlottesville: University Press of Virginia, 1972), 85, 95, 99–106; Franklin, *Black Self-Determination*, 16.

114. Meier, *A White Scholar and the Black Community, 1945–1965*, 11; David W. Southern, *Gunnar Myrdal and Black-White Relations: The Use and Abuse of An American Dilemma*,

1944–1969 (Baton Rouge: Louisiana State University Press, 1987), 20. For a detailed discussion of Bunche's role in Myrdal's project, see Holloway, "Editor's Introduction" in Bunche, *Brief and Tentative*, 1–38.

115. Holloway, "Editor's Introduction," 21.

116. Ralph J. Bunche, "Conceptions and Ideologies of the Negro Problem," *Contributions in Black Studies: A Journal of African and Afro-American Studies (1990–1992)*: 89.

117. Bunche, "Conceptions and Ideologies of the Negro Problem," 96–97. Here, Bunche defines conciliation and accommodation in reference to Washington.

118. Bunche, "Conceptions and Ideologies of the Negro Problem," 103.

119. Bunche, *Brief and Tentative*, 39–155.

120. Myrdal, *An American Dilemma*, 720.

121. Myrdal, *An American Dilemma*, 743.

122. August Meier, "The Emergence of Negro Nationalism: A Study in Ideologies," in Meier and Rudwick, *Along the Color Line*, 190–91, 212.

123. Meier, *Negro Thought in America*, 110.

124. Logan, *Negro in American Life and Thought*, 278.

125. See Francis L. Broderick, *W. E. B. Du Bois: Negro Leader in a Time of Crisis* (Stanford: Stanford University Press, 1959); Elliott Rudwick, *W. E. B. Du Bois: Propagandist of the Negro Protest* (New York: Atheneum, 1986); Marable, *W. E. B. Du Bois;* David Levering Lewis, *W. E. B. Du Bois: Biography of a Race* (New York: Henry Holt and Company, 1993). For one of the most refreshing side-by-side analyses of Du Bois and Washington by a Du Bois biographer, see Arnold Rampersad, *The Art and Imagination of W. E. B. Du Bois* (New York: Shocken, 1990), 81, 83, 87.

126. Peter Eisenstadt, introduction to Eisenstadt, ed., *Black Conservatism: Essays in Intellectual and Political History,* ix–x. For another discussion of Washington and the black conservative tradition, see Henry Lewis Suggs, "The Washington Legacy: A History of Black Political Conservatism in America, 1915–1944, in Eisenstadt, ed., *Black Conservatism,* 81–108.

127. Bracey, *Saviors or Sellouts,* 20.

128. Charles P. Henry, "Who Won the Great Debate—Booker T. Washington or W. E. B. Du Bois?" *The Crisis* 99 (February 1992): 17.

129. Julianne Malveaux, "Chapter VIII," in Carroll, ed., *Uncle Tom or New Negro?* 68–75; Moore, *Booker T. Washington, W. E. B. Du Bois, and the Struggle for Black Uplift,* 61–113.

130. Harlan, *Booker T. Washington: The Making of a Black Leader, 1856–1901,* 2.

131. Verney, *Art of the Possible,* 49.

132. Houston A. Baker Jr., *Modernism and the Harlem Renaissance* (Chicago: University of Chicago Press, 1987). Also see, Houston A. Baker Jr., "Meditation on Tuskegee: Black Studies and Their Imbrication," *Journal of Blacks in Higher Education* 9 (Autumn 1995): 52–59.

133. See, for instance, Harlan, *Booker T. Washington: The Making of a Black Leader, 1856–1901,* 229–53; James M. Cox, "Autobiography and Washington," *Sewanee Review* 85 (Spring 1977): 235–61; Robert B. Stepto, *From Behind the Veil: A Study of Afro-American Narrative* (Illinois: University of Illinois Press, 1979), 32–51; Hedin, "Paternal at Last," 95–102; Roger J. Bresnahan, "Implied Readers of Booker T. Washington's Autobiogra-

phies," *Black American Literature Forum* 14 (Spring 1980): 15–20; Baker, *Modernism and the Harlem Renaissance;* William E. Cain, "Forms of Self-Representation in Booker T. Washington's *Up From Slavery,*" *Prospects: An Annual of American Cultural Studies* 12 (October 1987): 200–222; James H. Evans, *Spiritual Empowerment in Afro-American Literature: Frederick Douglass, Rebecca Jackson, Booker T. Washington, Richard Wright, Toni Morrison* (Lewiston, N.Y.: Edwin Mellen, 1987); Charlotte D. Fitzgerald, "The Story of My Life and Work: Booker T. Washington's Other Autobiography," *Black Scholar* 21 (Fall 1991): 35; Donald B. Gibson, "Strategies and Revisions of Self-Representation in Booker T. Washington's Autobiographies," *American Quarterly* 45 (September 1993): 370–93; Carla Willard, "Timing Impossible Subjects: The Marketing Style of Booker T. Washington," *American Quarterly* 53 (December 2001): 624–69; William L. Andrews, ed., *Up from Slavery: Authoritative Text, Contexts, and Composition History, Criticism* (New York: Norton, 1996); Brundage, ed., *Up from Slavery by Booker T. Washington with Related Documents;* Brundage, ed., *Booker T. Washington and Black Progress;* Amanda Kemp, "'Your Arms Are Too Short to Box with Me': Encounters with Booker T. Washington, International Trickster," in Cunnigen, Dennis, and Glascoe, eds., *Racial Politics of Booker T. Washington,* 63–83; Scott Hicks, "W. E. B. Du Bois, Booker T. Washington, and Richard Wright: Toward an Ecocriticism of Color," *Callaloo* 29 (Winter 2006): 202–22. Identifying Washington as a forbearer of ecocriticism, Hicks provides one of the first analyses of Washington's musings on and relationship with nature.

134. The most recent exception is Brundage, ed., *Booker T. Washington and Black Progress,* 12–15.

135. John Hope Franklin, *From Slavery to Freedom: A History of Negro Americans,* 3rd ed. (New York: Vintage, 1969), 397.

136. Oliver C. Cox, "The Leadership of Booker T. Washington," *Social Forces* 30 (October 1951): 95; Franklin, *Black Self-Determination,* 193, 195.

137. Franklin, *Black Self-Determination,* 203.

138. Few scholars have analyzed Washington's "Sunday Evening Talks." See, for instance, Jane Gottschalk, "The Rhetorical Strategy of Booker T. Washington," *Phylon* 27 (4th Quarter 1966): 388–95; Robert Michael Franklin, *Liberating Visions: Human Fulfillment and Social Justice in African-American Thought* (Minneapolis: Fortress, 1990), 11.

139. Franklin, *Liberating Visions,* 11.

140. Wilson Jeremiah Moses, *Creative Conflict in African American Thought: Frederick Douglass, Alexander Crummell, Booker T. Washington, W. E. B. Du Bois, and Marcus Garvey* (New York: Cambridge University Press, 2004), 150.

141. Mrs. Booker T. Washington, "What Girls Are Taught, and How," in *Tuskegee and Its People: Their Ideals and Achievements,* ed. Booker T. Washington, 68–69, 80 (Freeport, N.Y.: Books for Libraries, 1971).

142. Jacqueline Anne Rouse, "Out of the Shadow of Tuskegee: Margaret Murray Washington, Social Activism, and Race Vindication," *JNH* 81 (Winter–Autumn 1996), 31–46.

143. Adele Logan Alexander, "Susannah and the Elders or Potiphar's Wife? Allegations of Sexual Misconduct at Booker T. Washington's Tuskegee Institute," in *Women of the American South: A Multicultural Reader,* ed. Christie Anne Farnham, 150–64 (New York: New York University Press, 1997).

144. Friedman, "Life 'In the Lion's Mouth,'" 344.

145. For a debate concerning the nature of black nationalism, see Bracey, Meier, and Rudwick, eds., *Black Nationalism in America*, xxv–lx.

146. Booker T. Washington, *Character Building: Being Addresses Delivered on Sunday Evenings to the Students of Tuskegee Institute* (New York: Doubleday, 1902), 241.

Chapter 6: Genocide and African American History

1. Toni Morrison, ed., *To Die for the People: The Writings of Huey P. Newton* (New York: Writers and Readers Publishing, Inc., 1995), 166, 168, 169, 172; Charlene Mitchell, introduction to *The Man Who Cried Genocide: An Autobiography,* by William L. Patterson (New York: International Publishers, 1991), ix.

2. Patterson, *Man Who Cried Genocide,* 218.

3. Molefi Kete Asante, "The African American Warrant for Reparations: The Crime of European Enslavement of Africans and Its Consequences," in *Should America Pay? Slavery and the Raging Debate on Reparations,* ed. Raymond W. Winbush, 9 (New York: Amistad, 2003).

4. Calvin H. Sinnette, "Genocide and Ecology," *Freedomways* 12 (First Quarter 1972): 34, 36.

5. Charles M. Wiltse, ed., *David Walker's Appeal* (New York: Hill and Wang, 1965), 16, 24, 25.

6. Frederick Douglass, "A Few Words to Our Own People," *North Star,* January 19, 1849.

7. Jacqueline Jones Royster, ed., *Southern Horrors and Other Writings: The Anti-Lynching Campaign of Ida B. Wells, 1892–1900* (Boston: Bedford Books, 1997), 75–76.

8. William Darity Jr., "Many Roads to Extinction: Early AEA Economists and the Black Disappearance Hypothesis," *History of Economics Review* 21 (Winter 1994): 48.

9. W. E. B. Du Bois, "The Future of the Negro Race in America," *The East and the West: Quarterly Review for the Study of Missions* 2 (1904): 4.

10. Darity, "Many Roads to Extinction," 54.

11. Du Bois, "Future of the Negro Race," 12–13.

12. Du Bois, "Future of the Negro Race," 13.

13. Marcus Garvey, "The Conspiracy of the East St. Louis Riot," in *The Marcus Garvey and Universal Negro Improvement Association Papers,* vol. 1, *1826–August 1919,* ed. Robert A. Hill, 213 (Berkeley: University of California Press, 1983).

14. Raphael Lemkin, "Genocide," in *Genocide: An Anthropological Reader,* ed. Alexander Laban Hinton, 27 (Malden, Mass.: Blackwell, 2002).

15. John Cooper, *Raphael Lemkin and the Struggle for the Genocide Convention* (New York: Palgrave Macmillan, 2008), 238–39.

16. Cooper, *Raphael Lemkin,* 57.

17. Roger W. Smith, "As Old As History," in *Will Genocide Ever End?* ed. Carol Rittner, John K. Roth, and James M. Smith, 32 (St. Paul: Paragon, 2002).

18. "Appendix 1: Text of the 1948 Genocide Convention," in *Genocide: Conceptual and Historical Dimensions,* ed. George J. Andreopoulos, 230 (Philadelphia: University of Pennsylvania Press, 1994).

19. Samuel Totten and Steven Leonard Jacobs, introduction to *Pioneers of Genocide*

Studies, ed. by Samuel Totten and Steven Leonard Jacobs, xi (New Brunswick: Transaction, 2002). For an intriguing discussion of the evolution of Lemkin-influenced definitions of genocide, see Ann Curthoys and John Docker, "Defining Genocide," in *The Historiography of Genocide,* ed. Dan Stone, 9–41 (New York: Palgrave Macmillan, 2008).

20. Anton Weiss-Wendt, "Problems in Comparative Genocide Scholarship," in Stone, ed., *Historiography of Genocide,* 42, 44; Dan Stone, introduction to *Historiography of Genocide,* 1.

21. Rouben Paul Adalian, "Fighting Words," in Totten and Jacobs, eds., *Pioneers of Genocide,* 19. For examples of anthologies published on genocide since the late 1990s, see, for instance, Alan S. Rosenbaum, ed., *Is the Holocaust Unique? Perspectives on Comparative Genocide* (Boulder, Colo.: Westview, 1998); Kurt Jonassohn with Karin Solveig Bjornson, eds., *Genocide and Gross Human Rights Violations* (New Brunswick: Transaction, 1998); Levon Chorbajian and George Shirinian, eds., *Studies in Comparative Genocide* (New York: St. Martin's, 1999); Israel W. Charny, ed., *The Encyclopedia of Genocide,* 2 vols. (California: ABC-CLIO, 1999); Alexandre Kimenyi and Otis L. Scott, eds., *Anatomy of Genocide: State-Sponsored Mass-Killings in the Twentieth Century* (Lewiston, N.Y.: Edwin Mellen, 2001); Alexander Laban Hinton, ed., *Annihilating Difference: The Anthropology of Genocide* (Berkeley: University of California Press, 2002); Hinton, ed., *Genocide;* Rittner, Roth, and Smith, eds., *Will Genocide Ever End?;* Totten and Jacobs, eds., *Pioneers of Genocide Studies;* David E. Lorey and William H. Beezley, eds., *Genocide, Collective Memory, and Popular Culture: The Politics of Remembrance in the Twentieth Century* (Wilmington, Del.: Scholarly Resources, 2002); Robert Gellately and Ben Kiernan, eds., *The Specter of Genocide: Mass Murder in Historical Perspective* (Cambridge: Cambridge University Press, 2003); Samuel Totten, William S. Parsons, and Israel W. Charny, eds., *Century of Genocide: Critical Essays and Eyewitness Accounts* (New York: Routledge, 2004); Adam Jones, ed., *Genocide, War Crimes and the West: History and Complicity* (London: Zed, 2004); Dinah L. Shelton, ed., *Encyclopedia of Genocide and Crimes against Humanity* (Farmington Hills, Mich.: Macmillan Reference, 2005); Mark Lattimer, ed., *Genocide and Human Rights* (Burlington, Vt.: Ashgate, 2007); Stone, ed., *Historiography of Genocide.*

22. Sven Lindqvist, preface to *"Exterminate the Brutes"* (New York: New Press, 1996).

23. Jurgen Zimmerer, "Colonial Genocide: The Herero and Nama War (1904–8) in German South West Africa and Its Significance," in Stone, ed., *Historiography of Genocide,* 323.

24. For a useful chronology of twentieth-century genocides, see Rittner, Roth, and Smith, "Chronology," in Rittner, Roth, and Smith, *Will Genocide Ever End?* 5–18.

25. "U.S. Accused in U.N. of Negro Genocide," *New York Times,* December 18, 1951, 13.

26. Raphael Lemkin, "Nature of Genocide; Confusion with Discrimination against Individuals Seen," *New York Times,* June 14, 1953, E10. For an intriguing discussion of Lemkin's racist attitudes, see Curthoys and Docker, "Defining Genocide," 19–21.

27. Irving L. Horowitz, "Science, Modernity and Authorized Terror: Reconsidering the Genocidal State," in Chorbajian and Shirinian, eds., *Studies in Comparative Genocide,* 25.

28. Helen Fein, "Genocide, Terror, Life Integrity, and War Crimes: The Case for Discrimination," in Andreopoulos, ed., *Genocide: Conceptual and Historical Dimensions,* 95.

29. Philip Dray, *At the Hands of Persons Unknown: The Lynching of Black America* (New York: Modern Library, 2002), viii, 49.

30. Andrew Austin, "Explanation and Responsibility: Agency and Motive in Lynching and Genocide," *Journal of Black Studies* 34 (May 2004): 728–29.

31. Karen Grisby Bates, "AIDS: Is It Genocide," *Essence,* September 1990, 76, 78, 116.

32. Lorene Cary, "Why It's Not Just Paranoia: An American History of 'Plans' for Blacks," *Newsweek,* April 6, 1992, 23.

33. Cathy J. Cohen, *The Boundaries of Blackness: AIDS and the Breakdown of Black Politics* (Chicago: University of Chicago Press, 1999); Dorie J. Gilbert and Ednita M. Wright, eds., *African American Women and HIV/AIDS: Critical Responses* (Westport, Conn.: Greenwood, 2003); Jacob Levenson, *The Secret Epidemic: The Story of AIDS* (New York: Pantheon, 2004); Gil L. Robertson, ed., *Not in My Family: AIDS in the African-American Community* (Agate, 2006).

34. Vanessa Northington Gamble, "Under the Shadow of Tuskegee: African Americans and Health Care," in *Tuskegee's Truths: Rethinking the Tuskegee Syphilis Study,* ed. Susan Reverby, 431, 435, 436 (Chapel Hill: University of North Carolina Press, 2000).

35. Stone, "Introduction," 2.

36. Leo Kuper, "Theoretical Issues Relating to Genocide: Uses and Abuses," in Andreopoulos, ed., *Genocide: Conceptual and Historical Dimensions,* 31; Adam Jones, *Genocide: A Comprehensive Introduction* (New York: Routledge, 2006), 23; John K. Roth, "The Politics of Definition," in Rittner, ed., *Will Genocide Ever End?* 27–28. For detailed discussions of definitions of genocide, see, for instance, Scott Straus, "Contested Meanings and Conflicting Imperatives: A Conceptual Analysis of Genocide," *Journal of Genocide Research* 3 (2001): 349–75; Jones, *Genocide,* 3–38.

37. Lorey and Beezley, eds., *Genocide, Collective Memory, and Popular Culture,* xv.

38. Peter du Preez, *Genocide: The Psychology of Mass Murder* (New York: Boyars/Bowderdean, 1994), 4, 73.

39. Frank M. Afflitto and Margaret Vandiver, "The Political Determinants of Ethnic Genocide," in *Anatomy of Genocide: State-Sponsored Mass-Killings in the Twentieth Century,* ed. Alexander Kimenyi and Otis L. Scott, 8–9 (New York: Edwin Mellen, 2001).

40. Kuper, "Theoretical Issues," 34.

41. Israel W. Charny, "Toward a Generic Definition of Genocide," 74–75.

42. "Appendix 1: Text of the 1948 Genocide Convention," 230.

43. Patterson, *Man Who Cried Genocide,* 11.

44. Kenneth Mostern, *Autobiography and Black Identity Politics: Radicalization in Twentieth-Century America* (New York: Cambridge University Press, 1999), 12.

45. Patterson, *Man Who Cried Genocide,* 13.

46. Patterson, *Man Who Cried Genocide,* 7, 8, 19, 18.

47. Patterson, *Man Who Cried Genocide,* 20, 23, 25.

48. Patterson, *Man Who Cried Genocide,* 25, 22, 24.

49. Patterson, *Man Who Cried Genocide,* 30, 36.

50. Patterson, *Man Who Cried Genocide,* 77, 91.

51. Gerald Horne, *Communist Front? The Civil Rights Congress, 1946–1956* (Cranbury, N.J.: Associated University Presses, 1988), 13.

52. Horne, *Communist Front?* 18, 22.

53. Patterson, *Man Who Cried Genocide,* 167, 170.

54. "Much-Needed Word," *Chicago Defender,* September 21, 1946, 14; Willard Townsend,

"The Other Side," *Chicago Defender*, October 25, 1947, 15; "Hope UN Genocide Ruling Will Cut U.S. Lynching," *Chicago Defender*, June 5, 1948, 6; "UN Law May Be Hard on Dixie," *New York Amsterdam News*, October 21, 1951, 6.

55. Patterson, *Man Who Cried Genocide*, 175.

56. Patterson, *Man Who Cried Genocide*, 177, 178, 179.

57. William A. Rutherford, "Mrs. Roosevelt Claims Progress," *New York Amsterdam News*, January 26, 1952, 18.

58. Patterson, *Man Who Cried Genocide*, 197, 199.

59. Rutherford, "Mrs. Roosevelt Claims Progress," 18.

60. Horne, *Communist Front?* 175.

61. Curthoys and Docker, "Defining Genocide," 16.

62. Patterson, ed., *We Charge Genocide*, xiv, xv.

63. Patterson, ed., *We Charge Genocide*, xvi.

64. Patterson, ed., *We Charge Genocide*, 49, 28.

65. Patterson, ed., *We Charge Genocide*, 1, 23.

66. Patterson, ed., *We Charge Genocide*, 23, 134, 8.

67. Patterson, ed., *We Charge Genocide*, 26.

68. Patterson, ed., *We Charge Genocide*, 9.

69. Patterson, ed., *We Charge Genocide*, 35.

70. Patterson, ed., *We Charge Genocide*, 43.

71. Patterson, ed., *We Charge Genocide*, 125, 126.

72. Patterson, ed., *We Charge Genocide*, 126.

73. Patterson, ed., *We Charge Genocide*, 134.

74. Patterson, ed., *We Charge Genocide*, 142, 177, 178.

75. Morrison, ed., *To Die for the People*, 172.

76. George Breitman, ed., *By Any Means Necessary: Speeches, Interviews, and a Letter by Malcolm X* (New York: Pathfinder, 1970), 57.

77. Malcolm X, "Not Just an American Problem, but a World Problem," in *Malcolm X: The Last Speeches*, ed. Bruce Perry, 180–81 (New York: Pathfinder, 1989).

78. Eugene Victor Wolfenstein, *The Victims of Democracy: Malcolm X and the Black Revolution* (New York: Guilford, 1993), 318, 319.

79. Alphonso Pinkney, *Red, Black and Green: Black Nationalism in America* (New York: Cambridge University Press, 1979), 71.

80. Floyd B. McKissick, "Genocide U.S.A., A Blueprint for Black Survival" (speech, Newark, N.J., July 21, 1967) in Samuel F. Yette, *The Choice: The Issue of Black Survival in America* (New York: Putnam's, 1971), 298.

81. Lonnie Kashif, "U.S. Fears to Sign Treaty Against Genocide," *Muhammad Speaks*, February 27, 1970, 3.

82. William L. Patterson, "We (Still) Charge Genocide," *Muhammad Speaks*, June 26, 1970, 23, 24.

83. Joe Walker, "Genocide Petition," *Muhammad Speaks*, July 3, 1970.

84. Lacey Fosburgh, "Black Clergy Issue a 'Declaration of Independence,'" *New York Times*, June 26, 1970, 16.

85. "Black Declaration of Independence," *New York Times*, July 3, 1970, 7.

86. Castellano Turner and William A. Darity, "Fears of Genocide Among Black Ameri-

cans as Related to Age, Sex, and Region," *American Journal of Public Health* 63 (December 1973): 1033.

87. Dick Gregory, "My Answer to Genocide," *Ebony,* October 1971, 66, 72.

88. Robert G. Weisbord, *Genocide? Birth Control and the Black American* (Westport, Conn.: Greenwood, 1975), 7, 12, 25.

89. Weisbord, *Genocide?* 52–53.

90. Weisbord, *Genocide?* 92.

91. Weisbord, *Genocide?* 142.

92. Weisbord, *Genocide?* 147, 152, 169.

93. Weisbord, *Genocide?* 178, 185, 186.

94. Walter C. Farrell Jr., Marvin P. Dawkins, and John Oliver, "Genocide Fears in a Rural Black Community: An Empirical Examination," *Journal of Black Studies* 14 (September 1983): 50.

95. Turner and Darity, "Fears of Genocide Among Black Americans as Related to Age, Sex, and Region."

96. Farrell, Dawkins, and Oliver, "Genocide Fears in a Rural Black Community," 62.

97. Sidney M. Willhelm, "The Economic Demise of Blacks in America: A Prelude to Genocide?" *Journal of Black Studies* 17 (December 1986): 243, 241–42. For Willhelm's earliest ideas on this topic, see Willhelm, *Who Needs the Negro?* (New York: Doubleday, 1971).

98. Willhelm, "Economic Demise," 234.

99. Willhelm, "Economic Demise," 247, 250.

100. William Darity Jr., "Racial Equality in the Managerial Age: An Alternative Vision to the NRC Report," *American Economic Review* 80 (May 1990): 249, 250.

101. Though the term "Maafa" gained prominence in Afrocentric camps during the 1990s, Ani first used the term earlier. See Marimba Ani, *Let the Circle Be Unbroken: The Implications of African Spirituality in the Diaspora* (Trenton, N.J.: Red Sea, 1980), 12.

102. Marimba Ani, *Yurugu: An African-Centered Critique of European Cultural Thought and Behavior* (New Jersey: African World Press, 1996), 427, 432, 478, 433, 434, 438.

103. Asante, "The African American Warrant for Reparations"; C. T. Keto, *The African-Centered Perspective of History* (Blackwood, N.J.: K. A. Publishing, 1989); Kobi K. K. Kambon, *African/Black Psychology in the American Context: An African-Centered Approach* (Tallahassee, Fla.: Nubian National Publishers, 1998), 530; Erriel D. Roberson, *The Maafa and Beyond* (Columbia, Md.: Kujichagulia, 1995); Nancy Boyd-Franklin, *Black Families in Therapy: Understanding the African American Experience* (New York: Guilford, 2006). John Henrik Clarke has mentioned the "black holocaust" in several of his publications. See, for instance, *Christopher Columbus and the Afrikan Holocaust: Slavery and the Rise of European Capitalism* (New York: A & B, 2002). S. E. Anderson is also among those to use the term "African holocaust." See *The Black Holocaust for Beginners* (New York: Writers and Readers, 1995).

104. Wade W. Nobles, "From Na Ezaleli to the Jegnoch: The Force of the African Family for Black Men in Higher Education," in *Making It on Broken Promises: Leading African American Male Scholars Confront the Culture of Higher Education,* ed. Lee Jones and Cornel West, 178 (Sterling, Va.: Stylus, 2002).

105. Delores P. Aldridge and Carlene Young, *Out of the Revolution: The Development of Africana Studies* (Lanham, Md.: Lexington, 2003), 250.

106. Robert Johnson and Paul S. Leighton, "African Americans: Victims of Indirect Genocide," in *Genocide,* ed. William Dudley, 159, 160, 161 (San Diego: Greenhaven, 2001).

107. Johnson and Leighton, "African Americans," 161, 162, 163, 164, 167.

108. Augusta C. Del Zotto, "Gendercide in a Historical-Structural Context: The Case of Black Male Gendercide in the United States," in *Gendercide and Genocide,* ed. Adam Jones, 158 (Nashville: Vanderbilt University Press, 2004).

109. Del Zotto, "Gendercide in a Historical-Structural Context," 160, 165, 166.

110. The staff of the *Washington Post, Being a Black Man: At the Corner of Progress and Peril* (New York: Public Affairs, 2007), 7.

111. James B. Stewart and Joseph W. Scott, "The Institutional Decimation of Black American Males," *Western Journal of Black Studies* 2 (Summer 1978): 82, 83, 89, 90, 91.

112. Jewelle Taylor Gibbs, ed., *Young, Black, and Male in America: An Endangered Species* (Dover, Mass.: Auburn House, 1988).

113. "National Office," "NBUF Fact Sheet," http://www.nbufront.org/html (accessed October 23, 2008).

114. Conrad W. Worrill, "Revisiting NBUF's Genocide Campaign, Reparations," *Chicago Defender,* October 22–23, 2007, 8.

115. Patterson, ed., *We Charge Genocide,* 195.

116. Curthoys and Docker, "Defining Genocide," 34.

Index

Wright, Richard, 26–27, 85–86
Wright, W. D., 44

Yo' Mama's Disfunktional! Fighting the Culture Wars in Urban America (Kelley), 10
Young, Black and Male in America: An Endangered Species (Gibbs), 194

Young, Carlene, 191, 192
Yurugu: An African-Centered Critique of European Cultural Thought (Ani), 190–91

Zimmerer, Jurgen, 165

PERO GAGLO DAGBOVIE is an
associate professor of history at
Michigan State University and the
author of *The Early Black History
Movement, Carter G. Woodson,
and Lorenzo Johnston Greene.*

The New Black Studies Series

Beyond Bondage: Free Women of Color in the Americas   *Edited by
David Barry Gaspar and Darlene Clark Hine*

The Early Black History Movement, Carter G. Woodson, and Lorenzo Johnston
Greene   *Pero Gaglo Dagbovie*

"Baad Bitches" and Sassy Supermamas: Black Power Action Films   *Stephane Dunn*

Black Maverick: T. R. M. Howard's Fight for Civil Rights and Economic Power
David T. Beito and Linda Royster Beito

Beyond the Black Lady: Sexuality and the New African American Middle Class
Lisa B. Thompson

Extending the Diaspora: New Histories of Black People   *Dawne Y. Curry,
Eric D. Duke, and Marshanda A. Smith*

Activist Sentiments: Reading Black Women in the Nineteenth Century
P. Gabrielle Foreman

Black Europe and the African Diaspora   *Edited by Darlene Clark Hine,
Trica Danielle Keaton, and Stephen Small*

Freeing Charles: The Struggle to Free a Slave on the Eve of the Civil War
Scott Christianson

African American History Reconsidered   *Pero Gaglo Dagbovie*

The University of Illinois Press
is a founding member of the
Association of American University Presses.

Composed in 10.5/13 Adobe Minion Pro
at the University of Illinois Press
Manufactured by Thomson-Shore, Inc.

University of Illinois Press
1325 South Oak Street
Champaign, IL 61820-6903
www.press.uillinois.edu